❖ The Wooden Spoon Bread Book

BOOKS BY MARILYN M. MOORE

Baking Your Own: Recipes and Tips for Better Breads
The Wooden Spoon Bread Book

The Wooden Spoon Bread Book

❖ *The Secrets of Successful Baking*

by Marilyn M. Moore

THE ATLANTIC MONTHLY PRESS New York

Library of Congress Cataloging-in-Publication Data
Moore, Marilyn M.
  The wooden spoon bread book.
  Includes index.
  TX769.M655   1987   641.8'15   86-32180

ISBN 0-87113-505-1

Published simultaneously in Canada
Printed in the United States of America

First printing

Design by Laura Hough

Atlantic Monthly Press
841 Broadway
New York, NY 10003

❖ *for Joe, who breaks bread with me*

❊ Acknowledgments and Thanks

To my editor, Joyce Johnson, who allowed me the freedom to develop my ideas without interruption, and whose experienced eye helped me see the final form.

To Jeanette Groves for acting as a sounding board early in the development of the writing.

To my daughter, Shirley Browne, for reading my typing to catch irregular usage before it became ingrained in the text.

To Selma Young for being as enthusiastic as I about the project and for continually suggesting new directions for me to travel.

To all of my tasters. Particularly the crew at the library who literally ate their way through the entire book: Louise Griner, Esther Jarnigan, Carol Arnold, and Hazel Donaldson.

To the following good cooks, who generously shared recipes from their personal files: Marge Carlson, Jeanette Groves, Shuiho Lee, Winifred Martin, Meena Verma Roy, Joseph K. Sherrard, Natalie Smith, Candace J. Underhill, Mercedita Osorio Wells, Melida Zarate, Irma Zook.

To the following commercial concerns, who sent me information about their products, recipes to test, and/or samples to try: Arrowhead Mills; Better Foods Foundation, Inc.; The Birkett Mills; Brookside Farm; Cuisinarts, Inc.; Deer Valley Farm; Elam Mills; General Foods Corporation; Great Grains Milling Company; The Great Valley Mills; H. Roth & Son; Jaffe Bros.; International Multifoods; KWC International Corporation; Kenyon Corn Meal Company; The Little Old Bread Man; Maid of Scandinavia Company; Mari-Mann Herb Co., Inc.; The National Buckwheat Institute; Paprikas Weiss Importer; Quaker Oats Company; Sassafras Enterprises; Sun-Diamond Growers of California; The Uhlmann Company; Walnut Acres; War Eagle Mill; Whole Grain Sales; and Williams-Sonoma.

Some of the material in *The Wooden Spoon Bread Book* appeared earlier in *Baking Your Own: Recipes and Tips for Better Breads* in slightly different form.

vii

Occasionally in the recipes brand names are used for the ingredients called for. This does not mean that these brands are the only brands that could be used successfully. They are mentioned when, in the opinion of the author, their choice might make a difference in the outcome.

❊ Contents

❋ Introduction

Ah, bread! It has consumed my life for the past year, as I have consumed what seemed like an endless wonderment of breads in a multitude of shapes, sizes, and flavors—each one to be tested and tasted over and over again. You'd think one would tire of such a pursuit, but I have not. Constant reading, thinking, and talking about bread only makes me want to read, think, and talk about it once again.

One of my friends, on hearing that I was working on the manuscript for this book, said, "I knew it! Bread again! No matter what else you do, you always come back to bread!" She is right, of course. I have, over the years, pursued various ventures. The most successful of these have always had something to do with bread.

When my children were small, their afterschool treat was buttered slices of whatever bread was coming from the oven that day. They were the first to taste and give an opinion of the bread that would later win their mother a trip to the Pillsbury Bake-Off.

On the community occasions when food had to be brought in for donations or sharing, mine has always been bread in some form or another. I've been told that I carry the perfume of the bread with me as I go about distributing my freshly baked loaves.

For a few years I had my own weaving and pottery shop where I regularly sold homemade bread one day a week as a way to lure customers. It never failed. It took some time, however, before I realized that the bread was developing more of a following than my woven goods and pots.

The memories of our lives are intertwined with the foods that we eat. When I was very, very young, living in Hawaii, there was a neighbor who made what I can remember as great mounds of bread. Sometimes the aroma of the baking would entice me to her back door and she would invite me in to share with her family in breaking one of the loaves. We always gathered around her large kitchen table, chattering as we wolfed down the warm and wonderful bread.

Later, when we were living in Fresno, California, my family frequented a restaurant that was located in the basement of one of the downtown buildings. The food there was brought in on platters that were placed in the center of the table. We always sat at one of the big, round tables with our aunts, uncles, and cousins. There was usually a dish of stewed chicken, followed by a variety of vegetables and legumes, and an offering of red meats. With every course there were crusty round loaves of white bread and ample glasses of a pleasant red wine. No one seemed to think that I was too young to partake of a small glass, and whenever I go to a restaurant, I still save a piece of the bread to be savored with the last of the wine.

While living in California, we would often travel down the state to visit my Grandma Nachtigal in the Bakersfield area. Grandma always had some of her delicious zweibach to serve at her meals. These were served cold with her very own chilled juices or soups made of fruits from the garden. Grandma's recipe for zweibach appears later in this book.

We lived for a time in Mobile, Alabama, where I learned to love cornbread baked in cast-iron pans in the shape of small ears of corn. There were also the good Southern biscuits and spoon breads, often served with gravy as well as butter and jelly. I am getting hungry all over again just writing about them!

People seem surprised when I tell them I did not learn to bake bread from my mother. Mother was very proficient in many things, but she did not have the patience to teach. My brother and sister and I were usually ushered out of her kitchen. It was not until after my husband and I started our own family that I decided to learn to bake bread. I wanted to fill our home with that yeasty aroma, bringing back beautiful memories of my childhood, and instilling some anew for the next generation. My first attempts were not completely successful. The written directions I had were less than explicit. As time went by, my technique improved. The more I baked, the more I wanted to bake. Soon I was giving classes and writing down ideas of my own.

When creating new recipes, I am reminded of something an art instructor once taught me. He said, "No matter how knowledgeable you are about your artistic medium, you will do far better work if you do not put everything you know into every piece you produce. Restraint in execution achieves the greatest results." Recipes, like painting or sculpture, benefit from a little restraint.

I like to keep my recipes simple and easy to understand, using a minimum number of ingredients. I hope the result of each one will bring you pleasure.

Marilyn M. Moore

❄ Potpourri

Some thoughts on the subject of bread

❄ THE JOY OF BREAD BAKING TODAY

Modern homemakers do not have to bake their own bread. There are plenty of loaves waiting on supermarket shelves for those who want them. Yet more and more people are enjoying the simple pleasures of mixing, baking, and serving their very own creations, made with the loving warmth of home fires.

There are some cooks who are baking bread for the very first time, and for an interesting reason. They have become fascinated with the newest piece of mass-produced kitchen equipment, the food processor. Up till now they have thought that making their own bread would be too much trouble. But if they can make it in their food processors, they feel it is a different story. There really isn't much difference, though, in the effort it takes to mix dough in an earthenware bowl or revolve it in the workbowl of a speed machine. What matters is your enjoyment in making it and eating it.

❖ WRITING YOUR OWN RECIPES

It is not unreasonable to think that you can write your own recipes. The same method of development can be used, whether it is for a bread or for some other food. The first step in becoming a recipe writer is to learn everything you can about the kind of food you're interested in. Study instructive books, such as this one, and the many that are listed in the bibliography at the back of this book. Talk to other people you know who are good cooks to see if you can determine what it is that sets them apart. Analyze the patterns you see in the recipes that you read and use. Then take a basic recipe and change one or more of the ingredients to develop something that has a different character. From then on, use trial and error, until you have something you consider worthwhile.

As an example, let's take a recipe for Basic White Bread. The ingredients are as follows:

> 1 package yeast
> ¼ cup warm water
> 2 cups milk
> 2 teaspoons salt
> 2 tablespoons butter
> 2 tablespoons sugar
> 6 to 6 ½ cups unbleached all-purpose flour

Change the *milk* to *orange juice.*
Change the *butter* to *oil.*
Change the *sugar* to *honey.*
Change *one-half of the flour* to *whole-wheat flour.*

Now you have Orange-Honey Wheat Bread.

Change the *orange juice* to *water.*
Change the *honey* to *molasses.*
Change the *whole-wheat flour* to *rye flour.*
Add *1 tablespoon caraway seed.*

Now you have Caraway Rye.

As you continue to try different things, you will build a foundation of experience and knowledge that will help you to make more daring changes. You will also find that whenever you create something new, you open the door to your ability to create even more.

While you work, keep extensive notes on everything you do. Something that does not work today may trigger a productive idea tomorrow. It is best not to work from memory. You may lose the formula for something that you dearly want to repeat.

❖ BREAD AND YOUR DIET

Although *The Wooden Spoon Bread Book* is not a diet book, some comments about the use of bread in your diet may be in order.

The feedback from my first book makes me realize that many readers do not consider bread to be something they should eat when dieting. The truth is, if you include good, wholesome bread as part of your daily diet, you might never have to go on a reducing diet again. Bread is an important part of a healthful balanced diet. If you have a problem with weight control, enjoy the white breads, wheat breads, the rye, and the sourdough. Use the quick breads, muffins, and biscuits to a lesser degree. The filled breads, sweet breads, and fried breads should be special-occasion treats, much like birthday cake or Christmas candy. If you are eating a moderate amount of honest bread and gaining weight, look somewhere else in your diet for the culprit. It is probably not the bread at all. Bread is a high-energy food that can help you develop strength and endurance without making you fat.* If you eliminate bread in favor of more protein, more fat, and more simple sugars, you are much more likely to become sluggish— and put on weight!

Salt can cause problems in the diet of some people. If you need to, you can make bread with no salt at all. The results are too bland for most of us, and lack of salt can affect the texture of some breads. If you are merely trying to cut down on salt to avoid potential problems, use one-half of the

---

*Robert Haas, *Eat to Win—The Sports Nutrition Bible* (New York: Rawson Associates, 1983), p. 10.

salt called for in any of the recipes. The flavor and the texture of such bread should be quite acceptable.

Cholesterol has received a lot of press in recent years. Everyone now knows that too much cholesterol can be life-threatening, and that saturated fats can contribute to the formation of cholesterol. So much so, that there are many of you who would never think of buying butter. You use margarine exclusively, hoping that you are thereby assuring your better health. I prefer to think of fat as fat, no matter what the source. A little bit of fat goes a long way. If I'm going to enjoy a little bit of fat, let it be butter. It tastes worlds better than any margarine ever produced. But if you have a definite health problem in this respect, by all means follow the advice of your doctor.

If you would like to cut down on the fats used in the preparation of homemade bread, try using some of the nonstick bakeware that is now available. I have successfully baked breads in nonstick bakeware without any greasing at all. The crust is not as good as that produced in the black metal pans I prefer, but it isn't bad.

If you are concerned about using sugar, simply use the recipes that call for small amounts or none at all. There is a sugar available called fructose, which is supposed to produce a metabolic reaction different from that caused by the more common sucrose.* If you have a bad reaction to sugar, you could check with your doctor or dietician about substituting fructose. The jury is still out on artificial sweeteners. I hesitate to recommend their use in cooking.

❈ THE IDEAL BREAD BAKER'S KITCHEN

The first thing to think about in planning the ideal bread-baker's kitchen is a kneading surface. Butcher block is the first choice and Eastern hard-rock maple with full-length edge grain is the best. Make it table height, or 30 inches. If you plan a table, it can serve meals as well as provide your kneading surface. If you do not plan a table, drop part of your counter top

---

*J. T. Cooper, *Dr. Cooper's Fabulous Fructose Diet* (New York: Fawcett Crest, 1979), p. 10.

to 30 inches. If you make a lot of pastry-type breads, such as croissants, you will want to plan a cool surface—marble for country-style, granite for Euro-style.

You will want a double sink for preparing foods and for washing out your mixing bowls and pans as you work. I prefer Elkay stainless steel. The counter space right around the sink should not have cabinets above. This is where you will use an electric mixer and a food processor for some of your breads. My recommendations for these appliances are a Kitchenaid mixer and a Cuisinart food processor. If you want to grind grain, get the grain-grinding attachment for the mixer.

You should plan a side-by-side refrigerator-freezer. I think Sub-Zero is best. You need freezer room for bread and grains for later use. The refrigerator section will store whole-grain flours, sourdough starters, and make-ahead doughs, in addition to everyday groceries.

The stove top should have down-draft exhaust. You need elbow room above, for working with large pots of jams and jellies. I like Jenn-Air. They offer a wide choice of interchangeable plug-in cooktop cartridges—black glass–ceramic, solid element, conventional, induction. They also make accessory units, my favorite being their nonstick griddle.

I suggest built-in conventional double ovens, and my choice is Kitchenaid in a 27-inch width. It has high-density insulation, a built-in smoke eliminator, and a moisture evaporation system. It comes in a wide range of color choices: black glass, brushed chrome, and white, almond, wheat, coffee, or avocado porcelain. All have see-through doors.

My choice for a microwave is the Omni 5 by General Electric. It not only will melt butter and heat liquids quickly for your doughs, it will make your morning toast, and its small size makes it easy to fit in. My choices for a trash compacter and dishwasher are Kitchenaid.

Open shelves will store your multicolored grains and your prettiest serving pieces to add to your decor. Closed cabinets can be used for packaged foods and most cookware.

If you keep and organize recipes, you should plan enough room on your desk for a computer. I choose the Macintosh for its easy formatting ability. Don't forget to plan shelves to keep your cookbooks handy.

Here are two drawings showing how these ideas can be fit into a kitchen space. One plan remodels an existing 20×22-foot garage to provide both kitchen and family living/dining. The other shows how the same kitchen equipment can be fit into a smaller 10×14-foot area.

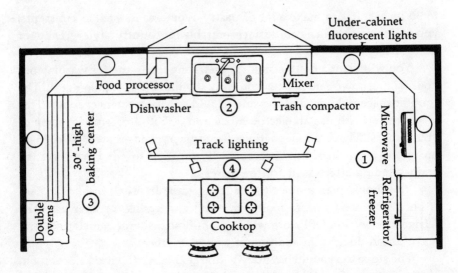

Under-cabinet fluorescent lights

Food processor

Mixer

Dishwasher   ② Track compactor

Microwave

30"-high baking center

Track lighting

① Refrigerator/freezer

③ Double ovens

④ Cooktop

◀ To new garage   To living room/dining room ▶

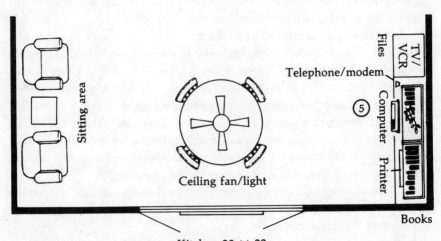

Files

TV/VCR

Telephone/modem

Sitting area

⑤ Computer

Printer

Ceiling fan/light

Books

Kitchen 20 × 22.

Notes:
1. Baking center and cooktop can be switched.
2. Computer must be away from flour dust. If you do not plan to have a computer, baking center can double as desk.
3. Circled numbers refer to elevation diagrams on facing page.

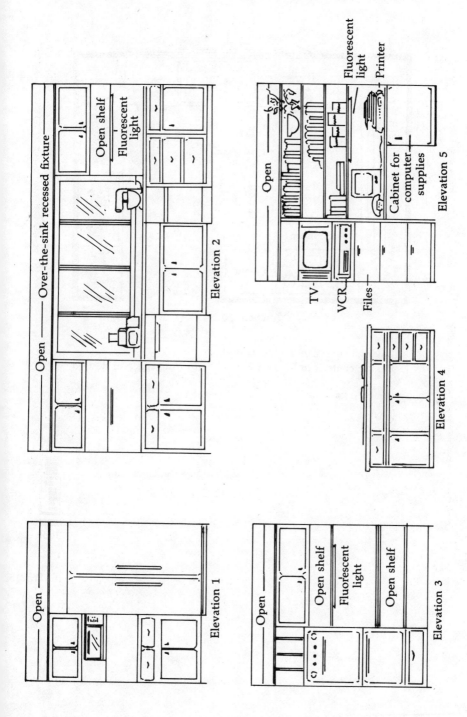

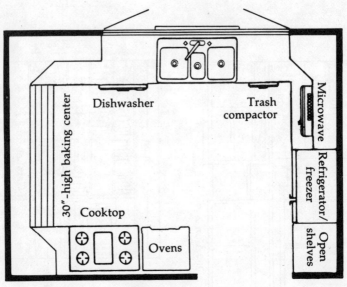

Kitchen: 10 × 14.

Notes:
1. Baking center can double as desk.
2. Baking center can be used for kitchen eating space, if desired.

✳ WHY THE WOODEN SPOON BREAD BOOK?

One night I thought about the answer to the question, "Why did you call your book *The Wooden Spoon Bread Book?"*

Perhaps I was simply being democratic. After all, more people own earthenware bowls and wooden spoons than food processors.

Perhaps it was because I think all bread bakers should serve their rightful apprenticeship with lowly utensils before allowing themselves the privilege of having machines make their bread. Indeed, when you get involved with hands-on breadmaking, you do experience the nuances of the dough and get a feel for its texture. But I would rather see you start making bread with a machine than not have you start at all.

Perhaps the title has something to do with the back-to-basics movement. Wooden-spoon breads certainly go right along with Mom's mashed potatoes and stove-top stew. There is a lot of old-fashioned good eating being "rediscovered" by culinary wizards in test kitchens all over the country. The fact is, however, that I was calling my bread-baking classes *The Wooden Spoon School of Bread* long before this rediscovery began.

When you get right down to it, I just really like the name, *The Wooden Spoon Bread Book.* Say it aloud to yourself. The words just roll off your tongue, leaving a comfortable, homey image in their wake. It is as simple as that.

❋ Getting Down to Business

*The ingredients, the utensils, the methods,
and all the little secrets of perfect bread*

SIDE-BY-SIDE BREADS	FAST-MIX WHITE BREAD
WHEAT BREAD FLOUR	MIXER FRENCH BREAD
BOHEMIAN FLOUR	BASIC DOUGH-HOOK WHITE BREAD
OLD-STYLE QUICK BREAD	STACKED CINNAMON LOAF
TO RENDER FRESH LEAF LARD	HERB-FLAVORED CHEESE BREAD
HOMEMADE WHEAT MALT	WHOLE-GRAIN FRENCH BREAD
THE LEARNING LOAF	FAST FOOD-PROCESSOR BREAD
MIXER WHITE BREAD	PROCESSOR BRAN BREAD

❖ THE INGREDIENTS OF BREAD

All bread is made with grain or flour and a liquid to bind it together. There are some basics which may or may not be added to that formula. They are leaveners, to make the bread rise; sweeteners, for the palate and to enhance fermentation in yeast bread; salt, for taste and to slow fermentation in yeast bread; fats, to tenderize the crumb and promote the keeping quality of the loaf; eggs, to add richness and color, and also to help the bread to rise; bread improvers, to enhance yeast development; and a variety of other flavorings and foods to add interest to the bread basket. In a discussion of the flours and grains, we shall start with the white flours.

White Flours

All-purpose flour is the flour most widely used in America's kitchens. It is a mixture of two kinds of milled wheat: hard wheat, which has a high protein content; and soft wheat, which has a low protein content. It has sufficient protein to result in a good gluten development for yeast breads, yet not so much as to be detrimental in quick breads. Although gluten is essential for the rising of a successful yeast bread, too much of it will make a quick loaf tough and unappetizing. Many bakers buy large bags of all-purpose flour for economy's sake. If you wish to economize, you may substitute all-purpose flour for the unbleached all-purpose flour called for throughout this book. Keep in mind that all-purpose flour may absorb slightly less liquid than the unbleached.

Unbleached all-purpose flour, as its name implies, has been spared chemical bleaching, and is usually more expensive than bleached flour. Unbleached flour requires time to age naturally. White bleached flour ages quickly, and can be shipped shortly after processing. When you convert time and space into money, you have a higher-priced product. Since bleaching chemicals destroy some of the fresh flavor of white wheat flour, my preference remains with the unbleached.

Bread flour has a higher protein content than the all-purpose. It is the proteins in flour that enable it to develop gluten. Bread flour, widely available in supermarkets since 1982, is a mixture of high-gluten flour and malted barley flour to which potassium bromate has been added. Potassium bromate is used by commercial bakeries as a dough conditioner. It is one of several gluten-oxidizing agents which have the effect of making the gluten more elastic. Some home bakers have expressed concern about the use of this chemical agent. The small amount added is less than what naturally occurs in many of our seafoods.[*] The potassium bromate remains inert until it interacts with the liquid in the dough. Then, because of its effect on the gluten, the dough has a greater ability to expand and the resulting loaf will be larger.

The malted barley flour that is added provides the right mix of natural enzymes needed to convert starch into the sugars needed for proper yeast growth. If flour has too much of a concentration of malted flour (enzymes), the dough will be sticky and the baked product may have gummy spots.

In my own baking, I alternate between unbleached all-purpose flour and bread flour. Since temperatures and humidity levels vary from day to day, I could not realistically compare the two by baking on consecutive days. I decided, therefore, to conduct a side-by-side test. I made two batches of bread, one with bread flour and the other with unbleached all-purpose flour. The bread flour I was using that day was Pillsbury's; the unbleached all-purpose flour was Gold Medal. I mixed, kneaded, let rise, punched down, shaped, let rise again, and baked the two side by side, using the same recipe for each. These were my findings:

1. The bread flour more readily absorbed the water in the recipe.
2. The unbleached batch required a little more flour.
3. The bread flour kneaded up into an elastic ball more quickly and easily, and was easier to punch down and shape.
4. During the first rising, the bread-flour batch seemed to expand a little more than the other.
5. After the second rising, the bread-flour loaf was noticeably higher. As the two rose, the unbleached all-purpose loaf had more of a tendency to spread out, rather than up.
6. After baking, the bread-flour loaf was obviously higher with a more pleasing rounded top.

---

[*]Joseph Amendola and Donald E. Lundberg, *Understanding Baking* (Chicago: Medalist Publications, 1970), p. 37.

Finally, I tasted the loaves warm, cold, and toasted. They were sampled both plain and with sweet butter. The two loaves were very close. The texture of the bread-flour loaf seemed a little better, not as toothy, while the flavor of the unbleached-flour loaf was slightly superior.

The test results are purely subjective, of course. If you want to conduct your own side-by-side test, perhaps you would like to use the recipe that I followed.

Side-By-Side Breads

To soften yeast, in a small mixing bowl combine

1 cup warm water
1 teaspoon sugar
1 ¼ teaspoons (or about ½ packet) active dry yeast

Stir into softened yeast mixture, in this order

1 teaspoon salt
1 teaspoon oil
2 ¼ to 2 ½ cups unbleached all-purpose flour or bread flour

Turn out on a floured surface and knead until smooth and elastic. Knead in additional flour, if needed. Place in a greased bowl, turning dough once to grease the top. Cover and let rise until doubled in bulk, 30 to 45 minutes. Punch dough down. Shape into an oblong loaf and place in a well-greased 8½×4½×2½-inch pan. Cover and let rise until almost doubled in bulk, 30 to 45 minutes. Before baking, brush top of loaf with a mixture of

1 egg
1 tablespoon water

With a sharp knife, make a slash in the top of the loaf. Bake in a preheated 375°F oven for 35 to 40 minutes. Cool on a wire rack. Makes 1 loaf.

Almost everyone is familiar with the reliable all-purpose flours and bread flours from the Pillsbury Company and from General Mills (Gold Medal). There are also some very good white or creamy white flours available from the smaller mills across the country. Elam's (Chicago) produces an all-purpose flour speckled with defatted wheat germ that makes a delicious bread. The Great Grains Milling Company (Scobey, Montana) offers a stone-ground golden-wheat flour with most of the bran removed. The Uhlmann Company (Kansas City) packages an unbleached, naturally white flour under the brand names of Heckers and Ceresota, both of which you will find to be reliable. Deer Valley Farm (Guilford, NY) lists several white flours, milled from spray-free Montana spring wheat. Arrowhead Mills (Hereford, TX) offers unbleached all-purpose flour milled from the hard red winter wheat grown in Deaf Smith County. Great Valley Mills (Telford, PA) lists both a hard unbleached flour for yeast bread and a soft unbleached flour for biscuits, muffins, and pancakes. Walnut Acres (Penns Creek, PA) offers a lovely unbleached wheat flour with most of the bran removed. There must be many more that are every bit as good as the ones mentioned here.

Another white flour worth mentioning is *cake flour*. Cake flour has a high-starch and a low-protein content, making it more suitable for cakes than for breads. It can be used in cakelike quick breads for a light product. Some bakers also use it to give pastries a delicate, flaky texture. To substitute cake flour for all-purpose flour, you will want to add 2 tablespoons of cake flour to every cup in the original recipe.

For more variety in your breadmaking, you might also try the whole-grain flours that are now available.

Whole-Grain Flours

When purchasing whole-grain flours for baking, it is better to select those which have been *stone ground* than those which have been commercially steel ground. If heat is produced during the grinding process, it destroys the vitamins in the grain by oxidizing the oil in the germ. When grain is ground by steel at a high heat, some of the vitamins must be added back after milling to replace what has been lost. Stone grinding wheels, or buhrstones, produce very little heat, preserving more of the grain's natural nutrients.

True whole-grain stone-ground flours contain all the parts of the complete grain: the endosperm, the bran, and the germ. It is the germ that contains the seed's oils, rich in vitamins and minerals. This richness, however, can cause improperly stored whole-grain flour to turn rancid. For the short term, whole-grain flours should be stored in the refrigerator. For long-term storage, use your freezer. Always bring your flour up to room temperature before use.

You can see why most supermarkets do not bother to stock whole-grain flours. You will want to check specialty shops, health-food stores, and some co-ops for the availability of good flour. Ask enough questions to determine that any flour supplied through these outlets is indeed fresh. The fact that a shingle has been hung outside the establishment proclaiming "health food" does not guarantee the freshness of the products sold. There are numerous reliable mail-order outlets that guarantee their products and welcome your inquiries (see Access).

The most commonly used whole-grain flours are: *whole-wheat flour* with its nutty taste; *rye flour* with its slightly bitter taste; and *cornmeal* with its sweet flavor and delightful crunch.

In addition to these more common grains, there are many others that merit your attention.

Other Grains and Flours

Whole-wheat pastry flour comes from whole-wheat kernels that have been finely milled to produce a lightly textured flour. It can be used in place of white flour in pies, biscuits, and pastries. You can make your own whole-wheat pastry flour by stirring more coarsely ground flour in a sieve held over a bowl. The flour that makes it through the mesh can be used in any of your lighter breads. The residue is called middlings. It can be added to doughs when extra fiber is desired.

Graham flour, named after Sylvester Graham, who first championed its use in his 1837 book, *Treatise on Bread and Bread Making,* is whole-wheat flour that has been sifted to remove the largest particles of bran. It can be used in all types of breadmaking, especially old-fashioned graham crackers.

Cracked wheat is made by cutting the wheat berry into small pieces. Softened by cooking or soaking in boiling water, it adds a chewy crunch and a nutty flavor to the loaf.

Gluten flour is produced by washing the starch from the endosperm of the wheat berry. What remains is a high-protein flour that is about 70 percent gluten. Gluten flour cannot be used alone, for it does not contain sufficient starch to make bread. It can be added to a low-gluten flour mixture for a lighter loaf. Bakers like it not only for its effect, but also for its flavor. I know of one who makes a large batch of bread weekly and uses gluten flour in every batch. For most bread recipes, the amount of wheat gluten to be added per cup of flour is: 1½ teaspoons wheat gluten per cup of whole-grain flour; 1 teaspoon wheat gluten per cup of unbleached all-purpose flour. Breads with significant amounts of bran, nuts, seeds, or nonwheat flours may need additional gluten.

Semolina flour is milled from the largest endosperm particles of hard durum wheat. It is widely used in the manufacture of pasta. It can also make a delightful cream-colored loaf of bread.

Bulgur is wheat that has been cracked, parched, and processed by steaming, then dried and left whole or ground. Finely ground bulgur can be added to bread dough without further preparation. Coarsely ground or whole bulgur should be soaked in hot water before such use.

Rye meal is simply coarsely ground whole-rye flour. Recipes for pumpernickel bread usually call for it. When it is not available, cornmeal added to rye flour can substitute.

The meal produced from a new hybrid corn called *hi-lysine* has a higher percentage of protein than the common corn. It also has an excellent flavor and can be used interchangeably with the more familiar meal. *Corn flour* is flour that is finely milled from whole-grain corn grits. It can be used to make tender pancakes and biscuits with a golden corn flavor.

Triticale flour is produced from a fairly new hybrid grain that is a cross between wheat and rye. This hybrid was discovered accidentally when closely planted fields of wheat and rye were found to cross-pollinate. Further investigation showed that the resulting grain was higher in protein than either parent. Triticale flour has a weak gluten content. With gentle kneading, a loaf of pure triticale can be coaxed into being. It is easier, however, to mix it with wheat flour to upgrade the gluten content of the dough.

Rolled oats are whole oat kernels pressed into flakes by heavy steel rollers. They can replace 1 cup of wheat flour in a 6-cup recipe for a chewy, earthy flavored bread. Homemade *oat flour* can be made by grinding rolled oats in a blender or food processor until fine. It can be used with wheat flour in muffins or loaf breads.

Potato flour is made from the starch of potatoes. A small amount of potato flour added to yeast dough acts as a natural bread improver. It triggers fermentation, makes the dough easier to knead, and prolongs the shelf life of the finished product. *Mashed potatoes,* used in small quantities, can be equally beneficial.

Rice, both the white and the more nutritious brown, should be cooked before adding to the dough. *Rice flour* is also available to use in your breadmaking.

Cooked *wild rice* is as delicious in bread as it is in a side dish. It is an aquatic grass rather than a true grain. Three-fourths of the entire wild-rice crop is grown in the state of Minnesota. Still harvested mostly by hand, wild rice remains expensive, all the more reason to include any leftovers in bread dough rather than throwing it out.

Ground from a three-cornered seed that is not a true grain, *buckwheat* produces a heavy, hearty-flavored flour. One-half cup will flavor a 9 × 5-inch loaf of yeast bread. People particularly love the flavor of buckwheat in pancakes. Buckwheat is high in lysine and has a higher protein content than most cereal grains. Dark buckwheat flour is nutritionally superior to light.

Available as a flour or meal, *barley* was at one time one of the most widely used grains in breadmaking. Many older English and European bread recipes call for barley flour. Barley meal can be used for 1 cup in a 6-cup yeast bread recipe. The resulting bread will be almost white with a slightly nutty barley flavor. Barley flour can be mixed with wheat flour for a loaf with a sweet barley flavor and a cakelike texture. Leftover cooked pearl barley can be added to your bread dough in small quantities for variety.

Millet is a very nutritious grain that has been little used in this country for baked goods. You are more likely to find it in domestic bird seed than in a bakery. As a flour and as millet meal, it can be added to a bread dough for a delightful loaf.

Milo flour is milled from sorghum, a grain that can be grown in climates too hot for wheat or rice. It is more commonly used as cattle feed than as a food for humans. It can be combined with wheat flour and used sparingly for a protein boost in your breads.

Amaranth dates back to 8,000 years ago, when it was grown by the Aztec Indians of Mexico. When sown, even under adverse conditions like drought, amaranth grows quickly and abundantly. For this reason, some believe it to be the potential supercrop grain of the future.* Amaranth flour is easily mixed with wheat flour to provide what can be considered a complete protein for breadmaking. If it is toasted for about 15 minutes at 325°F, it produces a marvelous nutty flavor.

Soy flour (low fat), ground from the ubiquitous soy bean, is remarkably high in protein with a correspondingly low fat content, making it desirable from a nutritional point of view. One tablespoon may be spooned into a cup before measuring white wheat flour to upgrade the protein content of the bread made from the mixture.

Peanut flour has at least sixteen times the protein value of wheat. Two tablespoons spooned into the cup before measuring will make quite a difference in the total protein of a bread made with wheat flour.

Pantry Mixes

I keep two flour mixes on hand that are called for in some of the recipes following. If you do a lot of baking, you will find it convenient to keep them in your pantry. If you bake infrequently, you may prefer to mix only what you need for a particular recipe.

✳. Wheat-Bread Flour

Combine in equal parts by volume or weight

> *stone-ground whole-wheat flour*
> *unbleached all-purpose flour or bread flour*

Mix well. Label and store in a cool place.

---

*Sheryl and Mel London, *Creative Cooking with Grains and Pasta* (Emmaus, PA: Rodale Press, 1982), p. 30.

❋ Bohemian Flour

Combine in equal parts by volume or weight

stone-ground rye flour
stone-ground whole-wheat flour
unbleached all-purpose flour or bread flour

Mix well. Label and store in a cool place.

Liquids

The most commonly used liquids for bread are *tap water* and *milk.* Water is used mostly in yeast breads; milk is used in both yeast breads and quick breads. Most tap water is trouble free, but some has an undesirable taste from the chemicals used in processing. If your tap water has enough chemical taste to bother you, try bottled water instead.

The acidity or alkalinity of your water can affect the development of the gluten and, in turn, the fermentation of your yeast. Too acid a condition can result in poor gluten development and a sticky dough. A highly alkaline water supply can toughen the gluten, thereby retarding yeast growth. A pH of 7 is considered a neutral acidity. The ideal water for bread baking is slightly more acid than neutral. A small quantity of vinegar can be added to alkaline water to make it more acid. Vinegar helps retard the molds that are likely to attack your homemade breads. Too much vinegar can tip the balance in the wrong direction, however, and cause the dough to be too sticky. Another way to confront a highly alkaline water supply is simply to use more yeast.*

When using milk, it doesn't matter whether it is whole, low fat, or skim. Whatever you have on hand to drink is okay. Some bakers use nonfat dry milk in bread. I prefer to use the liquid. Yeast breads made with milk will have a softer crumb than those made with water. Pasteurization has eliminated the sanitary need to scald and cool liquid milk before adding it to yeast dough, but since unscalded milk sometimes produces an overly soft loaf, I heat and cool the milk to eliminate the problem.

---

*Joseph Amendola and Donald E. Lundberg, *Understanding Baking* (Chicago: Medalist Publications, 1970), p. 43.

Potato water is water in which peeled potatoes have been boiled. This is a wonderful liquid for breadmaking. It adds a softness to the crumb, enhances fermentation, and helps retain the bread's freshness. Try to take advantage of the potato water produced whenever you boil potatoes for a meal.

Other liquids that can be used in your breads, separately or together, include: *buttermilk, cream, sour cream, yogurt, fruit* and *vegetable juices, whey, soup stock, tea, coffee,* and *beer.* Buttermilk, cream, sour cream, and yogurt help produce a rich and tender bread. Fruit and vegetable juices, while adding a variety of flavors, may dry out bread dough. They are best used in conjunction with some fat for tenderness. Whey is a by-product of cheese-making. If you make your own cheese, try using the whey in your breads. It will add nutrition and a mellow flavor. Soup stock, tea, and coffee can be used to add a distinctive flavor. Beer contributes a slightly bitter, robust flavor, very suitable for whole-wheat and rye doughs.

Leaveners

A leavener is anything that will cause a bread to rise. *Air* trapped in bread dough expands when heated, causing a rising of its own. *Moisture* turns to steam, creating the same effect. *Eggs* beaten and incorporated into dough will accentuate these effects. Although heat and steam act partially as leaveners, most breads call for yeast or a chemical leavener to help the bread rise.

Chemical leaveners used most frequently in the home kitchen are *baking soda* and *baking powder.* Baking soda is an alkali. When combined with an acid, it acts with a simple chemical action to form carbon dioxide. This gas formation proves very effective in producing light loaves of bread. Baking powder consists of an alkali and an acid combined with cornstarch, which prevents the absorption of moisture during storage. When added to a liquid mixture, the alkali and acid are able to do their work. In the past, when only single-acting baking powder was available, the chemical action commenced as soon as the powder was moistened. Double-acting baking powder, which delays part of the action until it can be activated by heat, is mainly what one finds on the supermarket shelf today.

Most commercial brands of this newer double-acting baking powder are treated with aluminum sulfate. It has a somewhat bitter aftertaste that

seems to increase if the baked goods age for a day or two. If you prefer
to avoid this chemical and its aftertaste, look for a brand that does not list
aluminum on the label. The only such brand I know of is Rumford. You
can substitute baking soda and cream of tartar for baking powder, if you
wish, and use the mixture as a single-acting baking powder. Simply measure 1 teaspoon baking soda (the alkali) and 2 teaspoons cream of tartar
(the acid) in place of 1 tablespoon baking powder. There is no need to mix
these ahead of time. They need only to be sifted in with the other dry
ingredients. Here is a sample recipe that uses this technique.

✤ Old-Style Quick Bread

*This recipe makes a large loaf. A slice of it, spread sparingly with butter and lightly
toasted in the oven, is delicious for breakfast.*

Preheat oven to 350°F. Grease and flour a 9×5-inch baking pan. Sift
together and set aside

> *3 cups unbleached all-purpose flour*
> *1 teaspoon salt*
> *1 teaspoon baking soda*
> *2 teaspoons cream of tartar*

In a large bowl, beat

> *2 eggs*

Beat into eggs, in this order

> *1 cup sugar*
> *½ cup oil*
> *1 teaspoon vanilla extract*
> *¾ teaspoon freshly grated nutmeg*

Stir into this batter, in this order

> *1 cup milk*
> *Sifted dry ingredients*

Quickly spoon batter into prepared pan. Place pan in oven and bake at
350°F for 60 to 70 minutes, or until loaf pulls away from sides of pan and

a wooden pick inserted in the center comes out clean. Cool in pan 5 minutes. Turn out on a rack to cool completely. Makes 1 loaf.

Yeast is surely one of the oldest of leaveners. Wild spores of yeast invaded the bread of early man, no doubt surprising him with its action.

Baker's yeast, for use in modern yeast bread, can be purchased in dried or cake form. Dried yeast has a much longer shelf life and produces outstanding results. I use it exclusively when testing recipes that call for yeast. Dried yeast is available in bulk or in small packages. The yeast contained in a small packet measures about 2½ teaspoons. For convenience, I prefer to think of this as a scant tablespoon. It is too much trouble to measure 2½ teaspoons every time you want to approximate one packet of premeasured yeast. A close measurement of this ingredient is not critical. Cake yeast is a moist form of yeast, sold in ⅗-ounce packages. It requires refrigeration to keep it fresh and viable and has a shorter shelf life than the dry. Check either type for a stamped date of recommended usage.

There are some new strains of yeast, labeled quick or fast, that produce results in about half the time usually required for rising. I have tried them and personally I do not care for the flavor of the breads produced. Some of my army of tasters, however, feel otherwise. Quick yeast may be substituted in the same measurements for the regular yeast called for. Expect the bread to rise in half the usual time.

Sweeteners

Sweeteners include *sugar, brown sugar, honey, molasses, maple syrup* and *corn syrup*. Brown sugar, honey, and molasses will all contribute some acid to your batters and are, therefore, sometimes chosen for breads to be leavened with baking soda. Liquid sugars, such as the syrups, honey, and molasses, can displace some of the liquid of a recipe, and an allowance should be made when using one of them in place of a solid sugar. When 1 cup of honey or molasses replaces 1 cup of sugar, the liquids should be reduced by approximately ¼ cup. Some bakers who like to feel they are eliminating a sugar problem from their diet will specify honey, date sugar, or turbinado sugar in their bread recipes. But sugar is sugar, no matter what the name. If you want to eliminate it, make your bread without it altogether. If you choose to use sugar, use the ones that appeal most to your taste. There is a popular misconception that sugar is needed for yeast growth. This is not the case. Yeast will grow in a moist, warm medium, fueled by flour alone. A small amount of sugar only enhances the process, while, in fact, too much sugar can deter it.

Salt

Salt flavors bread and inhibits the action of yeast. A bread made without salt will have a bland flavor. A yeast bread made without salt will have a porous texture and may rise faster than is desirable. A relatively small amount of salt added to a yeast dough inhibits the action of some of the enzymes in flour, thus preventing the breakdown of gluten bonds as the mass matures.* In the testing of these recipes, I have used Hain sun-evaporated sea-water salt. It is of a grind that is interchangeable with any of the more common table salts. If you prefer coarse kosher salt, you may want to include more salt than the recipe calls for.

Fats

The fats used in breads are *lard, solid vegetable shortening, butter, salad oil,* and *olive oil.* All of these add tenderness to the baked product and help prevent its becoming stale. Fats have a tendency to coat the yeast and flour particles in yeast dough, retarding their ability to produce the glutenous airy net-work essential for a light loaf. Too much fat mixed into yeast bread can cause a heavy loaf. One word about butter: The recipes in this book, unless specifically noted, have all been tested using *unsalted butter.* If only a small quantity of butter is called for, the substitution of lightly salted butter makes no difference. If a large amount of butter is called for, such a substitution can produce too salty a bread.

Fats are used in doughs of a pastry-type consistency to break up the network of gluten. After repeated folding and rolling, the dough becomes a stack of alternating fat and gluten layers. Baking results in an easily separated construction of flaky pastry. Butter is suitable for some pastry and is often chosen for its flavor.

Lard has a large crystalline structure which contributes to its effective-

---

*Harold McGee, *On Food and Cooking: The Science and Lore of the Kitchen* (New York: Scribner's, 1984), p. 305.

ness in forming a flaky consistency. Its status as a saturated animal fat has made it unpopular, and it is therefore not always kept in stock.

The best lard is leaf lard, rendered from the fat under the skin and surrounding the loin of the hog. It was first called leaf lard because it peeled off the carcass in what looked like leaves of fat. If you live in an area where hogs are raised, you may be able to acquire some pork fat and render fresh lard for your own use. In so doing, you will have the bonus of cracklings which can be added to your biscuits and corn bread, or used to make Crackling Flat Bread (see Index). I get my pork fat from the local meat locker, where they butcher the hogs raised in my home community.

❋ To Render Fresh Leaf Lard

Obtain pork fat from your local butcher or farmer. Cut the fat into small dice and place in a shallow roasting pan or Pyrex dish. Put the pan in a 250°F oven and cook, allowing the fat to slowly melt. From time to time, tilt the pan and spoon off any rendered drippings to remove them. Pour rendered fat through a fine strainer into a jar suitable for storage. Continue in this manner until only the cracklings remain. When you have removed all of the drippings, raise the temperature of the oven to 350°F to further crisp and brown the cracklings. Any drippings that may occur at this stage should be stored in a separate jar for use in frying chicken. Store the leaf lard in the refrigerator. Use the cracklings in corn breads or yeast doughs.

Shortening has a precreamed texture, making it an easy fat to use in any type of breadmaking. It will lend itself to the flakiness of pastries and can easily be creamed for inclusion in a cakelike bread.

When a fat such as shortening, lard, or butter is creamed with sugar, the sharp edge of the sugar crystals cut into it, creating tiny pockets of air and adding to the leavening of the loaf. Oil, on the other hand, will more easily penetrate a flour mixture, causing a softer batter to form. Quick breads made with oil will never have the lightness of those cooked with a creamed solid fat.

To grease baking pans, shortening, butter, and oil are most commonly used. I prefer shortening because it is so easy to use and because I do not object to the flavor of baked goods produced with its coating. Butter can be employed for a similar crusting with the richness of flavor that only butter can give. Lard is also suitable for the task, though rarely used in modern kitchens, for the reasons mentioned before. I prefer not to use oil. I don't care for the way it seeps into whatever dough or batter one is baking.

Eggs

Eggs add color and nutritional richness to bread doughs. They help both quick and yeast doughs to rise. Too many eggs, however, can cause a loaf of bread to dry out quickly. When eggs are beaten, they incorporate air which helps leaven dough. Egg whites are particularly suitable for this. A bread can be leavened by egg whites alone if they are beaten until stiff and folded into the batter right before baking. Four to five large eggs can displace one cup of liquid in a bread recipe. Large eggs were used to test these recipes.

Bread Improvers

There are several *bread improvers* that can help the home baker improve or accelerate yeast action. Do not try to use them all in one recipe. If you get a good result, you will want to know which bread improver did it for you. Although some bakers swear by one or the other of these, I seldom use them beyond experimental testing.

When looking through old bread-baker's manuals, you may come across references to *malt*. It may be referred to as barley malt, wheat malt, diastatic malt, malt syrup, malt flour, or malt extract. It is available at some health-food stores and through mail order. When buying commercially produced malt, inquire to find out if your malt is one of the diastatic malts. A diastatic malt is one that has been processed at a low temperature so as not to destroy all the enzymes inherent in the product. These enzymes are what can transform the starch in flour into maltose and dextrin, the fermentation foods for yeast growth.[*]

Wheat malt can be made at home. It is particularly useful in simple

---

[*] *Jane Nordstrom, The Barmy Bread Book (Santa Fe, NM: The Lightning Tree, 1974), p. 14.

country breads. In a complicated loaf, its delicate flavor will be lost. One teaspoonful of homemade wheat malt will improve and flavor the dough for two loaves. When using wheat malt in simple breads, you can eliminate any sugar called for.

❖ Homemade Wheat Malt

To make homemade wheat malt, you will have to sprout some wheat berries, dry them, and grind them into flour.

To sprout: Use a 1-quart jar fitted with a fine mesh lid, or fashion a lid with cheesecloth. Soak overnight in this jar filled with warm water

½ cup wheat berries

Drain soaked berries. Rinse in warm water. Drain again. Turn jar on its side and cover with a clean cloth to keep grain in the dark. Leave a small opening in the cloth to allow for air circulation. Repeat rinsing and draining three times a day for two or three days, until the new shoots are about as long as the kernels of grain.

To dry: Rinse and drain sprouted grain. Dry briefly on paper towels or a clean cloth towel. Spread on a large baking sheet. Dry in an oven set at 150°F for 8 to 10 hours. You will want the kernels to be brittle, but not exceptionally hard.

To grind: Grind dried sprouts in a food processor, blender, flour mill, or electric coffee grinder. Store under refrigeration in a tightly covered container. Keeps indefinitely. Makes about ½ cup Wheat Malt, enough for about 50 loaves of bread.

I first read about the use of *ginger* as a yeast improver in the 1960 edition of Ada Lou Roberts' book, *Favorite Breads from Rose Lane Farm.* Ms. Roberts had reportedly read about its use in one of her very old cookbooks. The recommended amount of ground ginger for this purpose is ⅛ teaspoon for each scant tablespoon of yeast. I use ground ginger on occasion in my yeast breads, although it is more for its old-fashioned charm than for practical reasons.

Ascorbic acid is a known catalyst for a network of yeast growth. It can be used in either a straight or sponge-type dough. It is advised that the baker allocate about 50 milligrams of vitamin C, or ascorbic acid, for a dough that will make three loaves of bread. Simply crush a 50-milligram tablet of vitamin C in your bowl before adding water to soften the yeast.*

Potassium bromate, a popular dough improver in the commercial baking industry, is one of the oxidizing agents that will exert its influence during the dough stage. It will remain dormant until yeast formation lowers the pH of the dough sufficiently to activate it. The home baker will find it premixed in some bread flours, as discussed earlier.

Additions for Variety's Sake

There are so many other things that can be added to your bread doughs that they defy a complete listing. *Herbs,* fresh or dried, and *spices* merit mentioning. Spices are at their best when freshly ground. If you buy them already ground, be sure they are fresh. Store all spices and herbs in airtight containers away from heat and sunlight. Date the containers when you buy them. If they are more than three months old, they probably need to be replaced.

Fruits and *some vegetables* make nice additions. By adding little dabs of this or that to bread, you can efficiently use up leftovers that might otherwise go to waste. *Dried fruits, nuts,* and *seeds* add texture as well as taste to your homemade breads.

Crumbs of bread, biscuits, crackers, or toast can replace up to 1 cup of flour in a 6-cup recipe. *Breakfast cereals,* either dry or cooked, may be added in the same ratio. *Cooked legumes* that can be used in breads include peas, beans, and lentils.

---

*Lloyd Moxon, *The Baking Book* (New York: Delair Publishing, 1981), p. 102.

❋ THE UTENSILS FOR BREADMAKING

Basic Needs

You probably already have the basic utensils needed to make bread. First and foremost you will want a sturdy *earthenware bowl* and a *wooden spoon*. A bowl with a 3- or 4-quart capacity will handle most doughs. I like to reserve my breadmaking wooden spoon only for that purpose. If I use a wooden spoon for stirring things on the stove top, it is a different one.

To prepare foods for inclusion in your dough, you will want a good sharp *knife,* which you can also use to slash your loaves before baking.

Measuring cups for both wet and dry ingredients are essential. For liquids, clear glass or plastic cups with spouts that have the measurements noted on their sides are best. Get the 1-cup, 2-cup, and 4-cup or quart sizes. For dry ingredients, you will want a nested set of exact containers for 1 cup, ½ cup, ⅓ cup, and ¼ cup. A set of *measuring spoons* will take care of smaller additions.

Basic *bread pans* should include one 9×5 inches, one 8½×4½×2½ inches, and one muffin tin with a 12-cup capacity.

Additional Things You May Want to Own

Earthenware bowls in various sizes can gradually be added to your collection. Try to find bowls that have steeply sloping sides to provide lift when the dough is rising. I have a 2-quart one from Sassafras called Batter-up that came packaged with its own wooden-handled stainless-steel whisk. It has become my favorite for one- and two-loaf recipes.

A *kitchen shears* is good for cutting foods, and for slashing and shaping dough.

Rubber spatulas are indispensable for getting out that last bit of batter or dough and can be acquired in a gradation of sizes to fit most needs. A *wire whisk* is helpful for whipping eggs and for mixing a batter or a sponge. *Pastry brushes,* both large and small, are used for glazing loaves.

Stainless-steel graters and *vegetable peelers* make their jobs less tedious. A small tool called a *lemon zester* will remove the peel from any citrus fruit with ease. A straight-edged *dough scraper* can be used to fold dough on a board and to divide or cut it into different shapes. Various *cookie, biscuit,* and *doughnut cutters* can also be put to use in the baker's kitchen.

Although you can use any smooth surface for kneading and the rolling or shaping of dough, you will find a *wooden surface* to be particularly warm and inviting for the task. *Marble* is good for working the doughs that need to stay chilled. Most modern caterers and chefs use polyurethane slabs because they are lightweight and may also be chilled.

Rolling pins are available in both wood and marble. Some bakers use textured ones to make crackers and shortbreads. The best source I know of for such pins is Maid of Scandinavia in Minneapolis.

Bread pans are almost endless in their variety. If you plan to make bread regularly, you will want to collect many of these. My favorite loaf pans are black metal with sloped sides, from Brick Oven of Chicago. They always produce a high-rounded loaf with a good crust. There are also numerous *stonewear* and *terra-cotta clay baking pots* available. The La Cloche from Sassafras is a stonewear pot with a bell-shaped top that forms its own miniature brick oven for baking crusty country loaves. *Granite-wear* (enameled steel) also bakes bread well.

If you have any *cast-iron baking pans* that are family heirlooms, hang onto them. There is nothing better for baking muffins or corn bread. Until quite recently, they were difficult to find new, and cooks who wanted them had to search them out at garage sales or antique shops. They are making a comeback, however, and may now be found in gourmet cookware shops and some department stores. If you buy new ones, be sure to season them by baking them with a coating of shortening before using them for bread. Shortening is better for this chore than oil. To season new cast-iron cookware: Wash with soap (not detergent) and warm water, rinse well, and dry. Coat with shortening. Place in a 250°F oven for 2 hours. Turn oven off. Let pan cool in the oven with the door ajar. Cast iron improves with age. Always wash with only hot water and dry well before storage. Paper towels are useful for drying cast-iron utensils.

Baguette pans make French loaves easy to shape. I recently found some blue steel pans in half-baguette lengths from Williams-Sonoma. These are imported from France, and are excellent for smaller loaves that can easily be gift wrapped.

There are pans that will completely enclose a dough for an evenly crusted loaf. Maid of Scandinavia lists several *nut-bread pans* that do this. They also have a *pullman loaf pan* which makes a perfectly shaped sandwich bread. The pain de mie *hinged round bread pan* from Cuisinarts, Inc., makes a nice round loaf in a size perfect for slicing into rounds for melba toast.

Bannetons are spiral-shaped baskets that can be used to form beehive-shaped loaves. The dough is allowed to rise in the basket, which has been coated with flour. It is then turned out onto a baking sheet to be cooked. Baskets with a more open weave may also be used if first lined with cloth.

Other specialty pans include *kugelhopf* or *bundt pans, brioche molds,* and *pizza pans.* You can also vary your bread shapes by forming them in *short-bread molds* or by baking them in small *madeleine pans.*

You can bake directly on *baking stones* or *quarry tiles* without using pans at all. Metal and wood *cooling racks* come in several sizes. The wood ones can double as attractive wall decorations in a country-styled kitchen. *Small grinders* are ideal for spices. Some *electric choppers* resembling miniature food processors do an efficient job with parsley and other herbs.

Last, but not least, to cut your bread, you will want to have a *serrated knife,* preferably high-carbon stainless steel. A scalloped design is better than one with fine serrations. If you wash your knife by hand, it will last a lifetime. In fact, I wash all my bread-baking equipment by hand, because I know that it improves with age, and that a dishwasher obliterates any aging it may have acquired.

Ovens

Though not really thought of as utensils, ovens are integral to the bread-baking process. A *conventional oven* works fine for bread baking. All the recipes in this book were tested in a conventional oven. Lucky is the bread baker who has double ovens. These enable you to bake more loaves at once, or to bake bread in one oven while baking something else in the other.

A *convection oven* has been touted as being exceptionally suited to bread baking. I have made many excellent loaves in a convection oven, but I cannot say they were superior to those baked in the conventional type. The convection oven also has a tendency to deflate even a slightly overrisen loaf, because there is a fan going constantly. This is not an insurmountable problem. If you have only a convection oven in which to bake, and if your bread is slightly overrisen, knead it down and allow it to rise again before baking. Most convection oven manufacturers suggest that breads be baked at a slightly lower temperature (about 25° less) than that used in a conventional range.

I have baked bread in a *microwave oven* and I wouldn't give you two cents for it. Microwave power will cook a bread, but it will not brown it. Indeed, it does little toward the development of a decent crust. Microwave manuals are replete with suggestions for toppings to cover up this problem. Forget it. Use your microwave for something else and free your conventional range for bread baking.

Grain Mills

Grain mills are not essential to breadmaking and most bakers prefer to buy their grain already ground into flour. You may grow your own grain, or live in an area where you can easily buy it directly from the farmer or elevator. Or you may simply prefer to buy your grain whole, and grind what you need when you need it. A good source book for information about some of the home grain mills available is *Home Food Systems,* by the editors of Rodale Press, 1981, Emmaus, PA. You would be wise to study such a book before investing in a mill of your own.

I find the grain-grinding attachment of my Kitchenaid mixer to have sufficient capacity for what little grinding I do. The Kitchenaid attachment will grind about 10 cups at a time into either a fine- to medium-textured flour or a coarse meal.

✿ THE METHODS OF MAKING BREAD

In order to understand what happens when we make bread, we need to explore the differences between a quick bread and a yeast bread. A *quick bread,* leavened with baking powder or baking soda, is quickly and gently mixed, and the gasses are instantly formed for its rising. Gluten should not be developed, since it can make the loaf tough. This is why some bakers will allow a quick-bread batter to stand in a pan for five minutes before baking; they will leave a pancake batter in the refrigerator overnight; rest a pastry between rollings of the dough, or a refrigerated fritter batter for an hour before frying. In all of these instances, resting the batter allows any gluten that may have developed to relax.

In a *yeast bread,* however, gluten is essential to the slow development of the dough. As yeast metabolizes, producing carbon dioxide, it feeds on the sugars in dough and those produced by the action of enzymes on the starch granules of the flour.

Gluten is the product of the interaction of two proteins found in flour. These proteins are glutenin and gliadin. They consist of long, straggly molecules. In the presence of water, and when agitated by mixing or kneading, these proteins will unfold and then intertwine into a tangled mass. There is both a physical and a chemical action that takes place. This bonding or crosslinking forms a glutenous network that holds the gas produced by the metabolism of the yeast.[*]

A yeast dough that is allowed to rise only once will have a few large pockets of gas. When the dough is reworked, the network is redefined so that the texture of the bread becomes less coarse with smaller, more numerous gas pockets.

Your glutenous yeast dough will have both a *plasticity* and an *elasticity.* The plasticity will allow you to stretch the dough by pressing on it with your hands or a rolling pin. The elasticity will cause it to spring back to its original shape as soon as you let go. If a dough becomes too springy to shape as desired, it can be covered and allowed to rest, thereby relaxing the developed gluten.

As you work your dough by *kneading* in an orderly fashion, the molecules become aligned in more or less the same direction. You will gradually develop a dough that is stiff, somewhat harder to manipulate, and with a smooth, satiny appearance. This is the point at which you will want to stop kneading. It is possible to overwork the dough, usually by processing it for too long a period in a food processor. It is unlikely that you will ever have the perserverance to knead a dough too long by hand. If it happens, the disulfide bonds deteriorate and the resulting bread will be flat.[†]

---

[*]Harold McGee, *On Food and Cooking: The Science and Lore of the Kitchen* (New York: Scribner's, 1984), pp. 293–94.
[†]McGee, pp. 296–97.

An important consideration in the development of a yeast dough is the growth of the *yeast* itself. Yeast must be rehydrated or softened in liquid before it can begin its growth. This is accomplished in warm water. For compressed or cake yeast, a temperature of 95°F is best; for dried yeast, 105°F. If the temperature of the water is too low, the yeast will not activate. If it is too high, the yeast will be killed. With experience you will be able to approximate the correct temperature by testing it with your hands. If you are unsure, you may use a thermometer for that purpose. After rehydration, the yeast is mixed with the remaining ingredients for the particular recipe you are using.

Given a good environment and proper food, yeast will multiply rapidly. This brings us to a consideration of both the sponge and the straight-dough methods for making bread. Most modern bread recipes advocate the *straight-dough method.* When it is used, one-half of the flour is added to the softened yeast along with the other ingredients called for. This is beaten well to develop the gluten. Then the remaining flour is gradually added to make a stiff dough.

With the *sponge method,* one-half of the flour is added to the softened yeast and beaten. The resulting sponge is covered and allowed to rise for a minimum of one hour to encourage development of the yeast before the sugars, fats, salts, or other ingredients are allowed to complicate the process. You may, if you wish, change almost any straight dough recipe to a sponge dough. A sponge dough may require less yeast, as it is allowed time to grow some of its own. It lets you develop some of the old-fashioned flavor missing from many of the more modern breads that are baked today.

With both methods, the second half of the flour is gradually added to make a somewhat stiff dough. This dough is then kneaded to further develop its texture. After kneading, it is allowed to rise one, two, or three times. The ideal temperature for this rising is between 70°F and 80°F. Many bakers recommend higher temperatures than this. I prefer the results of the cooler rising period, which is also slower. The slower the dough, the better the bread.

Each successive rising will take less time. You will want the dough to double or nearly double each time it rises. The novice baker often finds it difficult to determine when this has occurred. Poke two fingers into the risen dough. If risen enough, the depressions will remain when the fingers are withdrawn. If the dough has overrisen, it may fall. The maximum number of risings for a yeast dough is four or five, after which time the yeast will tire from lack of fresh food. The optimum number of risings is two or three. This gives the dough time to develop a full flavor while the yeast is still in the prime of its life.

After the last rising, the bread is baked. You will want to preheat your oven before baking. If you forget to do so, however, it is better to put the bread in and start the oven, rather than let the dough overrise. Baking in an oven that is not preheated may take slightly longer than baking in one that is already warm.

When first introduced to the warm oven, the yeast in the dough will have its last fling at rapid growth before being killed by the heat. The gasses trapped in the bread will expand as the starch sets to define the final shape. This last burst or rise is called *oven spring*.

Most breads are baked at a constant temperature. A *slackening oven* can be used, however, to approximate the old-fashioned baking process. In an old wood-fired range, the baking cavern was heated until ready for the loaves. Its readiness could be tested by tossing a small handful of flour onto the oven floor. The experienced baker knew just how long it would take to brown this flour. After the loaves were added, the oven was allowed to gradually cool, or slacken. The modern baker can practice the same technique with the advantage of precise thermostatic controls by reducing oven temperature during the overall baking time. The slackening oven can turn out marvelous bread with a superior crust.

When the bread has baked sufficiently, the crust will have browned and the loaf will have a hollow sound when tapped on the bottom. At this point, the outside of the loaf is drier than the interior. As the bread cools, the moisture slowly travels to the outside, equalizing this difference. The cooling loaf should be placed on a rack to elevate it and allow air to circulate around it so that no moisture can collect on its surface.

When completely cooled, the bread may be wrapped for storage. For the short term, it is best stored at room temperature in a tightly closed plastic sack. Otherwise, it should be wrapped tightly in aluminum foil, wrapped again in plastic, and frozen. Bread does not keep well in the refrigerator; refrigeration slows the development of mold, but it does not prevent staling. Any bread that contains meat, however, must be refrigerated to prevent spoilage.

To put all this information into practice, I have devised something called the Learning Loaf. It should be helpful to the beginning baker. ·

❉ The Learning Loaf

Here is an easy-to-handle one-loaf bread recipe that can be used for a learning experience. If you are timorous about trying your hand with yeast, try this recipe first. The small amount of dough is very easy to knead and should give you the confidence for later projects.

In a small, heavy saucepan, heat until scalded

1 cup milk

The milk is scalded when small bubbles begin to form on the sides of the pan. Combine in a mixing bowl, stonewear preferred

the scalded milk
2 tablespoons butter
2 tablespoons sugar
1 teaspoon salt

Stir to dissolve butter and sugar. Let cool until just warm. Meanwhile, place in a small container, such as a 1-cup liquid measuring cup

¼ cup warm water

The water should feel neither hot nor cold. Go ahead and stick your finger in to see how hot it is. (We know you washed your hands before you started.) Sprinkle into the water

1 teaspoon sugar
1 scant tablespoon (or 1 packet) active dry yeast

Stir the mixture to soften yeast and dissolve sugar, and let it stand for a while. This is called proofing the yeast. The yeast mixture should begin to grow, slowly rising in the cup. When the milk mixture has cooled down to warm (remember your finger thermometer?), stir in

softened yeast mixture
1 egg yolk
2 cups unbleached all-purpose flour or bread flour

Beat well, as this will develop the gluten in the dough. After you have beaten it awhile, beat it some more. Then stir in another

½ cup unbleached all-purpose flour or bread flour

Beat well. Stir in, ¼ cup at a time, another

¾ cup unbleached all-purpose flour or bread flour

Be sure to scrape the sides of the bowl, and stir in thoroughly with each ¼ cup addition. Always stir well before adding any new flour. If dough has enough flour incorporated, it will begin to pull away from the sides of the bowl. If not, it is too sticky. *If it is too sticky, add to dough

1 tablespoon unbleached all-purpose flour or bread flour

Again, be sure to scrape the sides of the bowl. Repeat from * as many times as necessary until the dough begins to pull away from the sides of the bowl. Make an 8-inch circle of flour on a bread board with

¼ cup unbleached all-purpose flour or bread flour

Turn the dough out onto the center of this. Rub a little flour between your hands and knead until the dough becomes smooth and begins to spring back when you let it go. To knead: Lift the back third of the dough and fold it over the remaining dough. Press this down with the heels of your floured hands. Turn the dough one-quarter turn. Lift the back third of the dough again and fold it over the remaining dough. Press this dough down also. Notice that you were not told to put any flour on top of your dough as you worked. You only want to be sure that the surface under the dough remains floured. If you put flour directly onto the dough's surface by sprinkling, you could force the dough to take in too much flour, resulting in a tough loaf of bread. When you are through kneading, the ball of dough should be as smooth as a baby's bottom.

Now wash the bowl in which you mixed the dough. With warm water, warm the bowl thoroughly. Dry completely, then grease liberally with shortening. Place the ball of dough into the bowl and press it into the grease. Turn the dough over so that the greased bottom is now on the top. Pull the sides under slightly until the ball rounds up again. Cover the top of the bowl with a slightly dampened cloth or with plastic wrap. This will keep the surface of the dough soft as it rises. Place the bowl on a counter away from any drafts. Let dough rise in the bowl for about 45 minutes. It should double in bulk during this time. If not, let it rise a little longer.

Remove the cloth or plastic wrap and knead the dough down in the bowl. To do this, plunge one fist into the center of the dough. Then use a gentler version of the kneading action to force the large bubbles of trapped air out of the dough. Take up the ball of dough and form it into a smooth, round shape in your hands. Using only enough flour on your bread board to prevent sticking, press the dough out with your hands or a rolling pin to a 6×9-inch rectangle. Brush off any flour that may have gotten onto the surface of the dough. Roll the dough up tightly, starting with the 6-inch side. Place the resulting loaf in a well-greased 9×5-inch baking pan, with the seam of the loaf facing down. Cover again and allow to rise for 30 to 45 minutes, or until the dough has risen to the top of the pan. Mix together

> *1 egg white*
> *1 teaspoon water*

Brush a layer of this mixture onto the top of the risen loaf. This will produce a nice glaze which will make your baked loaf most attractive. Save any leftover egg glaze in a small covered container in the refrigerator. It will keep for several days. Use it for glazing other breads, or incorporate it into scrambled eggs. Using a sharp knife, cut a slash down the center of the loaf. Be gentle, as you do not want to deflate the risen loaf. Place the loaf in a cold oven and set it to bake at 375°F. Bake for 35 to 40 minutes. Remove from oven. Put an oven glove over your hand. Turn the loaf out of the pan onto this hand, so that the top of the loaf is down. Tap the bottom of the loaf. It should sound hollow. If the bottom of the loaf is white, the loaf is not completely done, and should be put back in its pan and returned to the oven to bake 5 minutes longer. When fully baked, turn out onto a wire or wood rack to cool. Cool completely before wrapping to store. If you want to eat some of the bread while it is still warm from the oven, wait until you can handle it without protection. Otherwise, it will not be firm enough to slice. Makes 1 loaf.

Although bread dough is easily mixed in an earthenware bowl with a wooden spoon, it can also be made with an electric mixer or a food processor. Here is some helpful information for using these machines.

Electric-Mixer Breads

An electric mixer may be used to mix the dough for any conventional yeast bread up to the point where about half of the flour has been incorporated into the other ingredients. Then the bowl must be removed from the mixer and the remainder of the flour stirred in with a wooden spoon.

There is a second method, which I call the fast-mix method. Here, one-half of the flour is mixed with the other dry ingredients, including the active dry yeast. The liquid ingredients, including any solid shortening that may be used, are heated until quite warm. They then are added to the dry ingredients in the electric mixer and everything is beaten until smooth. Again, the remaining portion of flour is best incorporated by hand. If you wish, you may also apply the fast-mix method of adding ingredients to wooden-spoon mixing.

Here are three recipes for yeast bread that make use of an electric mixer. They were developed using a Sunbeam Mixmaster that is at least ten years old, but should work well with any standard mixer.

✶ Mixer White Bread

To soften yeast, in a small container combine

> ¼ cup warm water
> 1 scant tablespoon (or 1 packet) active dry yeast

In a saucepan, heat until milk is warm and shortening is almost melted

> 2 cups milk
> 2 tablespoons shortening
> 2 tablespoons sugar
> 2 teaspoons salt

Place heated ingredients in large bowl of mixer. Add to heated ingredients

> 2 cups unbleached all-purpose flour or bread flour

Beat on low speed until smooth. Add

> softened yeast mixture
> 1 cup unbleached all-purpose flour or bread flour

Beat until smooth on low speed. Then beat for 3 minutes on medium speed. Remove from mixer stand. To make a stiff dough, stir in with a wooden spoon

> 2 ¾ to 3 ¼ cups unbleached all-purpose flour or bread flour

Turn out on a floured surface and knead until smooth and elastic. Place in a greased bowl, turning dough once to grease the top. Cover and let rise until doubled in bulk, 1 to 1½ hours. Knead dough down in bowl and divide in half. Shape into loaves and place in well-greased 9×5-inch baking pans. Cover and let rise until almost doubled, 45 to 60 minutes. Before baking, brush tops of loaves with milk. With a sharp knife, cut a slash down the center of each loaf. Bake at 375°F for 35 to 40 minutes. Turn out on racks to cool. Makes 2 loaves.

❖ Fast-Mix White Bread

To soften yeast, in large mixer bowl combine

> 2 ½ cups unbleached all-purpose flour or bread flour
> 1 scant tablespoon (or 1 packet) active dry yeast
> 2 tablespoons sugar
> 2 teaspoons salt

In a large saucepan, heat until milk is warm (about 115°F) and butter is almost melted

> 2 ¼ cups milk
> 1 tablespoon butter, cut into 3 pieces

Add heated ingredients to mixer bowl and beat at low speed until smooth. Then beat at medium speed for 3 minutes. Remove bowl from mixer stand. To make a stiff dough, gradually stir in with a wooden spoon

> 3 to 3 ½ cups unbleached all-purpose flour or bread flour

Turn out on a floured surface and knead until smooth and elastic. Place in a well-greased bowl, turning dough once to grease the top. Cover and let rise until doubled in bulk, 1 to 1½ hours. Knead dough down in bowl and divide in half. Shape each half into a ball. Place in well-greased round pans. Cover and let rise until almost doubled in bulk, 45 to 60 minutes. Before baking, brush tops of loaves with melted butter. With a sharp knife, cut two slashes in the top of each loaf. Bake at 375°F for 35 to 40 minutes. Turn out on racks to cool. Makes 2 loaves.

❖ Mixer French Bread

To soften yeast, in large mixer bowl combine

> *1 ¼ cups warm water*
> *1 teaspoon sugar*
> *1 scant tablespoon (or 1 packet) active dry yeast*

Let stand for 1 full minute. Add

> *1 teaspoon salt*
> *1 teaspoon oil*
> *1 cup unbleached all-purpose flour or bread flour*

Beat at low speed until smooth. Add

> *½ cup unbleached all-purpose flour or bread flour*

Beat at low speed until smooth. Then beat at medium speed for 3 minutes. Remove bowl from mixer stand. To make a soft dough, gradually stir in with a wooden spoon

> *1 to 1 ½ cups unbleached all-purpose flour or bread flour*

Turn out on a floured surface and knead until smooth and elastic. Place in a well-greased bowl, turning dough once to grease the top. Cover and let rise until doubled in bulk, 45 to 60 minutes. Knead dough down in bowl. Divide dough into four parts. Shape each part into a long loaf and place in well-greased half-baguette pans or on a well-greased baking sheet. Cover and let rise until almost doubled in bulk, 30 to 45 minutes. Brush tops of loaves with a mixture or

> *1 egg*
> *1 teaspoon water*

Slash tops of loaves at an angle in several places down the loaf. Bake at 400°F for 30 to 35 minutes. Turn out on racks to cool. Makes 4 loaves.

There are no special recipes for quick breads made in an electric mixer. One should take care not to overmix these doughs.

Some heavy-duty mixers come equipped with a dough hook for mixing and kneading yeast doughs. One such brand known to bakers is the

Kitchenaid. The recipes given next were developed using a Kitchenaid, model K45SS.

With a dough hook at your command, you will be able to mix in all of the flour needed for a yeast batter or dough. There is little danger of overmixing or overkneading with a dough hook, and the texture of the bread produced is comparable to that of one kneaded by hand. A dough hook can be a boon to a baker with arthritis or other physical problems that make mixing and kneading by hand difficult.

❖ Basic Dough-Hook White Bread

Here is an easy recipe showing how simple it is to use a machine equipped with a dough hook.

To soften yeast, in the bowl of mixer combine

2 cups warm water
3 tablespoons sugar
1 scant tablespoon (or 1 packet) active dry yeast

Allow yeast to proof. Add to softened yeast mixture

2 teaspoons salt
3 tablespoons oil
4 ½ cups unbleached all-purpose flour

Attach bowl to mixer fitted with dough hook. Mix on low speed (speed 2 on Kitchenaid) until well blended, about 2 minutes. Stop machine and scrape down sides of bowl. Add

½ cup unbleached all-purpose flour

Mix at low speed until all flour is incorporated. With machine running add, ¼ cup at a time, enough flour for dough to cling to hook and clean sides of bowl

½ to 1 cup unbleached all-purpose flour

Continue running machine at this low speed until dough is smooth and elastic, 5 to 7 minutes. The dough may be slightly sticky to the touch. Transfer to a well-greased bowl, turning dough once to grease the top. Cover and let rise until doubled in bulk, 1 to 1½ hours. Punch dough down. Divide dough in half. Shape into loaves and place in well-greased 9×5-inch baking pans. Cover and let rise until almost doubled, about 1 hour. Bake in a preheated 400°F oven for 30 to 35 minutes. Turn out on racks to cool. Makes 2 loaves.

✖ Stacked Cinnamon Loaf

This cinnamon bread uses a novel shaping to stack the layers of butter and cinnamon sugar that give it its popular taste.

Place in mixer bowl

> *3 ½ cups unbleached all-purpose flour*
> *¼ cup sugar*
> *1 ½ teaspoons salt*
> *2 scant tablespoons (or 2 packets) active dry yeast*

Attach bowl to mixer fitted with the dough hook. Mix on low speed (speed 2 on Kitchenaid) until blended, about 1 minute. In a heavy saucepan, heat until liquids are hot (about 120°F) and butter begins to melt

> *1 cup milk*
> *½ cup water*
> *¼ cup butter, cut into 4 pieces*

Add hot liquids to the dry ingredients. Mix for 2 minutes. Stop machine and scrape down sides of bowl. Mix on low speed for an additional 2 minutes. With machine running add, ¼ cup at a time, enough flour for dough to cling to dough hook and clean sides of bowl

> *½ to 1 cup unbleached all-purpose flour*

Mix well after each addition. Continue to knead dough on low speed until smooth and elastic, 5 to 7 minutes. Transfer dough to a well-greased bowl, turning dough once to grease the top. Cover and let rise 30 minutes. Turn dough out on a lightly floured surface and toss until no longer sticky. Divide dough in half. *Roll one-half of dough into a 12-inch square. Brush top of dough with

> *1 tablespoon melted butter*

Sprinkle with a mixture of

¼ cup sugar
½ teaspoon cinnamon

Fold dough in from the sides to meet in the center. Fold dough in from the top and the bottom to meet in the center. Fold the package of dough in half and place on a buttered baking sheet. Repeat from * with second half of dough. Cover and let rise until doubled in bulk, about 1 hour. With a sharp knife, cut a long slash in the top of each loaf. Bake in a preheated 375°F oven for 30 to 35 minutes, or until lightly browned. Cool on wire racks. If desired, when slightly cooled, drizzle tops of loaves with

Vanilla Glaze

Makes 2 loaves.

Vanilla Glaze

Stir together until smooth

½ cup sifted confectioner's sugar
¼ teaspoon vanilla
1 tablespoon boiling water

Food-Processor Breads

Yeast bread can be made very quickly in a food processor. While there are several methods that can be used, the most foolproof is to start with the dry ingredients and work toward the wet. All of the dry ingredients, except the yeast, are placed in the workbowl fitted with the metal blade. The machine is pulsed on/off, or run for a brief period of time, to mix these ingredients thoroughly. Then the wet ingredients are added quickly while the machine is running. The processor will mix and knead the dough in less than a minute. The dough can then be allowed to rise in a greased bowl in the usual manner.

There are two major things to guard against when making processor yeast breads. Because of the powerful motor, it is possible to make a ball of dough that has too much flour in relation to liquid. This will result in a tough loaf of bread. Some bakers prefer to reserve a small amount of flour and then knead this in by hand on the traditional floured board. That way they can get the feel of the dough.

Again, because of the powerful motor, it is possible to heat the dough while mixing, thereby limiting the power of the yeast. To avoid this, you can dissolve the yeast in a small amount of warm water, add this to the flour mixture, and then pour in the remainder of the liquid, which should be cool.

Conversely, if your food processor does not have a powerful motor, it may not handle bread doughs at all. Check your manufacturer's instructions.

Most food processors handle only enough dough for one 9×5-inch loaf. However, some of the larger models can hold two or three times that amount. Large amounts of dough are mixed with a plastic dough blade. Most bakers I talk to prefer to use the metal blade, and so make just one loaf at a time.

If your food-processor yeast dough seems to have too much flour in it, you may do this: Tear the dough into small pieces. Return the pieces of dough to the workbowl. Add a small amount of liquid. Process just until dough is again a ball. Check. Repeat until dough consistency is correct. If it appears to be too wet, you can add a spoonful of flour at a time, reprocessing after each addition.

Because of the capabilities of the machine, a food processor can make unique breads. Fresh ginger root can be grated or ground for a novel gingerbread. A peanut-butter bread could begin with the peanuts themselves. Use your imagination to produce something unusual.

Below are several recipes I developed while demonstrating how to make bread in the food processor. I used model DLC-X from Cuisinarts, Inc.

❖ Herb-Flavored Cheese Bread

This bread was developed for a demonstration featuring cheese breads and hearty winter soups.

Fit the food processor with the shredding disc. Shred into the workbowl

4 ounces extra-sharp cheddar cheese, such as Kraft's Cracker Barrel

Change to the metal blade. Add to the workbowl

3 cups unbleached all-purpose flour or bread flour
1 teaspoon herb salt
1 tablespoon sugar

Pulse on/off to mix dry ingredients. To soften yeast, in a small container combine

¼ cup warm water
1 scant tablespoon (or 1 packet) active dry yeast

Add to workbowl

softened yeast mixture
1 tablespoon oil
1 egg

With machine running, through the feed tube add

¾ cup cold water

Process until a ball of dough forms on the blade. If necessary, add more flour and process again. Or add more water, if necessary, and process again. Process for 10 seconds longer to knead the dough. Turn into a greased or an oiled bowl, turning dough once to grease the top. Cover and let rise until doubled in bulk, 45 to 60 minutes. Knead dough down in bowl. Shape into an oblong loaf and place in a well-greased 9×5-inch baking pan. Cover and let rise until almost doubled in bulk, 30 to 45 minutes. Bake at 375°F for 35 to 40 minutes. Turn out on a rack to cool. Makes 1 loaf.

✳ Whole-Grain French Bread

During my training to become a consumer advisor for Cuisinarts, Inc., my district advisor told me that Abby Mandel and Carl Sontheimer had successfully experimented with grinding grain in a food processor. They discovered that an overnight soak would soften the grain so that it could be ground easily. Dry, unsoaked grain has a tendency to bounce around in the workbowl, preventing its transformation into flour.

Fit workbowl with the metal blade. Place in workbowl

2 ¼ cups unbleached all-purpose flour or bread flour
1 cup grain, such as wheat, that has been soaked and drained (measured before
soaking)

Process until grain is finely ground. This may take several minutes. If you like crunchy bread, stop processing before the grind is fine. It may turn out to be crunchier than it appears at this stage. Add to workbowl

1 teaspoon salt
1 teaspoon sugar

Pulse on/off to mix well. To soften yeast, in a small container combine

½ cup warm water
1 scant tablespoon (or 1 packet) active dry yeast

Add to workbowl

softened yeast mixture
1 teaspoon oil

With machine running, add through feed tube

½ cup cold water

Process until a ball of dough forms on the blade. Add more flour if necessary and process again. Or, if necessary, add more liquid and process again. Process for an additional 10 seconds. Turn into a greased or an oiled bowl, turning dough once to grease the top. Cover and let rise until doubled in bulk, 45 to 60 minutes. Knead dough down in bowl and divide in half. Shape each half into a long loaf and place in well-greased baguette pans. Cover and let rise until almost doubled in bulk, 30 to 45 minutes. Cut several slashes at an angle in the tops of the loaves. Bake at 400°F for 30 to 35 minutes. Turn out on racks to cool. Makes 2 loaves.

To Soak Grain

Using three parts water to one part grain, cover grain with hot water. Let stand for about 12 hours. Drain well. One cup dry grain will measure 1¾ to 1⅞ cups after soaking. Refrigerate in a small Ziploc plastic sack. The soaked grain will keep in the refrigerator for about 5 days.

❖ Fast Food-Processor Yeast Bread

I offer this recipe with some misgivings. It could be called the fastest bread in the West. It hardly has time to develop a personality of its own.

Butter an 8½×4½×2½-inch baking pan. Place in the workbowl fitted with the metal blade

2 ⅔ *cups unbleached all-purpose flour or bread flour*
1 teaspoon salt
1 tablespoon sugar
1 tablespoon butter

Process just until butter is incorporated and seems to disappear. To soften yeast, in a measuring cup with a pouring spout combine

1 cup lukewarm water
1 package fast-rising yeast

With the machine running, pour softened yeast mixture through the feed tube as fast as the flour will take it up to form a ball of dough. Continue processing for 5 seconds. Remove dough from processor bowl. With buttered hands shape into an oblong loaf and place in prepared pan. Set the pan on a wire rack over a bowl of warm water. Cover the whole thing with a towel and let rise for 20 to 25 minutes. Meanwhile, preheat oven to 375°F. When bread has risen, bake in preheated oven for 35 to 40 minutes. Turn out on a rack to cool. Makes 1 loaf.

Quick breads can also be mixed in the food processor. The same general rule applies. Work from dry to wet. If you are using a solid shortening, the shortening can be cut into the dry ingredients after they are mixed. Then the liquid ingredients can be added all at once. Pulse on/off to mix. If you are using eggs, it is simpler to whisk them and other liquid ingredients in a side bowl before adding them to the dry. If you wish, you may add the eggs with the other liquid ingredients and process just until all dry ingredients are moistened. With this method, however, you risk overmixing.

Here is a typical recipe for a food-processor quick bread.

❖ Processor Bran Bread

• Fit food processor with the metal blade. Place in the workbowl

> *1 cup unbleached all-purpose flour*
> *1 ½ cups Kellogg's All-Bran cereal*
> *¼ cup brown sugar*
> *½ teaspoon salt*
> *1 teaspoon baking soda*

Process until All-Bran cereal is coarsely ground. In a side bowl, beat

> *1 egg*

Stir into egg

> *¼ cup oil*
> *1 cup buttermilk*

Add liquid ingredients to workbowl. Pulse on/off to mix. Turn into well-greased 8×8-inch baking pan. Bake in preheated 350°F oven for 35 to 40 minutes, or until a wooden pick inserted in the center comes out clean. Serve warm. Makes 9 servings.

❖ THE SECRETS OF PERFECT BREADS

Here, for your quick reference, are all the little secrets to help you make perfect breads every time.

For Every Kind of Bread

1. Always have your ingredients assembled and at room temperature before beginning any baking. Cold eggs can cause a problem with some recipes. If you forget to remove your eggs from the refrigerator ahead of time, they can be warmed in a small bowl of lukewarm water for 5 to 10 minutes before use.

2. For measuring liquid ingredients, use cups that have their gradations printed on the side. Sight the level you want by bringing your eyes flush with that point. If you sight the level from either above or below, you may be measuring more or less than you desire.

3. For measuring dry ingredients, use cups that contain exactly the amount you are measuring with a flush rim for leveling off. For all dry ingredients except brown sugar, simply spoon into the measuring cup until overflowing. Level the material by moving a straight-edged table knife across the top of the container. Brown sugar should be packed into the measuring cup before leveling off at the top.

4. When using salt, spices, and chemical leavenings in your breads, it is always better to sift them together. This will ensure an even distribution of these materials.

Taking the Mystery Out of Yeast Breads

1. The recipes in this book use active dry yeast. Cake yeast may be substituted, if you wish. One ⅗-ounce cake of yeast is interchangeable with one packet, or scant tablespoon, of active dry yeast. The yeast should be softened in a warm liquid, such as water, at about 105°F. If you are unsure of the temperature, use a thermometer. You will soon learn to judge by feel alone. Too cool a temperature will retard yeast growth. Indeed, if cold, it may prevent its starting at all. Too hot a temperature will kill it and stop its action.

2. Proofing your yeast means letting it grow only until you are convinced it is indeed alive. Sugar or flour must be added before it will foam, but it will change character when combined only with a warm liquid. If you want to see a definite change, add a pinch of sugar to the proofing yeast, even if the recipe does not call for it. After it is softened, it should begin action within 3 to 5 minutes. If not, discard it and start over. You will find active dry yeast to be very reliable.

3. Batter should be beaten vigorously when the softened yeast has been combined with the liquid and the first half of the flour. If beating by hand, use a wooden spoon, tilt your bowl slightly, and beat with a rotary motion.

4. The second half of the flour should be stirred in, about ½ cup at a time. The total amount needed will vary from kitchen to kitchen and from day to day. Some flours simply absorb more liquid than others. When your dough is becoming stiff and beginning to clean the sides of the bowl, turn it out to knead.

5. At the beginning of the kneading process, the dough is sticky. Be sure the surface is well floured. You may wish to coat your hands with flour and toss the dough over and over on the floured surface until no longer sticky.

6. In kneading, you will incorporate some additional flour, but do not try to mix in large quantities of flour at this time. It will only result in a poorly mixed dough and a tough loaf of bread. For a good description of the kneading process, see the Learning Loaf, page 34.

7. Place the kneaded dough in a well-greased bowl. Press the dough into the grease. Turn the dough over so the greased part is at the top. Pull the sides of the dough down to round the greased top.

8. Cover the dough with a slightly moistened clean cloth or plastic wrap and let rise in a warm, draft-free place for the desired time. If you have a drafty kitchen, you will have to improvise. Your dough may be placed in an unlit oven to rise, provided that a pilot light does not make the oven too warm. Remember that too high a temperature will kill your yeast. The ideal temperature range is 70 to 80°F. If your kitchen is cold and your oven has no pilot light, place a pan of hot water in the bottom of the oven. If enough humidity forms in this enclosed space, you will not have to cover the dough while it rises. The dough should double in bulk during the first rising.

9. At the end of the first rising period, punch down the dough. Make a fist and plunge it into the center of the dough. Repeat the plunging process around the edges of the dough.

10. To shape a ball of dough for a round loaf, pull down the sides of the dough as you rotate the emerging ball. Tuck the sides under as you place it in the pan. To shape an oblong loaf, pull two sides of the dough down until a loaf shape emerges. Tuck the sides under as you place it in your pan.

11. During the second rising, the dough should almost double in bulk, but not get larger than that or it may collapse in baking. If you think your dough has gotten too large, punch it down, reshape, and allow it to rise a third time. Your bread will not suffer.

12. At the end of the baking time, test for doneness. Turn the loaf out onto a protected hand. The bottom crust should be evenly golden. Tap the bottom of the loaf—a hollow sound signals it is done. If not, return it to the pan and bake a few minutes longer.

13. Turn the baked loaves out on wire racks to cool. Avoid drafts while cooling. After loaves are cooled completely, seal tightly in plastic bags.

14. To freeze extra loaves: Wrap tightly in foil. Seal foil-wrapped loaves tightly in plastic bags. When ready to use, allow to return to room temperature before unwrapping. To serve a frozen loaf of bread as a hot, freshly baked loaf, heat it unwrapped in a 350°F oven for about 30 minutes. However, bread which has been frozen will dry out more quickly than fresh.

The How-To of Quick Breads

1. As their name implies, quick breads are quick and easy. Requiring no yeast or rising periods before baking, they are leavened by baking powder, baking soda, and beaten eggs. They have a cakelike crumb and their batters take well to the addition of fruits, nuts, and seasonings.

2. Although this is not as critical as with muffins, pancakes, and waffles, it is advisable not to overbeat your quick-bread batter. Gentle blending is all that is needed after the dry ingredients and liquids are combined.

3. A crack down the center is characteristic of quick breads baked in a loaf pan. This can be minimized by pressing down gently on the center of the batter in the pan with a wooden spoon or spatula.

4. Quick breads are done when they pull slightly away from the sides of the pan, and a toothpick inserted in the center comes out clean.

5. Freshly baked quick breads crumble easily. If you make your quick loaves several hours, or even one day ahead, you will find them easier to slice.

6. After baking and cooling, wrap loaf quick breads in foil. They may be stored in the refrigerator or on the kitchen counter.

7. Quick coffeecakes are intended for immediate consumption. They do not keep well past one day. The rule here is to bake and enjoy!

The Secrets of Delicate Muffins

1. Sift dry ingredients separately. Beat liquid ingredients together. Then add the liquid to the dry, or the dry to the liquid, and mix both gently and quickly. There will be some lumps. If your batter is smooth, you have probably beaten too vigorously, and your muffins may turn out tough.

2. Fill greased muffin cups one-half to two-thirds full. Filling above this may cause an overflow during baking.

3. Remove muffins from cups with a fork a few moments after baking. Serve at once. They, too, should be eaten immediately.

Tips for Better Biscuits

1. Always sift the dry ingredients together. This is to insure the even distribution of leavening in your dough.

2. Cut shortening or butter into the dry ingredients with a pastry blender or two table knives. Combine until mixture resembles coarse cornmeal.

3. Add liquid to the mixture all at once and stir with a fork. When mixed adequately, the dough will clean the sides of the bowl. Do not overmix.

4. The dough should be transferred to a lightly floured surface and kneaded gently and quickly. Just a few strokes insures a flaky product.

5. Roll or pat out to the desired thickness. Be gentle.

6. Cut straight down with a biscuit cutter dipped in flour, avoiding any twisting motion.

7. Baking sheets for biscuits need not be greased, unless the recipe so states. Biscuits placed 1 inch apart will be crusty all over. Place them closer together for softer sides.

Pointers for Perfect Pancakes

1. Beat batter just enough to moisten the dry ingredients. It is normal to have lumps in this batter.

2. Preheat the griddle to the proper temperature before use. A griddle

with a thermostat is most helpful. Lacking that, test with a few drops of water. If little beads of water dance around, the heat is perfect.

3. You may want to grease the griddle before baking your first batch of pancakes. It is rarely necessary as you continue to bake. A seasoned griddle should not require greasing at all as long as the batter contains at least 2 tablespoons of fat for every cup of liquid.

4. Pour the batter gently onto the griddle, using ¼ cup of batter per cake. Turn the pancakes when the rim of each cake is full of broken bubbles and the whole top has bubbles, some of which are broken. Turn only once. It should take less time to bake the second side. Serve at once on a warmed plate.

How to Bake the Best Waffles

1. Stir the batter with a few gentle strokes, only long enough to moisten the dry ingredients. Overbeating and overmixing will make your waffles tough.

2. Be sure to preheat the waffle iron. Again, if you have no heat indicator, sprinkle a few drops of water on the heated grids. The water will dance if the iron is ready.

3. A seasoned waffle iron does not require greasing. To season a new iron: Brush grids with oil, close iron, and heat to baking temperature. The first waffle baked will soak up any excess oil.

4. Cover about two-thirds of the surface of the iron with batter. Close the lid and do not peek until all steaming stops. If the iron resists opening, it may indicate the waffle is not quite done. Bake slightly longer and try again.

5. Remove your perfectly baked waffle with a fork and serve on a warmed plate.

⁂ One Baker's Dozen

The author's favorites from a lifetime of baking

French Bakery Baguettes
Best-Ever Bran Muffins
Whole-Wheat Raisin Bread
Fitness-Formula Bread
Fresh Tomato Bread
Strawberry Brunch Bread
San Francisco Sourdough Bread
German Sourbrot
Dusty Potato Bread
Home-Style Hamburger and Hot-Dog Buns
Quick Wheat Coffee Cake
Buttermilk Biscuits
Blueberry Muffins

❋ ONE BAKER'S DOZEN

Since I am continually asked what my favorite bread recipes are, I decided one day to try to list them, using a baker's dozen as the limiting number. It was not an easy task. It reminded me of trying to select one puppy or one kitten from a litter, when all have an enticing allure. But decisions are a part of life, and I managed finally to come up with some. I offer my selections, with an explanation of why they were chosen as the first recipe chapter in this book.

For me, French Bakery Baguettes are a must, because I love having French bread any and all the time. Best-Ever Bran Muffins are one of our most frequently served breakfast foods. Whole-Wheat Raisin Bread makes great breakfast toast. Fitness-Formula Bread is baked for diet days. Fresh Tomato Bread celebrates the garden I love. Strawberry Brunch Bread is absolutely delicious, and we use it often in place of birthday cake for our summer birthdays. San Francisco Sourdough provides superb herb-buttered toast to accompany our grilled meats and fish. German Sourbrot represents my German heritage. Dusty Potato Bread has to be mentioned as a family favorite. Home-style Hamburger and Hot-dog Buns service all the hamburgers, hot dogs, and brats that come from the grill. Quick Wheat Coffeecake has been served at too many family brunches to be left out. Buttermilk Biscuits make the list because of my preference for anything baked with buttermilk. And Blueberry Muffins—well, the whole family loves blueberries, and these muffins are really the very best.

As I look back over these selections, I am struck by the fact that none is particularly fancy or rich. But then neither am I.

❋ French Bakery Baguettes

Everyone wants to make bread that tastes like it came from a good French bakery. Most recipes that try for authenticity advise baking on stone or quarry tiles. The instructions tell you to mist the oven or use a pan of hot water in the bottom of the oven to create steam. This recipe makes an excellent French bread without all the fuss of the stone or the steam. The same basic recipe can be adapted for Italian Bread.

In a large bowl, combine

1 ½ cups unbleached all-purpose flour
1 ½ cups warm water
1 scant tablespoon (or 1 packet) active dry yeast

Beat well. Cover and let this sponge stand for 2 to 3 hours. Stir down sponge. Stir into sponge, in this order

1 cup warm water
2 teaspoons salt
2 cups unbleached all-purpose flour

Beat well. To make a soft dough, gradually add

2 to 3 cups unbleached all-purpose flour

Turn out on a floured surface. Knead gently for a full 10 minutes, dusting the surface with additional flour to prevent sticking. This gentle kneading will develop a skin on the dough. Place in a well-greased bowl, turning dough once to grease the top. Cover and let rise until doubled in bulk, 1 to 1½ hours. Knead dough down in bowl. Cover and let rise until doubled again, about 1 hour. Press dough down in bowl to deflate. Divide dough into four parts in this manner: First press your fingertips into dough to make dividing lines. Then, with your fingers, carefully divide the dough along these lines, keeping the skin of the dough intact. Press or roll each part into a long oval. Starting with a long side, roll up into a long loaf. Keep rolling loaf back and forth until it is 12 inches long. Line four baguette pans with well-floured cloths. Place rolled loaves into cloth-lined pans. Cover loosely with a floured towel and let rise until doubled in size, about 1 hour. One at a time, roll loaves gently onto large baking sheets that have been lightly greased and sprinkled with cornmeal. You should be able to place two loaves on one sheet. Allow ample space between loaves to insure a hard crust all around. Brush tops of loaves with a mixture of

1 egg white
1 teaspoon water

With a kitchen shears, slash across the tops of the loaves in several places.
*Place loaves in an oven preheated to 450°F. Reduce heat to 400°F and bake

---

*The baking of this bread depends on the capacity of your oven(s). If you do not have room for all four loaves at one time, try shaping two of the loaves after the first rising

for 30 minutes. Turn off oven and leave loaves for 10 additional minutes
to dry out inside of loaves. Remove from oven. Place on wire racks that
have been propped up on water glasses to let air circulate freely on all sides.
Cool. Makes 4 loaves.

To Make Small, Round Italian Loaves

When adding salt to the sponge, also pour in 2 teaspoons olive oil. Mix
and knead as described above. Instead of greasing the rising bowl, lubricate
it with 1 teaspoon olive oil. After second rising, divide dough into four
parts, as described above. Shape each part into a round ball. You do this
by gently pulling the sides down and under, keeping the skin of the dough
intact. Pinch the ball together on the underside. Place these balls on a large
baking sheet that has been generously sprinkled with cornmeal. Leave
ample space between loaves to produce a hard crust all around. The loaves
have a tendency to "grow" together in the oven. Cover lightly with a
floured cloth and allow to rise until doubled in bulk, about 1 hour. Before
baking, brush tops of loaves with the egg-white glaze. With a kitchen
shears, make two slashes in the top of each loaf. Bake and cool as described
for baguettes. Makes 4 loaves.

❖ Best-Ever Bran Muffins

*We have tried many variations of bran muffins over the years. This is the hands-
down favorite of them all. The brown sugar and butter flavors give a richness to the
batter that is unusual for a bran muffin. For those trying to increase their daily fiber
intake, each of these muffins contains 2 tablespoons bran.*

Preheat oven to 400°F. Grease a 12-cup muffin pan. Sift together and set
aside

1 cup unbleached all-purpose flour
1 tablespoon baking powder
½ teaspoon salt

---

and bake the loaves in two batches. Alternately, let half of the dough rise for a third
time before shaping and bake the loaves in succession. Always punch down the dough
between risings.

In a large bowl, combine

>   1 ½ cups Kellogg's All-Bran cereal
>   ½ cup brown sugar
>   ¼ cup butter
>   1 cup scalded milk

Stir to dissolve butter and sugar. Let cool until just warm. Beat into all-bran mixture

>   1 egg

Add dry ingredients to the all-bran mixture, stirring only until dry ingredients are moistened. Spoon into prepared muffin cups. Bake at 400°F for 20 to 25 minutes. Serve warm. Makes 12 muffins.

❖ Whole-Wheat Raisin Bread

>   *A sponge is a wet dough that is mixed and allowed to ferment. The use of a sponge in this bread dough brings out the full flavor of the raisins while it allows them to plump. It also gives the stone-ground whole-wheat flour ample time to absorb moisture before the rest of the flour is added to the dough.*

In a large bowl, combine

>   2 cups warm water
>   1 scant tablespoon (or 1 packet) active dry yeast
>   2 cups stone-ground whole-wheat flour
>   1 cup raisins

Beat well to develop gluten. Cover and let stand for 4 to 8 hours to make a sponge. Stir down sponge. Stir in

>   ¼ cup brown sugar
>   ¼ cup orange juice
>   ¼ cup oil
>   2 teaspoons salt
>   1 egg yolk

To make a stiff dough, gradually add

>   3 to 4 cups unbleached all-purpose flour or bread flour

Turn out on a floured surface and knead until smooth and elastic. Place in a well-greased bowl. Turn dough once to grease the top. Cover and let rise until doubled in bulk, 1 to 1½ hours. Knead dough down in bowl. When making this for everyday use, I shape two loaves that are twisted; when making it for a family reunion weekend, I prefer to shape the dough into one braid similar to that used for challah. The directions for these two shapings are given below. After shaping, cover and let rise until almost doubled in bulk, 45 to 60 minutes. Before baking, brush tops of loaves with a mixture of

1 egg white
1 teaspoon water

Bake in a preheated 375°F oven for 35 to 40 minutes. Turn out on racks to cool. Makes 1 or 2 loaves.

To Shape Twists

Divide dough into four parts. Roll each part into a 15-inch rope. Using two of the ropes, twist gently together and place on one long side of a well-greased large rectangular baking sheet. Make a second twist with the remaining two ropes and place on the other long side of the same baking sheet.

To Shape Braid

Divide dough into four parts. Roll each part into a 20-inch rope. Using three of the ropes, braid gently and place diagonally across a well-greased large rectangular baking sheet. Pinch the ends together and tuck them under just slightly. Pinch the remaining rope in the center to form two ropes that are 10 inches long. Roll these to lengthen them into 18-inch ropes. Twist these two ropes gently together and place the twist on top of the braid, tucking the ends under.

❖ Fitness-Formula Bread

This is a good dietary bread because it is low in fat, salt, and sugar. Its baguette shape lends itself to small servings when the need arises to cut back on quantities.

To soften yeast, in a large bowl combine

> *2 ½ cups warm water*
> *1 scant tablespoon (or 1 packet) active dry yeast*

Stir into softened yeast mixture, in this order

> *1 teaspoon sugar*
> *1 teaspoon wheat germ*
> *1 teaspoon bran*
> *1 teaspoon salt*
> *1 teaspoon oil*
> *3 cups Bohemian Flour (see Pantry Mixes, page 18)*
> *OR*
> *3 cups Wheat-Bread Flour (see Pantry Mixes, page 18)*

Beat well. To make a stiff dough, gradually add

> *3 to 3 ½ cups Bohemian Flour*
> *OR*
> *3 to 3 ½ cups Wheat-Bread Flour*

Turn out on a floured surface and knead until smooth. Place in a greased bowl, turning dough once to grease the top. Cover and let rise until doubled in bulk, 1 to 1½ hours. Knead dough down in bowl. Divide into four parts. Roll each part into a cylinder, about 12 inches long. *Place in well-greased baguette pans. Cover and let rise until almost doubled in bulk, 45 to 60 minutes. Bake at 375°F for 35 to 40 minutes. Cool on wire racks. Makes 4 long loaves.

❊ Fresh Tomato Bread

Fresh tomato juice is delicious and easy to prepare. You simply peel and quarter red-ripe garden tomatoes and then press them through a sieve or a food mill. One day I found I had made more than I cared to drink, so I put the extra juice into a bread. The resulting loaves had the color of fired terra-cotta clay. Parsley and oregano added a freshness without overpowering the delicate tomato taste.

---

*If you want to avoid this fat, place loaves on nonstick baking sheets.

To soften yeast, in a small container combine

> *¼ cup warm water*
> *1 scant tablespoon (or 1 packet) active dry yeast*

In a medium-sized mixing bowl, combine

> *1 cup fresh tomato juice*
> *1 tablespoon finely chopped fresh Italian parsley*
> *1 tablespoon finely chopped fresh oregano*
> *2 tablespoons sugar*
> *2 tablespoons oil*
> *1 teaspoon salt*
> *1 egg yolk*
> *softened yeast mixture*
> *2 cups unbleached all-purpose flour or bread flour*

Beat well. To make a soft dough, gradually add

> *1 to 1 ½ cups unbleached all-purpose flour or bread flour*

Turn out on a floured surface and knead until smooth. Place in a well-greased bowl, turning dough once to grease the top. Cover and let rise in a warm place for 45 to 60 minutes. Knead dough down in bowl and divide in half. Roll each half to a long loaf, about 12 inches. Place loaves in well-greased baguette pans. Cover and let rise until almost doubled, about 30 minutes. Brush tops of loaves with a mixture of

> *1 egg white*
> *1 teaspoon water*

Slash tops of loaves down the center with a sharp knife. Bake in a preheated 375°F oven for 35 to 40 minutes. Turn out on racks to cool. Makes 2 loaves.

�֎ Strawberry Brunch Bread

Some years the weather is just right and the strawberry crop is unbelievable. One such year I decided to make Strawberry Brunch Bread with my overabundant berries. I now make it every summer when the berries are in season.

Preheat oven to 350°F. Grease and flour a 9-inch fluted tube pan. Sift together and set aside

1 ¾ cups unbleached all-purpose flour
½ teaspoon baking soda
½ teaspoon baking powder
½ teaspoon salt
½ teaspoon ginger
½ teaspoon cinnamon

In a large bowl, beat

2 eggs

Beat into the eggs, in this order

1 cup sugar
½ cup oil
1 tablespoon lemon juice

Stir in

*1 ½ cups firmly packed sliced fresh garden strawberries

Add the flour mixture and stir just until the dry ingredients are moistened. Fold in

⅔ cup firmly packed flake coconut

Turn into prepared pan. Bake at 350°F for 1 hour, or until a wooden pick inserted in the center comes out clean. Cool in pan 10 minutes, then turn out onto a wire rack to cool further. Store on a covered cake plate or wrap in foil. Makes 12 servings.

To serve: Fill center of bread with sliced fresh strawberries. Cut into servings at the table.

*I use an old-fashioned flat potato masher to firm the strawberries. The intent is not to mash them, but to be sure you are not just measuring air. I slice the berries about ¼ inch thick.

❖ San Francisco Sourdough Bread

This recipe has been adapted for bread-baking students who want to learn how to make sourdough bread, but do not want the responsibility of always having to keep a sourdough starter on hand. It is one of my personal favorites.

Three days before baking day, mix in a glass quart container

1 cup unbleached all-purpose flour
1 cup warm water
1 tablespoon sugar

Cover loosely with plastic wrap or a clean cloth. Set on kitchen counter out of the sun. Stir well three times a day. By the third day the mixture should smell sour. Your sourdough starter is then ready to use. To soften yeast on baking day, in a large mixing bowl combine

2 ¼ cups warm water
2 scant tablespoons (or 2 packets) active dry yeast
1 tablespoon sugar

Allow yeast to proof. Add to yeast mixture

sourdough starter (all of it)
1 tablespoon salt
4 ½ cups unbleached all-purpose flour

Beat well. Cover and let this sponge rise for 1 hour. Keep an eye on it— do not allow it to overflow. If it threatens to, stir it down a little. Mix together and stir into the sponge

½ teaspoon baking soda
1 cup unbleached all-purpose flour

To make a soft dough, gradually add

4 to 4 ½ cups unbleached all-purpose flour

Turn out on a floured surface and knead until smooth. Cover with a cloth and let rest 20 minutes. Divide dough into three or four parts. Shape into balls and place in well-greased round pans which have been sprinkled with cornmeal. Cover and let rise until doubled in bulk, 45 to 60 minutes. Place a large, flat pan on the bottom rack of the oven and fill with boiling water. Place loaves on center rack and bake at 400°F for 40 to 45 minutes. Carefully remove pan of water for last 5 minutes of baking time to brown bottoms of loaves. Cool on wire racks. Makes 3 or 4 loaves.

❖ German Sourbrot

This recipe includes its own starter for a wonderful peasant loaf of wheat and rye.

Three or four days before baking, combine in a large bowl

> *2 cups warm water*
> *1 scant tablespoon (or 1 packet) active dry yeast*
> *2 cups Bohemian Flour (see Pantry Mixes, page 18)*

Beat well. Cover and let ferment on kitchen counter for 3 or 4 days. Stir several times a day. To soften yeast on baking day, in another large bowl combine

> *½ cup warm water*
> *1 scant tablespoon (or 1 packet) active dry yeast*

Stir into softened yeast mixture, in this order

> *fermented sourdough sponge*
> *1 tablespoon salt*
> *1 tablespoon oil*
> *2 tablespoons molasses*
> *2 cups Bohemian Flour*

Beat well. To make a stiff dough, gradually add

> *1 ½ to 2 ½ cups Bohemian Flour*

Turn out on a floured surface and knead until smooth and elastic. Place in a greased bowl, turning dough once to grease the top. Cover and let rise until doubled in bulk, about 1 hour. Knead dough down in bowl and divide in half. Shape each half into a ball and place in well-greased round pans. Cover and let rise until almost doubled, 45 to 60 minutes. Before baking, brush tops of loaves with a mixture of

> *1 egg*
> *1 tablespoon water*

With a sharp knife, cut a cross in the top of each loaf. Bake in a preheated 375°F oven for 40 to 45 minutes. Cool on wire racks. Makes 2 loaves.

❖ Dusty Potato Bread

This old family recipe was given to me by my husband's mother. It is simple, but outstanding.

To soften yeast, in a large mixing bowl combine

2 cups warm potato water (water in which peeled potatoes have been boiled)
1 scant tablespoon (or 1 packet) active dry yeast

Allow yeast to proof. Stir in

3 tablespoons sugar
1 tablespoon salt
3 cups unbleached all-purpose flour

Beat well to develop gluten. Stir in

2 tablespoons melted shortening, cooled until just warm

To make a soft dough, gradually add

2 ½ to 3 cups unbleached all-purpose flour

Turn out on a floured surface and knead until smooth. Place in a greased bowl, turning dough once to grease the top. Cover and let rise until doubled in bulk, 1 to 1½ hours. Knead dough down in bowl. Divide dough in half. Shape into balls and place in well-greased round pans. Cover and let rise until almost doubled, 45 to 60 minutes. Before baking, dust loaves lightly with flour. Bake at 400°F for 35 to 40 minutes. Cool on wire racks. Makes 2 loaves.

❖ Home-Style Hamburger and Hot-Dog Buns

These buns are perfect for family picnics. They are so much better than anything available at the market.

To soften yeast, in a mixing bowl combine

> *2 cups warm water*
> *2 tablespoons sugar*
> *2 scant tablespoons (or 2 packets) active dry yeast*

Let stand 5 minutes. Stir in

> *1 egg*
> *2 tablespoons wheat germ*
> *2 tablespoons oil*
> *2 teaspoons salt*
> *3 cups Wheat-Bread Flour (see Pantry Mixes, page 18)*

Beat well to develop gluten. To make a stiff dough, gradually add

> *2 ½ to 3 ½ cups Wheat-Bread Flour*

Turn out on a floured surface and knead until smooth. Place in a greased bowl, turning dough once to grease the top. Cover and let rise until doubled in bulk, 45 to 60 minutes. Knead dough down in bowl and divide in half. Shape and bake as described below. Makes 8 hamburger buns and 8 hot-dog buns, or 16 of either type.

To Make Hamburger Buns

Divide one-half of dough into eight pieces. Roll each piece into a ball. Place four balls of dough in a well-greased 8 × 8-inch baking pan. Repeat with the other four pieces of dough, using a second pan. Press each ball of dough into a 4-inch circle, so that sides of circles are almost touching. Cover and let rise until almost doubled, 30 to 45 minutes. Before baking, brush tops of buns with a mixture of

> *1 egg*
> *1 tablespoon water*

Sprinkle tops liberally with

> *sesame seeds*

Bake at 400°F for about 20 minutes, or until golden brown. Cool on wire racks.

To Make Hot-Dog Buns

Divide one-half of dough into eight pieces. On a lightly floured surface, roll each piece to a length of 5½ inches. Lay four of the buns side by side in a well-greased 8 × 8-inch baking pan. Lay the remaining four in a second well-greased 8 × 8-inch baking pan. Flatten rolls slightly so that buns are almost touching. Cover and let rise until almost doubled, about 30 minutes. Before baking, brush tops of buns with

> *melted butter*

Bake at 400°F for 20 to 25 minutes, or until golden brown. Cool on wire racks.

❖ Quick Wheat Coffee Cake

> *If you want to feel virtuous about eating coffee cake, bake this one. The whole-wheat flour, wheat germ, raisins, and nuts make this sweet cake extra nutritious.*

Preheat oven to 375°F. Grease an 8 × 8-inch baking pan. Sift together and set aside

> *¾ cup unbleached all-purpose flour*
> *1 tablespoon baking powder*
> *½ teaspoon salt*
> *3 tablespoons sugar*

Stir in

> *1 tablespoon wheat germ*
> *1 cup whole-wheat flour*
> *1 cup raisins*

Beat together in a large bowl

> *1 cup milk*
> *1 egg*
> *3 tablespoons oil*

Stir dry ingredients into the milk mixture. Pour into prepared pan. Combine and sprinkle over the top

> *½ cup sugar*
> *1 tablespoon cinnamon*
> *½ cup finely chopped walnuts or pecans*

Dot the top with

> *2 tablespoons butter*

Bake at 375°F for 25 to 30 minutes, or until a wooden pick inserted in the center comes out clean. Serve warm. Makes 9 servings.

❖ Buttermilk Biscuits

> *To my mind, buttermilk makes the best biscuits on earth.*

Preheat oven to 450°F. Sift together into a large bowl

> *2 cups unbleached all-purpose flour*
> *1 tablespoon baking powder*
> *¼ teaspoon baking soda*
> *¾ teaspoon salt*

Cut into dry ingredients, using a pastry blender or two table knives

> *⅓ cup shortening*

Stir in with a fork just until dough cleans sides of bowl

> *¾ cup buttermilk*

Knead lightly on a lightly floured surface. Pat or roll to ½-inch thickness. Cut with a floured biscuit cutter and place on an ungreased baking sheet. Bake at 450°F for 12 to 15 minutes. Makes 8 large or 16 small biscuits.

❖ Blueberry Muffins

Blueberry muffins should be slightly sweet, and these are. Use them in a mixed basket of breads for brunch or luncheon.

Preheat oven to 400°F. Grease a 12-cup muffin pan. Combine and set aside

*¼ cup sugar
1 cup fresh blueberries*

Sift together into a large bowl

*1 ½ cups unbleached all-purpose flour
¼ cup sugar
2 teaspoons baking powder
½ teaspoon salt*

In another bowl, beat

2 eggs

Stir into beaten eggs

*½ cup milk
¼ cup melted butter, slightly cooled*

Add milk mixture all at once to the dry ingredients, stirring only until dry ingredients are moistened. Gently stir in

sugared blueberries

Spoon into prepared muffin cups. Sprinkle tops lightly with

sugar

Bake at 400°F for 20 to 25 minutes. Serve warm with sweet butter. Makes 12 muffins.

An Honest Loaf

All of the white and nearly white loaves to grace your table

Perfect White Bread
Buttermilk Bread
Farmhouse French Bread
Butter-and-Egg Braid
Cut Vienna Loaf
Golden Raisin Loaf
Garden-Fresh Herb Bread
Cottage Casserole Bread
Toasted Flour Bread
Chicken-Butter Bread
Gluten Loaf
Adobe-Oven Bread
Batch Bread

❖ AN HONEST LOAF

White breads are extremely versatile, and thus allow for many variations. By increasing sugar and butter, for example, you can make your
bread decadently rich. You can also alter your dough's character by using
water instead of milk, and vice versa, and there is variety in the different
shapes dough can assume. Bread baked in a 9×5-inch baking pan will
appear to be entirely different from the same dough baked in long sau-
sage-shaped baguettes. Whether bread is glazed before or after baking
can also determine the appearance the loaf has when it emerges from the
oven.

I offer here a sampling of recipes for white breads. Although they
include explicit directions for mixing, shaping, glazing, and panning, I
hope you will experiment by varying these on successive bakings. The
doughs for white breads are the easiest to handle. They will lend themselves quite readily to any amendments you may care to make. You will,
if you enjoy being inventive, find yourself with more than a bakery full
of loaves from which to choose.

❖ Perfect White Bread

*This is always the first bread made by my students in The Wooden Spoon School
of Bread—perhaps because it is so easy to execute. The two-loaf recipe enables us to
learn how to shape a loaf with one-half of the dough. The other half can be used
to make some kind of unusually shaped larger bread or, if the students are so inclined,
little breads or rolls. It is fun to encourage people to be creative with a piece of dough.
Sometimes the "fun loaf" is less successful than expected. In such cases, we always
have the traditionally shaped loaf to fall back on for serving to our family and friends.
The second loaf, although sometimes less than perfect, is never inedible.*

To soften yeast, in a large bowl combine

2 cups warm water
2 scant tablespoons (or 2 packets) active dry yeast
1 teaspoon sugar

Allow yeast to proof. Stir in, in this order

⅓ cup sugar
⅓ cup oil
2 teaspoons salt
3 cups unbleached all-purpose flour or bread flour

Beat well. To make a stiff dough, gradually add

3 to 3 ½ cups unbleached all-purpose flour or bread flour

Turn out on a floured surface and knead until smooth. Place in a greased bowl, turning dough once to grease the top. Cover and let rise until doubled in bulk, 45 to 60 minutes. Knead dough down in bowl and divide in half. Shape into oblong loaves and place in well-greased 9×5-inch baking pans. Cover and let rise until almost doubled, 30 to 45 minutes. Bake at 375°F for 35 to 40 minutes. Cool on wire racks. Makes 2 loaves.

✻ Buttermilk Bread

I love the tender texture of this loaf, typical of a bread made with buttermilk.

In a large mixing bowl, combine

¼ cup brown sugar
¼ cup butter
2 teaspoons salt
1 ¾ cups hot buttermilk

Stir to dissolve butter and brown sugar. Let cool until just warm. Meanwhile, to soften yeast, in a small container combine

¼ cup warm water
1 scant tablespoon (or 1 packet) active dry yeast

Allow yeast to proof. When buttermilk mixture has cooled down to warm, stir in

softened yeast mixture
2 ½ cups unbleached all-purpose flour

Beat well. To make a soft dough, gradually add

2 ½ to 3 ½ cups unbleached all-purpose flour

Turn out on a floured surface and knead until smooth. Place in a greased bowl, turning dough once to grease the top. Cover and let rise for 1 to 1½ hours, or until doubled in bulk. Knead dough down in bowl and divide in half. Shape into oblong loaves and place in well-greased 8½ × 4½ × 2½-inch baking pans. Cover and let rise 45 to 60 minutes, or until almost doubled. Before baking, brush tops of loaves with

melted butter

Bake at 375°F for 35 to 40 minutes. Cool on wire racks. Makes 2 loaves.

❖ Farmhouse French Bread

This old-fashioned French Bread recipe has a strong, salty flavor, good with bland cheese, fruit, and cold beer.

To soften yeast, in a large bowl combine

2 cups warm water
1 scant tablespoon (or 1 packet) active dry yeast

Allow yeast to proof. Stir in

1 tablespoon sugar
1 tablespoon salt
3 cups unbleached all-purpose flour or bread flour

Beat well. Cover and let stand 15 minutes. Uncover. To make a stiff dough, gradually add

2 to 3 cups unbleached all-purpose flour or bread flour

Turn out on a floured surface and knead until smooth. Place in a greased bowl, turning dough once to grease the top. Cover and let rise until doubled in bulk, 45 to 60 minutes. Knead dough down in bowl and divide in half. Shape into balls and place in well-greased round pans. Cover and let rise until almost doubled, 45 to 60 minutes. Before baking, brush tops of loaves with a mixture of

> 1 tablespoon cold water
> ½ teaspoon salt

Bake at 375°F for 35 to 40 minutes. Cool on wire racks. Makes 2 loaves.

❖ Butter-and-Egg Braid

> *A truly glorious bread. The egg wash makes the high-risen braids shine with a golden glow.*

In a large mixing bowl, combine

> ½ cup sugar
> ½ cup butter
> 1 tablespoon salt
> 1 ½ cups scalded milk

Stir to dissolve butter and sugar. Let cool until just warm. Meanwhile, to soften yeast, combine in a small container

> ½ cup warm water
> 2 scant tablespoons (or 2 packets) active dry yeast

Allow yeast to proof. When milk mixture has cooled down to warm, stir in

> softened yeast mixture
> 2 eggs
> 4 cups unbleached all-purpose flour or bread flour

Beat well. To make a soft dough, gradually add

> 3 to 4 cups unbleached all-purpose flour or bread flour

Turn out on a floured surface and knead until smooth. Place in a greased bowl, turning dough once to grease the top. Cover and let rise until doubled in bulk, 1 to 1½ hours. Knead dough down in bowl and divide in half. Divide each half into three pieces. Roll each piece to a strip about 12 inches long. On a lightly greased baking sheet, gently and loosely braid three strips together. Do not stretch. Pinch ends together to fasten and tuck fastened ends under. Repeat with remaining dough. Place in a cold oven with a pan of hot water on the rack below the loaves. Let rise until almost doubled, about 30 minutes. After the rising period, remove the pan of water from the oven. Beat together and brush over braids

1 egg
2 tablespoons cold water

Bake at 375°F for 30 to 35 minutes. Cool on wire racks. Makes 2 large braids.

❖ Cut Vienna Loaf

The use of egg white alone gives this bread a full-bodied Vienna flavor without coloring the loaf. The shaping of the loaf is surprisingly easy. Your guests who partake of this loaf will be impressed with your professionalism.

To soften yeast, in a large bowl combine

½ cup warm water
1 scant tablespoon (or 1 packet) active dry yeast
1 tablespoon sugar

Let stand 5 minutes. Stir in, in this order

4 egg whites, about ½ cup
1 cup warm water
2 teaspoons salt
1 tablespoon oil
3 cups unbleached all-purpose flour

Beat well. To make a stiff dough, gradually add

2 to 3 cups unbleached all-purpose flour

Turn out on a lightly floured surface and knead until smooth. Place in a well-greased bowl, turning dough once to grease the top. Cover and let rise until doubled in bulk, 1 to 1½ hours. Punch dough down and knead lightly in bowl. Divide dough in half. Working with one-half at a time, press out to a slightly flat oval. Roll up tightly into an oval loaf. Holding your hands at the ends, roll loaf back and forth a couple of times to taper it. Place on a well-greased baking sheet. Cover and let rise until almost doubled, 45 to 60 minutes. Before baking, brush tops of loaves with a mixture of

> 1 egg white
> 1 teaspoon water

Sprinkle liberally with poppy seeds. With a vertically held kitchen shears, make alternating cuts on either side of exact center, forming a crisscross pattern down each loaf. Bake in a preheated 350°F oven for 35 to 40 minutes, or until well-browned. Cool on wire racks. Makes 2 loaves.

❖ Golden Raisin Loaf

> *This recipe was developed as the blond cousin to the more familiar Raisin Cinnamon bread. It's a refreshing change for your morning toast.*

To soften yeast, in a large mixing bowl combine

> 2 cups warm water
> 2 scant tablespoons (or 2 packets) active dry yeast
> ¼ teaspoon ginger

Allow yeast to proof. Stir in

> ½ cup oil
> ½ cup honey
> 2 teaspoons salt
> grated rind of 1 lemon
> 3 ½ cups unbleached all-purpose flour or bread flour

Beat well. Stir in

> 1 cup golden seedless raisins

To make a soft dough, gradually add

> 3 to 4 cups unbleached all-purpose flour or bread flour

Turn out on a floured surface and knead until smooth. Place in a greased bowl, turning dough once to grease the top. Cover and let rise until doubled in bulk, 45 to 60 minutes. Knead dough down in bowl and divide in half. Shape into oblong loaves and place in well-greased 9×5-inch baking pans. Cover and let rise until almost doubled, 30 to 45 minutes. Bake at 375°F for 35 to 40 minutes. After removing from pans, brush tops of loaves with

> *1 tablespoon melted butter*

Sprinkle with a combination of

> *1 teaspoon sugar*
> *¹⁄₁₆ teaspoon ginger*

Cool on wire racks. Makes 2 loaves.

❖ Garden-Fresh Herb Bread

> *In the summer when the herb garden is flourishing, I love to throw a snippet of a fresh herb into whatever bread dough I am making. This combination is one of my favorites.*

To soften the yeast, in a large mixing bowl combine

> *2 cups warm water*
> *2 scant tablespoons (or 2 packets) active dry yeast*
> *1 teaspoon sugar*

Allow yeast to proof. Stir in

> *1 tablespoon instant chicken bouillon*
> *¹⁄₄ cup brown sugar*
> *¹⁄₄ cup oil*
> *3 cups unbleached all-purpose flour or bread flour*

Beat well. Blend in

> *2 tablespoons finely chopped fresh chives*
> *2 tablespoons finely chopped fresh Italian parsley*
> *2 tablespoons finely chopped fresh dill*
> *2 tablespoons freshly grated Parmesan cheese*

To make a stiff dough, gradually add

> *3 to 3 ¹⁄₂ cups unbleached all-purpose flour or bread flour*

Turn out on a floured surface and knead until smooth. Place in a greased bowl, turning dough once to grease the top. Cover and let rise until doubled in bulk, 45 to 60 minutes. Knead dough down in bowl and divide in half. Shape into balls and place in well-greased round pans. Cover and let rise until almost doubled, 30 to 45 minutes. Bake at 350°F for 40 to 45 minutes. Cool on wire racks. Makes 2 loaves.

❖ Cottage Casserole Bread

Here is an easy one-rise bread with a flavor and tenderness that only comes from using sour cream.

To soften yeast, in a large mixing bowl combine

¼ cup warm water
1 scant tablespoon (or 1 packet) active dry yeast

Allow yeast to proof. Stir in

3 tablespoons sugar
½ teaspoon celery salt
½ teaspoon onion salt
1 teaspoon dill seed
1 cup sour cream, at room temperature
1 egg
1 ½ cups unbleached all-purpose flour

Beat well. To make a soft dough, gradually add

1 to 2 cups unbleached all-purpose flour

Turn out on a floured surface and knead until smooth. Shape into a ball and place in a well-buttered 1½-quart casserole. Brush top of dough with

1 tablespoon melted butter

Cover and let rise until doubled in bulk, 45 to 60 minutes. Bake at 375°F for 35 to 40 minutes. Cool on a wire rack. Makes 1 loaf.

❖ Toasted Flour Bread

Back in the days when flour was not allowed to ripen or mellow, bakers found that toasting it helped avoid the gumminess commonly produced by unaged flour. This technique also gave bread a rich, toasty flavor. Try it for this recipe and for others. It could become your "secret ingredient." Flour dehydrates when toasted, so don't forget to use more liquid than normal.

In a mixing bowl, combine

> *1 ½ cups warm water*
> *1 scant tablespoon (or 1 packet) active dry yeast*
> *1 tablespoon sugar*

Stir to soften yeast. Allow yeast to proof. Stir into softened yeast mixture, in this order

> *1 tablespoon oil*
> *1 teaspoon salt*
> *2 cups Toasted Flour*

Beat well. To make a stiff dough, gradually add

> *1 to 1 ½ cups Toasted Flour*

Turn out on a surface floured with unbleached all-purpose flour and knead until smooth. Place in a greased bowl, turning dough once to grease the top. Cover and let rise until doubled in bulk, 45 to 60 minutes. Knead dough down in bowl and divide in half. Roll each half into an 8-inch square. Then, starting with one corner, roll into a tapered loaf. Place on a well-greased baking sheet. Cover and let rise until almost doubled, 30 to 45 minutes. Before baking, dust tops of loaves with

> *Toasted Flour*

Bake in a preheated 400°F oven for 35 to 40 minutes. Cool on wire racks. Makes 2 loaves.

To Toast Flour

Toasted Flour is best used in simple breads where other ingredients will not mask its subtle flavor.

Spread the flour you want to toast in a large, flat pan, such as a jelly-roll pan. Bake at 325°F until a pale bisque color. Stir flour about every 5 minutes. The time it takes to toast will vary with the flour used. Usually, 20 minutes is sufficient. Cool toasted flour thoroughly before using. Sift cooled flour to remove any lumps.

❖ Chicken-Butter Bread

Fat from fresh chickens can be rendered, as can fat from other fresh poultry, such as turkeys, ducks, or geese. The best-quality fat comes from the bird's cavity. Fats from the outer parts and any fats rendered from a stockpot will not be as light in color or firm in texture. They are, however, the most easily available. Here your rendered chicken fat, referred to as chicken butter, *makes a tasty loaf of bread.*

In a large bowl, combine

¼ cup chicken butter
2 teaspoons salt
3 tablespoons sugar
¼ cup stone-ground cornmeal
2 cups scalded milk

Stir to dissolve chicken butter, salt, and sugar. Let cool until just warm. Meanwhile, to soften yeast, in a small container combine

1 scant tablespoon (or 1 packet) active dry yeast
¼ cup warm water
1 teaspoon sugar

When chicken butter mixture has cooled to just warm, stir in

softened yeast mixture
3 cups unbleached all-purpose flour or bread flour

Beat well. To make a soft dough, gradually add

2 to 3 cups unbleached all-purpose flour or bread flour

Turn out on a floured surface and knead until smooth and elastic. Place in a well-greased bowl, turning dough once to grease the top. Cover and let rise until doubled in bulk, 1 to 1½ hours. Knead dough down in bowl and divide in half. Shape into oblong loaves and place in well-greased 9× 5-inch baking pans. Cover and let rise until almost doubled, 60 to 75 minutes. Before baking, brush tops of loaves with

1 teaspoon melted chicken butter

With a sharp knife, slash tops of loaves down the center. Bake at 375°F for 35 to 40 minutes. Turn out on racks to cool. Makes 2 loaves.

To Render Chicken Fat

Dice chicken fat and cover with water in a heavy saucepan. Heat over medium heat until fat has separated from the solids. Press pieces with the back of a spoon now and then to speed up the process. Strain through a sieve and refrigerate the strained liquid. The fat will rise to the top and can be removed easily after chilling. Remove chicken fat and store in a covered container in the refrigerator. It may be used in baking in place of regular butter. Substitute about ¾ cup chicken fat for every cup of butter.

To Render Chicken Fat From Stockpot

Place in a large stockpot

3 pounds chicken backs and necks
3 quarts cold water

Bring to a boil. Skim the surface several times to remove any scum that accumulates. Reduce heat, cover, and simmer for 3 hours. Remove bony meat pieces with a slotted spoon. Strain remaining liquid and cool. After liquid has partly cooled, refrigerate. Sort out the remaining solids to salvage any bits of meat from the skin and bones. You should have about 2 quarts stock, 1½ cups meat, and ½ cup chicken fat. When stock is chilled, remove and store chicken fat in a covered jar or crock in the refrigerator. Add vegetables and seasonings to stock and chicken pieces to make an economical soup.

❖ Gluten Loaf

Wheat gluten is basically wheat flour with the starch removed through a washing procedure. It can be added to any dough in small quantities for beautiful, well-risen breads.

Stir together thoroughly and set aside

> *3 cups unbleached all-purpose flour*
> *3 tablespoons wheat gluten*

In a large mixing bowl, combine

> *2 cups scalded milk*
> *¼ cup butter*
> *¼ cup sugar*
> *2 teaspoons salt*

Stir to dissolve butter and sugar. Let cool until just warm. Meanwhile, to soften yeast, in another container combine

> *¼ cup warm water*
> *1 scant tablespoon (or 1 packet) active dry yeast*
> *1 teaspoon sugar*
> *¼ teaspoon ginger*

When milk mixture has cooled down to warm, stir in

> *softened yeast mixture*
> *flour-gluten mixture*

Beat well to develop gluten. To make a stiff dough, gradually add

> *2 to 2 ½ cups unbleached all-purpose flour*

Turn out on a floured surface and knead for 7 to 10 minutes. Place in a well-buttered bowl, turning dough once to butter the top. Cover and let rise until doubled in bulk, 1 to 1½ hours. Punch dough down in bowl and knead lightly. Divide dough in half. Shape into loaves and place in well-buttered 8½×4½×2½-inch loaf pans. Cover and let rise until almost doubled, 45 to 60 minutes. Before baking, brush tops of loaves with

> *melted butter*

With a sharp knife, cut a deep slash down the center of each loaf. Bake in preheated 375°F oven for 35 to 40 minutes. Turn out on racks to cool. Makes 2 loaves.

❖ Adobe-Oven Bread

> *Some of the Indians of the Southwest still bake their bread in conical or beehive-shaped adobe ovens called* hornos. *A fire is built on the oven floor. When the oven has been sufficiently heated, the fire is raked out and the ashes quickly swept aside. Then the bread is placed directly on the oven floor and a covering is placed over the opening. The bread is baked in a gradually slackening oven, which produces the best crusts. I wish I could build such an oven for myself. But adobe would be unable to withstand Illinois weather. Lacking the real thing, I bake my Adobe-Oven Bread in a conventional oven on a preheated baking stone, and I gradually slacken the oven temperature. If you have a baking stone, you might try it.*

In a large, flat bowl, combine

> *3 cups unbleached all-purpose flour or bread flour*
> *2 tablespoons toasted cornmeal*
> *1 teaspoon salt*

Rub into the flour mixture

> *2 tablespoons lard or shortening*

To soften yeast, in a small container combine

> *¼ cup warm water*
> *1 scant tablespoon (or 1 packet) active dry yeast*
> *1 teaspoon sugar or honey*

When yeast mixture is nice and bubbly, after 2 or 3 minutes, make a well in the center of the flour mixture and pour the yeast into it. Begin working flour in from the sides and gradually add when needed

1 cup warm water, more or less

Turn out on a floured surface and knead the dough until smooth and elastic. Place in a well-greased bowl, turning the dough once to grease the top. Cover and let rise until doubled in bulk, 45 to 60 minutes. Punch dough down. Shape into a ball. On a surface sprinkled liberally with toasted cornmeal, press out to an 8-inch circle. Fold the circle in half. Cut into the circle about two-thirds of the way through, starting from the curved side toward what was the center of the circle. Cut it in four or five places. Place the shaped loaf on a wooden paddle or flat baking sheet that has been liberally sprinkled with cornmeal. Gently spread the loaf to open up the places where it has been cut. Cover and allow to rise until almost doubled, 30 to 45 minutes. Meanwhile, preheat oven to 475°F with the rack in the lowest position and the baking stone on the rack. When the loaf has risen, quickly sprinkle the baking stone with cornmeal. Transfer the loaf directly to the baking stone, using a series of quick jerks to dislodge the loaf from the wooden paddle. Immediately turn the oven down to 400°F. After 15 minutes, reduce heat to 375°F. After 15 more minutes, reduce the heat to 350°F. Bake for an additional 15 minutes. Remove from oven and cool on a wire rack. Makes 1 loaf.

To Toast Cornmeal

Use toasted cornmeal from Great Valley Mills, or toast your own.

In a dry skillet, over medium to medium-high heat, stir cornmeal until it turns a golden brown. Watch this carefully. Once it starts to toast, it can burn quickly. Cool before using.

✳ Batch Bread

Here is a big bread recipe suitable for a large family, a boardinghouse, or a small restaurant. You will need an entire 5-pound bag of flour for this. Use a very large bowl or stockpot for mixing this dough. I use a bowl with a 4-quart capacity. When

I have run out of room in that, I dump the remainder of the flour on the counter and transfer the dough to the center of the flour. I then work the flour into the dough by hand.

To soften yeast, in a very large bowl combine

> *½ cup warm water*
> *2 tablespoons (or 3 packets) active dry yeast*

Let stand 5 minutes. Stir in, in this order

> *6 cups warm water or scalded milk cooled to warm*
> *1 cup sugar*
> *1 cup oil*
> *2 tablespoons salt*
> *1 egg*
> *1 cup stone-ground whole-wheat flour*
> *approximately ½ of 5-pound bag unbleached all-purpose flour or bread flour*

Measure the amount of flour you need by sight. Beat this batter vigorously with a sturdy wooden spoon for at least 5 minutes. Cover and let rise for 1 hour. If the sponge threatens to overflow, stir it down. To make a stiff dough, gradually add

> *approximately ½ of 5-pound bag unbleached all-purpose flour or bread flour*

Knead in any extra flour until smooth. Place in a well-greased bowl, turning dough once to grease the top. If your bowls are not large enough, divide the dough in half and place in two prepared bowls. Cover and let rise until doubled in bulk, 1 to 1½ hours. Knead dough. Divide dough into 6 or 18 parts. Shape each part into an oblong loaf. If making 6 loaves, place them in well-greased 9×5-inch baking pans. If making 18 loaves, place them in well-greased 5½×3×2-inch baking pans. Cover and let rise until almost doubled, 30 to 60 minutes. The time may vary with the size of the loaf. Brush tops of loaves with a mixture of

> *1 egg*
> *2 tablespoons water*
> *1 teaspoon sugar*

Using a sharp knife, make a slash down the center of each loaf. Bake the larger loaves at 375°F for 35 to 40 minutes; the smaller loaves at 400°F for 20 to 25 minutes. Cool on wire racks. Makes 6 large or 18 small loaves.

Note: If you want to make this bread, but have only one oven for baking, do this: Divide dough in half. Shape one-half and return the other to a greased bowl for another rise. Shape the second half about the time the first batch is ready to go in the oven. The second batch will be rising while the first bakes.

❋ A Mixed Bag of Grain

Whole wheat, rye, and everything else under the sun

Honey-Wheat Bread
Honey-Bear Bread
Wheat-Berry Bread
Wheat-Germ Wheat Bread
Fall-Harvest Herb Loaf
Shredded-Wheat Bread
Whole-Wheat Potato Bread
Brown Rice-'n-Wheat Bread
Brown Rice-'n-Rye Bread
Swedish Limpa
Bohemian Limpa
Bohemian Rye Bread
Beer Rye Bread
Papa's Pumpernickel
Onion Rye Bread
Buttermilk Rye
Light Lemon Rye
Triticale Loaf
Toasted Amaranth Loaf
Ezekiel Bread
Barley Bread
Red Cheddar Loaf
Coffee-Bran Bread
Wheat-Germ Bread
Banana Wheat Bread
Orange-Honey Banana Bread
Old-Fashioned Oatmeal Bread
Bacon Corn Pones
Alabama Corn Sticks
Hush Puppies
Ba-Corn Bread
Buttermilk Corn Bread
Field Hands' Corn Bread
Southern Spoon Bread
Buttermilk Spoon Bread
Cheddar-Cheese Spoon Bread
Bacon Spoon Bread
Oatmeal Spoon Bread

✵ A MIXED BAG OF GRAIN

There are many arguments for whole-grain bread versus white bread. Such bread is higher in fiber, and fiber is very important for a healthy digestive system. The lack of it can lead to a number of disorders. Such lack may even predispose us to colon cancer.* Whole-grain breads contain a greater amount of the B vitamins than do white loaves. By adding more B vitamins to our diets, we may enjoy a better memory, more energy, and better mental and emotional health.† Whole-grain breads, because they are complex carbohydrates and contain more fiber, are much more filling than white breads. One does not desire as much to eat.‡

Although you no doubt agree with all of these reasons, I would suggest to you that you try the recipes in this chapter, not just because they are good for you, but because they are so tasty. The wonderful nutty flavors you find in whole-wheat breads are reason enough to bake them. The distinctive tastes of rye breads and the crunchy sweet flavors of corn breads can be downright addictive. Some of the lesser utilized grains, such as amaranth and triticale, are not only high in nutritional value, they are delectable.

✵ Honey-Wheat Bread

I always ask my bread-baking students to make this bread twice, using 100 percent whole-wheat flour the second time. The sponge method applied to whole-wheat flour produces a nicely textured loaf.

To soften yeast, in a large mixing bowl combine

2 1/2 cups warm water
2 scant tablespoons (or 2 packets) active dry yeast

---

*Carlton Fredericks, *Carlton Fredericks High-Fiber Way to Total Health* (New York: Pocket Books, 1976), p. 27.

†Charles Gerras, ed., *Rodale's Basic Natural Foods Cookbook* (Emmaus, PA: Rodale Press, 1984), p. 793.

‡Sheryl and Mel London, *Creative Cooking with Grains and Pasta* (Emmaus, PA: Rodale Press, 1982), p. 5.

Allow yeast to proof. Stir in

½ cup oil
½ cup honey
1 tablespoon salt
4 cups Wheat-Bread Flour (see Pantry Mixes, page 18)

Beat well. Cover and let this sponge rise 45 to 60 minutes. Stir down sponge. To make a stiff dough, gradually add

4 to 4 ½ cups Wheat-Bread Flour

Turn out on a floured surface and knead until smooth. Place in a greased bowl, turning dough once to grease the top. Cover and let rise until doubled in bulk, 1 to 1½ hours. Knead dough down in bowl. Divide dough into three parts. Shape into oblong loaves and place in well-greased 8½ × 4½×2½-inch baking pans. Cover and let rise 45 to 60 minutes, or until almost doubled. Bake at 375°F for 35 to 40 minutes. Cool on wire racks. Makes 3 loaves.

❋ Honey-Bear Bread

Sometimes, to amuse my granddaughter, I make Honey-Wheat Bread in the shape of teddy bears. If you have a child at your house, you might like to do the same.

Follow Honey-Wheat Bread recipe. When ready to shape, divide dough into four equal parts. You will use two parts for the bear bodies. Cut one of the remaining parts in half for heads. The last part should be cut into 14 pieces.

Shape all pieces of dough into round balls. Place large balls (bodies) on greased baking sheets. Flatten the medium-sized balls slightly and attach for heads.

Use two of the smallest remaining balls for noses. Poke your finger into the dough in the bottom half of each head and place noses. Flatten the remaining small balls slightly and use for ears, arms, and legs. Attach all parts.

Cover and let rise until almost doubled in bulk, 45 to 60 minutes. With a sharp, pointed tool, make small indentations for eyes, nose, and belly button. Place raisins in all indentations, placing the eyes just above the nose. Brush over all a mixture of

1 egg
1 tablespoon water

Take care not to let egg wash run down into the seams where honey-bear parts have been joined. Bake in a preheated 375°F oven for 30 to 35 minutes. Cool on wire racks. Makes 2 Honey Bears.

❖ Wheat-Berry Bread

Cook a pot of wheat berries. Use some of them in place of rice at dinner time or for breakfast cereal. Save one cup for Wheat-Berry Bread.

To soften yeast, in a large bowl combine

2 cups warm water
1 scant tablespoon (or 1 packet) active dry yeast
1 teaspoon sugar

Allow yeast to proof. Stir into softened yeast mixture

1 cup cooked wheat berries, at room temperature
3 tablespoons oil
3 tablespoons honey
2 teaspoons salt
1 egg yolk
3 cups Wheat-Bread Flour (see Pantry Mixes, page 18)

Beat well. To make a stiff dough, gradually add

2 1/2 to 3 cups Wheat-Bread Flour

Turn out on a floured surface and knead until smooth. If any wheat berries pop out of the dough, poke them back in. Place dough in a greased bowl, turning dough once to grease the top. Cover and let rise until doubled in bulk, about 1 hour. Knead dough down in bowl. Divide dough in half. On a lightly floured surface, roll each half to an 8-inch square. Starting with one corner of square, roll to an oblong loaf. Place on a well-greased baking sheet. Cover and let rise until almost doubled in bulk, 30 to 45 minutes. Before baking, brush tops of loaves with

> *1 egg white, beaten*

Using a sharp knife, make seven equally spaced slashes across the tops of the loaves. Bake in a preheated 375°F oven for 35 to 40 minutes. Cool on wire racks. Makes 2 loaves.

To Cook Wheat Berries

Lightly toast wheat berries by stirring over medium heat in a heavy skillet. Place in a heavy saucepan

> *2 cups toasted wheat berries*
> *6 cups water*
> *1 teaspoon salt*

Bring to a boil. Reduce heat, cover and simmer until berries are soft, but not mushy, about 1 hour. Remove with a slotted spoon. Will make about 5 cups.

❖ Wheat-Germ Wheat Bread

> *I can't think of a better way to start the day than with a couple of slices of this nutritious bread toasted and served with hot chocolate, freshly sliced oranges, and bananas.*

To soften the yeast, in a large mixing bowl combine

> *2 cups warm water*
> *2 scant tablespoons (or 2 packets) active dry yeast*
> *1 teaspoon sugar*

Allow yeast to proof. Stir in

> *¼ cup wheat germ*
> *¼ cup brown sugar*
> *¼ cup oil*
> *2 teaspoons salt*
> *1 egg*
> *3 cups Wheat-Bread Flour (see Pantry Mixes, page 18)*

Beat well. To make a stiff dough, gradually add

> 2 ½ to 3 cups Wheat-Bread Flour

Turn out on a floured surface and knead until smooth. Place in a greased bowl, turning dough once to grease the top. Cover and let rise until doubled in bulk, 45 to 60 minutes. Knead dough down in bowl and divide in half. Shape into oblong loaves and place in well-greased 9×5-inch baking pans. Cover and let rise until almost doubled, 30 to 45 minutes. Bake at 375°F for 35 to 40 minutes. Cool on wire racks. Makes 2 loaves.

❋ Fall-Harvest Herb Loaf

I hate to put my garden to bed for the winter and each fall I put it off as long as I can, always hoping for one more garden-fresh ripe tomato or pepper. One fall I noticed small volunteer seedlings of dill sprouting from the seeds dropped by the summer's stalks. There were also fresh green spears of garlic. I added these sproutings along with some Italian parsley and oregano to a hearty wheat bread made with sour milk, the result of which was so good, it has to be included here. Feel free to substitute whatever fresh herbs you have in your fall garden. We think the garlic is essential!

To soften yeast, in a medium-sized bowl combine

> ¼ cup warm water
> 1 scant tablespoon (or 1 packet) active dry yeast

Stir into the softened yeast mixture, in this order

> 1 cup sour milk
> 1 egg yolk
> 1 tablespoon oil
> 1 tablespoon honey
> 1 teaspoon salt
> 1 tablespoon chopped fresh dill
> 1 tablespoon chopped fresh oregano
> 1 tablespoon chopped fresh Italian parsley
> 1 tablespoon chopped fresh garlic
> 2 cups Wheat-Bread Flour (see Pantry Mixes, page 18)

Beat well. To make a soft dough, gradually add

1 ¼ to 1 ½ cups Wheat-Bread Flour

Turn out on a floured surface and knead until smooth. Invert a bowl over the dough to prevent its drying out. Let stand 30 minutes. Knead again lightly. Shape into an oblong loaf and place in a well-greased 9×5-inch baking pan. Cover and let rise until almost doubled in bulk, 30 to 45 minutes. Brush top of risen loaf with

beaten egg white

Bake at 375°F for 35 to 45 minutes. Cool on a wire rack. Makes 1 loaf.

To Sour Milk

Pasteurized milk, such as we use today, cannot be soured naturally. In order to produce a soured pasteurized milk, one must add an acid to the milk and allow it to stand until curdled, or clabbered.

Place in the bottom of a measuring cup

1 tablespoon lemon juice or white vinegar

Fill the cup with

milk, at room temperature

Stir and let the mixture stand about 5 minutes, or until curdled.

❖ Shredded-Wheat Bread

This is one of my very favorite wheat breads. The shredded wheat adds a nutty flavor to the loaf. I use Nabisco Shredded Wheat.

Combine in a large mixing bowl

3 large shredded-wheat biscuits, broken into pieces
⅓ cup brown sugar
¼ cup butter
2 teaspoons salt
1 ½ cups scalded milk

Stir to dissolve butter and sugar. Let cool until just warm. Meanwhile, to soften yeast, in a quart container combine

> *½ cup warm water*
> *2 scant tablespoons (or 2 packets) active dry yeast*
> *1 teaspoon sugar*
> *¼ teaspoon ginger*

Allow yeast to proof. When shredded-wheat mixture has cooled down to warm, stir in

> *softened yeast mixture*
> *1 ½ cups Wheat-Bread Flour (see Pantry Mixes, page 18)*

Beat well. To make a stiff dough, gradually add

> *1 ½ to 2 ½ cups Wheat-Bread Flour*

Turn out on a floured surface and knead until smooth. Place in a greased bowl, turning dough once to grease the top. Cover and let rise until doubled in bulk, 45 to 60 minutes. Knead dough down in bowl and divide in half. Shape into balls and place in well-greased round pans. Cover and let rise until almost doubled, 30 to 45 minutes. Bake at 375°F for 35 to 40 minutes. Cool on wire racks. Makes 2 loaves.

❖ Whole-Wheat Potato Bread

This tender wheat and potato bread is sure to become a favorite. Use a mealy baking potato.

In a covered saucepan, boil gently until potatoes are soft and break apart

> *1 cup peeled, finely diced potatoes*
> *2 cups water*

Remove pan from heat and stir into potato mixture

> *3 tablespoons shortening*
> *3 tablespoons molasses*
> *1 tablespoon salt*

Set potato mixture aside to cool. Meanwhile, to make a sponge, in a large mixing bowl combine

   1 cup warm water
   2 scant tablespoons (or 2 packets) active dry yeast
   1 tablespoon sugar
   1 ½ cups Wheat-Bread Flour (see Pantry Mixes, page 18)

Cover this sponge and let stand. When potato mixture has cooled down to just warm, stir it into sponge with

   2 ½ cups Wheat-Bread Flour

Beat well. To make a soft dough, gradually add

   2 to 3 cups Wheat-Bread Flour

Turn out on a floured surface and knead until smooth, incorporating as much additional flour as necessary to prevent sticking. Place in a greased bowl, turning dough once to grease the top. Cover and let rise until doubled in bulk, 45 to 60 minutes. Punch dough down. Divide into three parts. Shape each part into a ball and place in well-greased round tins. Place loaves, uncovered, in a cold oven on the center shelf. Place a large, flat pan of very hot tap water on the bottom or bottom shelf of the oven. Close door and let loaves rise in this moist atmosphere until almost doubled, 30 to 45 minutes. Carefully remove both the risen loaves and the pan of water from the oven. Turn oven on to 375°F. Sift a fine layer of white flour over the tops of the loaves. With a sharp knife, cut a cross in the top of each loaf. Bake at 375°F for 35 to 40 minutes. Cool on wire racks. Makes 3 loaves.

✖ Brown Rice-'N-Wheat Bread

This is a good way to use up leftover rice. The texture of the rice in this loaf is particularly pleasing, especially when toasted.

To soften yeast, in a large mixing bowl combine

   2 cups warm leftover coffee
   2 scant tablespoons (or 2 packets) active dry yeast

Allow yeast to proof. Stir in

¼ cup oil
¼ cup molasses
2 teaspoons salt
1 cup cooked brown rice
3 cups Wheat-Bread Flour (see Pantry Mixes, page 18)

Beat well. To make a stiff dough, gradually add

2 to 3 cups Wheat-Bread Flour

Turn out on a floured surface and knead until smooth. Place in a greased bowl, turning dough once to grease the top. Cover and let rise until doubled in bulk, 45 to 60 minutes. Knead dough down in bowl. Divide into two or three parts. Shape into balls and place in well-greased round pans. Cover and let rise until almost doubled, 30 to 45 minutes. Before baking, brush tops of loaves with

1 to 2 tablespoons cold coffee

Bake at 375°F for 35 to 40 minutes. Cool on wire racks. Makes 2 or 3 loaves.

❖ Brown Rice-'N-Rye Bread

To make Brown Rice-'N-Rye Bread, substitute Bohemian Flour for the Wheat-Bread Flour (see Pantry Mixes, page 18). Proceed as for Brown Rice-'N-Wheat Bread.

❖ ABOUT RYE FLOURS AND BREADS

Rye flour is not endowed with the glutenous properties of wheat, and one can have problems when trying to use it like a wheat flour. Rye flour can cause dough to be quite sticky and the resulting loaf may be rather dense.

Rye flours vary considerably from source to source. Some are coarsely ground, more like a rye meal. Others have been bolted, or sifted, until most of the bran and the germ have been removed. You may find one flour more troublesome than another. Here are some tips to help you.

Rye doughs ferment readily and lend themselves well to souring, as in an overnight sponge. Souring improves the texture and flavor of the breads produced and helps prevent the development of a wet, gummy dough. Doughs that are not to be soured overnight may benefit from a quick, shortcut souring, accomplished by adding an acid liquid, like vinegar.

Rye dough responds well to a gentle, somewhat lengthy kneading. Should it become sticky while being kneaded, cover it and let it rest for a few minutes before resuming the kneading process.

Rye doughs should not be forced to rise quickly, either by adding more yeast, or by placing the dough in too warm a proofing atmosphere. A 70°F temperature is all that is needed, especially for the second rising, after the loaves are shaped. If you have trouble at that temperature, try placing the covered loaves in the refrigerator to retard the rising process.

Rye breads are better sliced after they have cooled completely. The heavier breads will slice more readily on the second day.

If you feel you simply cannot handle a heavy rye dough, make one with a small amount of rye flour—one-third rye to two-thirds wheat or white is a good proportion. You can gradually work toward the heavier rye as you become more comfortable handling the dough.

Use a generous hand with caraway seeds, up to 1 tablespoon per loaf. It is the caraway flavor that most people associate with rye, anyway.

❖ Swedish Limpa

There are countless variations of sweet and spicy limpa, the favorite bread of many Swedish-Americans. Our version uses Orange-Zest Syrup.

In a large bowl, combine

> *2 cups scalded milk*
> *Orange-Zest Syrup (see recipe below)*
> *¼ cup butter*
> *¼ cup brown sugar*
> *1 tablespoon salt*
> *2 teaspoons anise seed, lightly crushed*
> *1 teaspoon ground cardamon*

Stir to dissolve butter and sugar. Let cool until just warm. Meanwhile, to soften yeast, in another container combine

½ cup warm water
2 scant tablespoons (or 2 packets) active dry yeast
1 teaspoon brown sugar

Allow yeast to proof. When milk mixture has cooled down to warm, stir in

softened yeast mixture
2 cups rye flour
2 cups unbleached all-purpose flour or bread flour

Beat well. To make a rather stiff and sticky dough, gradually add

2 to 3 cups unbleached all-purpose flour or bread flour

Turn out on a well-floured surface and knead until smooth. Place in a well-buttered bowl, turning once to butter the top. Cover and let rise until doubled in bulk, 45 to 60 minutes. Punch dough down. Divide into three parts and shape each part into a ball. Place in buttered baking tins. Cover and let rise until almost doubled, 30 to 45 minutes. Brush tops of loaves with a mixture of

1 tablespoon melted butter
1 teaspoon brown sugar

Bake in a preheated 375°F oven for 35 to 40 minutes. Cool on wire racks. Makes 3 loaves.

Orange-Zest Syrup

Use a lemon zester to remove the zest from

3 oranges

Chop or cut zest into small pieces (about ¼ inch long). In a saucepan, simmer the orange zest in a solution of

½ cup sugar
¼ cup water

Cook the mixture over medium heat until the zest is translucent and the syrup is about the consistency of corn syrup.

❖ Bohemian Limpa

Bohemian Limpa has the same flavor as Swedish Limpa, but the texture is more reminiscent of a peasant bread.

Follow the directions given for Swedish Limpa, substituting Bohemian Flour (see Pantry Mixes, page 18) for the rye and unbleached all-purpose flours.

❖ Bohemian Rye Bread

This unpretentious peasant-type loaf is the very best kind of bread to serve with a hearty winter soup.

In a large mixing bowl, combine

>   *3 tablespoons brown sugar*
>   *3 tablespoons shortening*
>   *3 tablespoons molasses*
>   *2 teaspoons salt*
>   *2 cups scalded milk*

Stir to dissolve brown sugar and shortening. Let cool until just warm. Meanwhile, to soften yeast, in a small container combine

>   *¼ cup warm water*
>   *¼ teaspoon ginger*
>   *1 scant tablespoon (or 1 packet) active dry yeast*

Allow yeast to proof. When milk mixture has cooled down to warm, stir in

>   *softened yeast mixture*
>   *3 cups Bohemian Flour (see Pantry Mixes, page 18)*

Beat well. To make a soft dough, gradually add

3 to 3 1/2 cups Bohemian Flour

Turn out on a floured surface and knead until smooth. Place in a greased bowl, turning dough once to grease the top. Cover and let rise until doubled in bulk, 1 to 1½ hours. Knead dough down in bowl and divide in half. Shape into balls and place in well-greased round pans. Cover and let rise until almost doubled, 45 to 60 minutes. Bake at 375°F for 40 to 45 minutes. Cool on wire racks. Makes 2 loaves.

❖ Beer Rye Bread

This bread is best when made with a dark beer, but it can be made with light, if that is all that you have on hand. A good bet to serve when the ball game's on.

To soften yeast, in a large mixing bowl combine

½ cup warm water
2 scant tablespoons (or 2 packets) active dry yeast

Allow yeast to proof. Stir in

1 ½ cups dark beer, heated until warm
¼ cup brown sugar
¼ cup oil
1 tablespoon caraway seeds
2 tablespoons molasses
2 teaspoons salt
3 cups Bohemian Flour (see Pantry Mixes, page 18)

Beat well. To make a stiff dough, gradually add

2 ½ to 3 ½ cups Bohemian Flour

Turn out on a floured surface and knead until smooth. Place in a greased bowl, turning dough once to grease the top. Cover and let rise until doubled in bulk, 1 to 1½ hours. Knead dough down in bowl and divide in half. Shape into balls and place in well-greased round pans. Cover and let rise until almost doubled, 45 to 60 minutes. Bake at 375°F for 35 to 40 minutes. Cool on wire racks. Makes 2 loaves.

❖ Papa's Pumpernickel

My dad could never walk past a delicatessen. When he came out, he usually had a large sack of goods. Among the cheeses and meats he might have purchased, there would always be a container of pickled pig's feet and a loaf of pumpernickel bread. This recipe is for him.

To form a sponge, in a mixing bowl combine

1 ½ cups warm potato water (including any potato sediment that may be
    floating in the water)
1 scant tablespoon (or 1 packet) active dry yeast
1 tablespoon brown sugar
1 ½ cups stone-ground whole-rye flour (sometimes labeled rye meal or
    pumpernickel flour)

Beat until smooth. Cover and let stand 30 minutes. Stir into the sponge

1 teaspoon salt
2 teaspoons caraway seeds
1 tablespoon brown sugar
1 tablespoon soft butter

To make a stiff, sticky dough, gradually add

1 to 1 ½ cups bread flour

Turn out on a floured surface and toss until no longer sticky. Knead gently for 5 minutes. Cover and let rest 20 minutes. Divide dough in half. Roll each half into a rope about 15 inches long. Place in well-greased baguette pans. Cover and let rise until doubled in bulk, 45 to 60 minutes. Brush the tops of the loaves with a mixture of

1 egg
1 tablespoon water

With a sharp knife, make one long slash down the center of each loaf. Bake in a preheated 375°F oven for 35 to 40 minutes, or until well-browned. Cool on wire racks. After cooling completely, slice as thin as possible and serve with cheese from the deli. Makes 2 long loaves.

❈ Onion Rye Bread

This easy-to-prepare one-loaf recipe is best eaten soon after it is made.

To make a sponge, in a mixing bowl combine

> 1 cup warm water
> 1 scant tablespoon (or 1 packet) active dry yeast
> 1 tablespoon brown sugar
> 2 tablespoons instant minced or chopped onions
> 1 cup Bohemian Flour (see Pantry Mixes, page 18)

Beat until smooth. Cover and let rise for 1 hour. If sponge falls, don't worry. Stir down. Stir in

> 3 tablespoons brown sugar
> 2 tablespoons oil
> 1 tablespoon apple cider vinegar
> 1 teaspoon salt

To make a stiff, sticky dough, gradually add

> 1½ cups Bohemian Flour, more or less

Turn out on a floured surface and toss until no longer sticky. Knead gently for 5 minutes. Cover and let rest 25 minutes. Divide dough in half. Roll each half into a rope 15 inches long. Twist the two ropes together and place the twisted dough on a well-greased or nonstick baking sheet. Join the ends of the twisted dough to form a wreath-shaped loaf. Try to make the twist appear continuous. Cover and let rise until doubled in bulk, 45 to 60 minutes. Before baking, brush the top of the loaf with a mixture of

> 1 egg
> 1 teaspoon water

Bake in a preheated 350°F oven for 40 to 45 minutes, or until well-browned. Cool on a wire rack. Makes 1 loaf.

❖ Buttermilk Rye

The flavors of buttermilk and nutmeg come together well in this slightly tangy loaf.

To soften yeast, in a mixing bowl combine

  ¼ cup warm water
  1 scant tablespoon (or 1 packet) active dry yeast

Stir into softened yeast mixture, in this order

  2 cups buttermilk
  2 teaspoons salt
  ½ teaspoon freshly grated nutmeg
  ½ cup brown sugar
  ¼ cup melted butter, cooled slightly
  3 cups Bohemian Flour (see Pantry Mixes, page 18)

Beat until smooth. To make a stiff dough, gradually add

  2 to 2 ¼ cups Bohemian Flour

Turn out on a floured surface and toss until no longer sticky. Knead gently for 5 minutes. Place in a buttered bowl, turning dough once to butter the top. Cover and let rise until doubled in bulk, 1 to 1½ hours. Punch dough down and divide in half. On a lightly buttered surface, pat or roll out each half to a 9-inch square. Starting with one corner, roll into a tapered loaf. Place, seam side down, on a buttered or nonstick baking sheet. If the sheet is large, you can place both loaves on one. Be sure to separate them by a couple of inches. Cover and let rise until almost doubled in bulk, about 1 hour. Before baking, brush tops of loaves with

  melted butter

With a very sharp knife, make a slash down the center of each loaf. Bake in a preheated 350°F oven for 35 to 40 minutes, or until well-browned. Cool on wire racks. Makes 2 loaves.

❖ Light Lemon Rye

It is the very lightness of this rye bread that makes it special, so if your rye flour is heavy with bran, stir it through a sieve.

Stir together and set aside

> *4 cups bread flour*
> *2 cups light rye flour*

In a large mixing bowl, combine

> *2 cups scalded milk*
> *¼ cup butter*
> *½ cup honey*
> *2 teaspoons salt*

Stir to dissolve butter and honey. Let cool until just warm. Meanwhile, to soften yeast, in a small container combine

> *¼ cup warm water*
> *1 scant tablespoon (or 1 packet) active dry yeast*
> *1 teaspoon sugar*

When milk mixture has cooled down to warm, stir in, in this order

> *softened yeast mixture*
> *1 tablespoon lemon juice*
> *grated rind of 1 lemon*
> *3 cups of the flour mixture*

Beat well. Gradually add

> *remaining flour mixture*

Turn out on a floured surface and toss until no longer sticky. Knead gently for 5 minutes. Place in a well-buttered bowl, turning dough once to butter the top. Cover and let rise until doubled in bulk, 1 to 1½ hours. Punch dough down and divide in half. Shape into oblong loaves and place in well-buttered 9×5-inch baking pans. Brush tops of the loaves with

> *melted butter*

Cover and place in the refrigerator to rise slowly to the top of the pans, about 2 hours. Remove from the refrigerator and uncover. Brush tops of loaves generously with

> *melted butter*

Allow to stand 30 minutes. Meanwhile, preheat oven to 375°F. Bake at 375°F for 35 to 40 minutes, or until well-browned. Cool on wire racks. Makes 2 loaves.

❖ Triticale Loaf

> *Triticale has a delicate flavor all its own. The graham flour used here complements without overpowering it. The dough is allowed but one rise.*

To soften yeast, in a mixing bowl combine

> *1 ¼ cups warm water*
> *1 scant tablespoon (or 1 packet) active dry yeast*
> *1 tablespoon honey*

Allow yeast to proof. Stir in, in this order

> *1 tablespoon oil*
> *1 teaspoon salt*
> *1 ½ cups graham flour*

Beat well. To make a stiff dough, gradually fold in

> *1 ¼ to 1 ½ cups Arrowhead Mills triticale flour*

Turn out on a floured surface and knead just until smooth. Shape into an oblong loaf and place in a well-greased 9×5-inch baking pan. Cover and let rise until doubled in bulk, 45 to 60 minutes. Bake in a preheated 350°F oven for 40 to 45 minutes, or until well-browned. Cool on a wire rack. Makes 1 loaf.

❖ Toasted Amaranth Loaf

The light toasting brings out the nutty flavor of amaranth flour. Amaranth can easily be used in whole-wheat or white-flour recipes, replacing, as it does here, one-third to one-fourth of the flour called for.

Preheat oven to 325°F. On a dry baking sheet spread

> *¾ cup Arrowhead Mills amaranth flour*

Toast this in the oven for 10 to 15 minutes. Watch closely so that it does not burn. Remove from oven and cool the flour before using. In a mixing bowl, to dissolve butter and sugar combine

> *1 cup scalded milk*
> *2 tablespoons brown sugar*
> *2 tablespoons butter*
> *1 teaspoon salt*

Let cool until just warm. Meanwhile, to soften yeast, in another container combine

> *¼ cup warm water*
> *1 scant tablespoon (or 1 packet) active dry yeast*

When milk mixture has cooled down to warm, stir in, in this order

> *softened yeast mixture*
> *toasted amaranth flour*
> *1 cup graham flour*

Beat well. To make a soft dough, gradually add

> *¾ to 1 ¼ cups graham flour*

Turn out on a floured surface and knead until smooth. Shape into a round ball and place on a buttered baking sheet. Flatten the ball to a 9-inch diameter. Cover and let rise until doubled in bulk, 45 to 60 minutes. Pierce dough deeply with the tines of a fork in any pattern that pleases you. Brush the top of the dough with

> *melted butter*

Let the loaf recover while preheating oven, about 15 minutes. Bake in a preheated 375°F oven for 30 to 35 minutes, or until well-browned. Cool on a wire rack. Makes 1 loaf.

❖ Ezekiel Bread

Ezekiel Flour is mixed according to the Biblical instructions in Ezekiel 4:9: "Take thou also unto thee wheat, and barley, and beans, and lentils, and millet, and spelt, and put them in one vessel, and make thee bread thereof . . ." According to the American Heritage Dictionary of the English Language, *Triticum spelta is a hardy wheat, grown mostly in Europe. As grains and legumes gain new popularity in a health-conscious America, Ezekiel flour represents one of the easiest ways to offer them together*

To soften yeast, in a mixing bowl combine

½ cup warm water
1 scant tablespoon (or 1 packet) active dry yeast
1 tablespoon honey

Stir into softened yeast mixture, in this order

1 cup warm water
1 tablespoon oil
1 tablespoon apple cider vinegar
1 teaspoon salt
3 cups Arrowhead Mills Ezekiel Flour

Beat well. To make a stiff dough, gradually add

½ to 1 cup unbleached all-purpose flour

Turn out on a floured surface and knead until smooth. Shape into an oblong loaf and place in a well-greased 9×5-inch baking pan. Cover and let rise until doubled in bulk, 45 to 60 minutes. Bake in a preheated 350°F oven for 40 to 45 minutes, or until well-browned. Cool on a wire rack. Makes 1 loaf.

❋ Barley Bread

This bread is composed almost entirely of barley flour, which gives it a hauntingly sweet flavor. Use of the sponge technique avoids the dense loaf one might expect from such a formulation.

To make a sponge, in a mixing bowl combine

> *2 cups warm water*
> *1 tablespoon brown sugar*
> *1 scant tablespoon (or 1 packet) active dry yeast*
> *1 cup unbleached all-purpose flour or bread flour*

Set this sponge aside and allow to ferment for 20 to 30 minutes. Meanwhile, in a large shallow bowl, combine

> *5 cups barley flour*
> *2 teaspoons salt*

With your fingers, rub into this flour mixture

> *2 tablespoons butter*

Make a well in the center of the flour mixture. Pour into that well

> *the fermented sponge*

Gradually work the dry ingredients into the sponge until a cohesive dough is formed. Turn the dough out onto a lightly floured surface and knead until smooth. Form the dough into a smooth ball and place in the bottom of a well-greased Dutch oven. Brush the top of the dough with

> *melted butter*

Cover with the lid of the Dutch oven and allow to rise until doubled in bulk, 1 to 1½ hours. Preheat stove oven to 450°F. When dough has risen, place Dutch oven in preheated stove oven and reduce heat to 400°F. Bake for 45 to 60 minutes at 400°F, or until well-browned. Cool on a wire rack. Makes 1 loaf.

❖ Red Cheddar Loaf

We were tailgating at an Illinois game one day, and, of course, I had brought along some freshly made bread. After tasting it, one of the local canning company executives asked me if I could bake bread with one of their products. This is what I made for him—with Joan of Arc Tomato Juice.

To soften the yeast, in a medium-sized mixing bowl combine

> ¾ *cup warm tomato juice*
> *1 scant tablespoon (or 1 packet) active dry yeast*

Allow yeast to proof. Stir in

> *2 tablespoons sugar*
> *2 tablespoons soft butter*
> *1 teaspoon seasoned salt*
> ¼ *teaspoon red or cayenne pepper*
> ¼ *teaspoon paprika*
> *1 egg*
> *1 cup shredded sharp cheddar cheese*
> *1 cup unbleached all-purpose flour or bread flour*

Beat well. To make a stiff dough, gradually add

> *1 ½ to 2 cups unbleached all-purpose flour or bread flour*

Turn out on a floured surface and knead until smooth, kneading in additional flour if needed to prevent sticking. Place in a buttered bowl, turning dough once to butter the top. Cover and let rise until doubled in bulk, 45 to 60 minutes. Knead dough down in bowl. Shape into an oblong loaf and place in a well-greased 8½ × 4½ × 2½-inch baking pan. Cover and let rise 30 to 45 minutes, or until almost doubled. Bake at 350°F for 35 to 40 minutes. Cool on a wire rack. Makes 1 loaf.

❖ Coffee-Bran Bread

This is the best yeast-risen bran bread I have ever made. You can substitute Wheat-Bread Flour for the unbleached all-purpose flour, if you wish (see Pantry Mixes, page 18).

In a large mixing bowl, combine

> *1 tablespoon instant coffee*
> *1 cup bran or all-bran cereal*
> *½ cup brown sugar*
> *½ cup butter*
> *1 tablespoon salt*
> *2 cups scalded milk*

Stir to dissolve butter and sugar. Let cool until just warm. Meanwhile, in a quart container combine

> *½ cup warm water*
> *2 scant tablespoons (or 2 packets) active dry yeast*
> *1 teaspoon sugar*
> *¼ teaspoon ginger*

Allow yeast to proof. When bran mixture has cooled down to warm, stir in

> *softened yeast mixture*
> *3 ½ cups unbleached all-purpose flour or bread flour*

Beat well. To make a stiff dough, gradually add

> *3 ½ to 4 ½ cups unbleached all-purpose flour or bread flour*

Turn out on a floured surface and knead until smooth. Place in a greased bowl, turning dough once to grease the top. Cover and let rise until doubled in bulk, 1 to 1½ hours. Knead dough down in bowl. Divide dough into three parts. Shape into oblong loaves and place in well-greased 8½× 4½×2½-inch baking pans. Cover and let rise until almost doubled, 45 to 60 minutes. Before baking, brush tops of loaves with a solution of

> *1 teaspoon instant coffee*
> *2 tablespoons warm water*

Bake at 375°F for 35 to 40 minutes. Cool on wire racks. Makes 3 loaves.

❖ Wheat-Germ Bread

Serve this bread plain or toasted with a vegetarian meal. If desired, substitute Wheat-Bread Flour for unbleached all-purpose flour (see Pantry Mixes, page 18).

To dissolve yeast, in a large mixing bowl combine

2 ½ cups warm water
2 scant tablespoons (or 2 packets) active dry yeast

Allow yeast to proof. Stir in

½ cup oil
½ cup molasses
1 tablespoon salt
1 cup wheat germ
3 cups unbleached all-purpose flour or bread flour

Beat well. To make a soft dough, gradually add

4 to 5 cups unbleached all-purpose flour or bread flour

Turn out on a floured surface and knead until smooth. Place in a greased bowl, turning dough once to grease the top. Cover and let rise until doubled in bulk, 1 to 1½ hours. Knead dough down in bowl. Divide dough into three parts. Shape into balls and place in well-greased round pans. Cover and let rise until almost doubled, 45 to 60 minutes. Bake at 375°F for 35 to 40 minutes. Cool on wire racks. Makes 3 loaves.

❖ Banana Wheat Bread

If you think that bananas are only good for quick breads, you might be surprised by what follows. Using the inevitable blackened fruit, I developed this and the next recipe to vary their use. The aroma of the loaves while baking foretells a delicious outcome.

To soften yeast, in a large bowl combine

1 cup warm water
1 scant tablespoon (or 1 packet) active dry yeast

Stir into softened yeast mixture, in this order

> *2 tablespoons brown sugar*
> *2 tablespoons oil*
> *1 teaspoon salt*
> *½ teaspoon ground cardamom*
> *1 egg*
> *1 cup mashed fully ripe banana*
> *2 cups Wheat-Bread Flour (see Pantry Mixes, page 18)*

Beat well. To make a soft dough, gradually add

> *2 to 3 cups Wheat-Bread Flour*

Turn out on a floured surface and knead until smooth. Place in a well-greased bowl. Turn dough once to grease the top. Cover and let rise until doubled in bulk, 1 to 1½ hours. Knead dough down in bowl and divide in half. Flatten each half into a 9-inch square. Starting with one corner, roll to a tapered loaf. Place on well-greased baking sheets. Cover and let rise until almost doubled, 45 to 60 minutes. Before baking, glaze tops of loaves with

> *1 beaten egg*

With a kitchen shears, make several slashes across the tops of the loaves. Bake at 375°F for 40 to 45 minutes. Turn out on wire racks to cool. Makes 2 loaves.

❖ Orange-Honey Banana Bread

To soften yeast, in a large bowl combine

> *¼ cup warm water*
> *1 scant tablespoon (or 1 packet) active dry yeast*

Stir into softened yeast mixture, in this order

> *¾ cup orange juice, at room temperature*
> *2 tablespoons oil*
> *2 tablespoons honey*
> *1 teaspoon salt*

½ cup mashed fully ripe banana
2 teaspoons caraway seeds
2 cups Bohemian Flour (see Pantry Mixes, page 18)

Beat well. To make a stiff dough, gradually add

1 to 2 cups Bohemian Flour

Turn out on a floured surface and knead until smooth. Place in a greased bowl, turning dough once to grease the top. Cover and let rise until doubled in bulk, 1 to 1½ hours. Knead dough down in bowl. Divide dough in half. Shape each half into a round ball. Place both balls of dough on a large, well-greased baking sheet. Cover and let rise until almost doubled, 45 to 60 minutes. Before baking, brush tops of risen loaves with

orange juice

With a kitchen shears, cut a cross in the top of each loaf. Bake at 375°F for 40 to 45 minutes. Turn out on wire racks to cool. Makes 2 loaves.

✦ Old-Fashioned Oatmeal Bread

For those who love oatmeal, in their bowl or in their bread, this is excellent toasted and spread with honey-butter.

In a large mixing bowl, combine

1 cup old-fashioned rolled oats
½ cup brown sugar
½ cup butter
1 tablespoon salt
2 cups scalded milk

Stir to dissolve butter and brown sugar. Let cool until just warm. Meanwhile, in a quart container combine

½ cup warm water
2 scant tablespoons (or 2 packets) active dry yeast
1 teaspoon sugar
¼ teaspoon ginger

Allow yeast to proof. When oatmeal mixture has cooled down to warm, stir in

> *softened yeast mixture*
> *3 ½ cups unbleached all-purpose flour or bread flour*

Beat well. To make a stiff dough, gradually add

> *3 ½ to 4 ½ cups unbleached all-purpose flour or bread flour*

Turn out on a floured surface and knead until smooth. Place in a greased bowl, turning dough once to grease the top. Cover and let rise until doubled in bulk, 1 to 1½ hours. Knead dough down in bowl. Divide dough into three parts. Shape into balls and place in well-greased round pans. Cover and let rise until almost doubled, 45 to 60 minutes. Before baking, brush tops of loaves with

> *1 tablespoon milk*

Sprinkle with

> *1 tablespoon brown sugar*

Bake at 350°F for 40 to 45 minutes. Cool on wire racks. Makes 3 loaves.

❖ Bacon Corn Pones

> *Corn pones are a typical Southern bread. They are fast to make and full of Southern corn flavor.*

Position oven rack in top third of oven. Preheat oven to 400°F. Lightly grease two baking sheets. In a large bowl stir together

> *3 cups Quaker yellow cornmeal*
> *1 teaspoon baking powder*
> *½ teaspoon baking soda*
> *¾ teaspoon salt*
> *1 teaspoon sugar*

Add and stir into dry ingredients, just until moistened

> *¼ cup crisply fried crumbled bacon*
> *3 tablespoons bacon drippings*

1 ¼ cups buttermilk
1 cup water

Let stand 3 minutes. Stir again briefly. Using ¼ cup batter per patty, ladle onto prepared baking sheets. Each patty will spread somewhat like a cookie. If the batter is too thin, it will spread too much, but the pone will be delicious anyway. The batter will thicken as it stands. Stir batter occasionally if it appears to be settling. Bake in preheated 400°F oven for 15 to 18 minutes, or until lightly browned. Makes 16 corn pones.

❖ Alabama Corn Sticks

If you have never tasted corn sticks baked in a cast-iron corn-stick pan, you have missed one of life's greatest taste treats. If you have new cast-iron pans, be sure to season them before use (see page 29).

Preheat oven to 400°F. Place well-greased cast-iron corn-stick pans in the oven to heat while you mix the batter, about 3 minutes.

Stir together in a mixing bowl

1 ½ cups yellow cornmeal
¼ cup unbleached all-purpose flour
2 teaspoons baking powder
½ teaspoon baking soda
½ teaspoon salt
1 teaspoon sugar

Stir together and then stir into dry ingredients

2 eggs, beaten
1 cup buttermilk

Carefully retrieve heated corn-stick pans and spoon batter into them until they are about two-thirds full. Return to oven and bake at 400°F for 15 to 25 minutes, or until lightly browned. The number of corn sticks made depends on the size of your pans.

❖ Hush Puppies

The first hush puppies I enjoyed were at the Dog River Hunting and Fishing Club near Mobile, Alabama. This small club's membership really did like to fish. Sometimes the manager could be cajoled into frying the day's catch for a lucky angler. Hush puppies and fried fish would then be served in a dining room sparsely furnished with bare wooden tables. Pitchers of ice water and beer were set on the table to wash it all down.

Those early hush puppies had no onions in them, and to this day I prefer mine without. If you feel differently, simply add ¼ to ½ cup finely chopped onions and fry as directed.

Stir together in a mixing bowl

> *1 cup Quaker yellow cornmeal*
> *¼ teaspoon baking soda*
> *½ teaspoon baking powder*
> *½ teaspoon salt*

Stir together and then stir into dry ingredients

> *1 egg*
> *1 cup buttermilk*

Mix well. Let the batter sit while heating oil. Gently drop by tablespoons into oil heated to 350°F, frying no more than three or four at a time. Fry for about 3 minutes, or until golden brown, turning once. Drain on paper towels. Serve hot. Makes 24 hush puppies.

Note: If you fry your fish in a skillet, you may use that same skillet for the hush puppies. Just coat with ¼ inch of oil.

❖ Ba-Corn Bread

This light-textured bread has an exceptional flavor.

In a large mixing bowl, combine

> *1 cup yellow cornmeal*
> *½ cup sugar*

½ cup butter
1 tablespoon salt
2 cups boiling water

Stir to dissolve butter and sugar. Let cool until just warm. Meanwhile, in a quart container combine

½ cup warm water
2 scant tablespoons (or 2 packets) active dry yeast
1 teaspoon sugar

Allow yeast to proof. When cornmeal mixture has cooled down to warm, stir in

softened yeast mixture
3 cups unbleached all-purpose flour or bread flour

Beat well. To make a stiff dough, gradually add

4 to 5 cups unbleached all-purpose flour or bread flour

Turn out on a floured surface and knead until smooth. Place in a greased bowl, turning dough once to grease the top. Cover and let rise until doubled in bulk, 1 to 1½ hours. Knead dough down in bowl. Divide dough into three parts. Roll each part into a 6×10-inch rectangle. Sprinkle each with

2 slices crisply fried crumbled bacon

Press bacon firmly into dough. Starting with 6-inch side, roll to form an oblong loaf. Place in well-greased 8½×4½×2½-inch baking pans. Cover and let rise until almost doubled, 45 to 60 minutes. Before baking, brush tops of loaves with bacon drippings. Bake at 375°F for 35 to 40 minutes. Cool on wire racks. Makes 3 loaves.

�֎ Buttermilk Corn Bread

Buttermilk and cornmeal were meant for each other. This is as fine a marriage as you will ever find. Serve with a steaming bowl of chunky chili.

Preheat oven to 400°F. Grease a 9×12-inch glass baking dish. Sift together and set aside

> 2 cups unbleached all-purpose flour
> 2 teaspoons baking powder
> 1 teaspoon baking soda
> ¾ teaspoon salt

Beat together in a large bowl, in this order

> 2 eggs
> ¾ cup sugar
> 2 cups buttermilk
> ¼ cup melted butter, slightly cooled
> 1 cup stone-ground yellow cornmeal

Stir dry ingredients into the buttermilk mixture. Turn into prepared pan. Bake at 400°F for 25 to 30 minutes, or until a wooden pick inserted in the center comes out clean. Serve warm. Makes 12 servings.

✖ Field Hands' Corn Bread

When fall arrives in our part of the country, the landscape becomes a patchwork of corn and beans. Bringing in the mottled crop means that the crews work long into the night, their tractor lights snaking across the slowly flattened fields. The tireless workers welcome a hearty meal to keep them going, and nine times out of ten it includes sweet corn.

Bread made with freshly picked sweet corn presents a welcome change from the standard "corn on the cob." This version has a soft texture and can be spooned directly onto plates while still hot from the oven. Butter lovers can melt a dollop on their serving, but the bread is equally good without it. It can be made with either white or yellow corn.

Preheat oven to 425°F. Butter an 8×8-inch baking dish. Cut from the cob, scraping the cob to remove the pulp

5 ears freshly picked sweet corn

You should have 2¼ to 2½ cups corn kernels and pulp. Set this aside. In a medium-sized mixing bowl, beat

3 eggs

Stir into eggs, in this order

¾ cup milk
2 tablespoons sugar
¾ teaspoon salt
1 tablespoon baking powder
reserved corn

Stir into corn mixture, ¼ cup at a time

¾ cup unbleached all-purpose flour

Add and stir just until blended

¼ cup melted butter, slightly cooled

Pour the batter into the prepared pan and bake at 425°F for about 30 minutes. Serve at once. Makes 6 to 9 servings.

❄ ABOUT SPOON BREADS

Legend has it that spoon breads came into existence because a confused plantation cook forgot whether she was making corn bread or mush and ended up with a bread she had to eat with a spoon. I rather doubt that story. But whatever their origins, spoon breads are delicious light breads, to be eaten right from the oven, often with butter and strawberry preserves. They are commonly found on the menus of inns and hotels all over the South, but because of our growing interest in regional cooking, they are becoming more popular throughout the country.

The eggs used in spoon breads can be separated, and the whites beaten and folded in at the last minute. Made this way, the bread comes out similar to a souffle in texture. If the eggs are not separated, the bread will have more of a custard consistency. I prefer to separate the eggs, however, as it is the bread's light quality that makes it special.

Spoon breads can be baked in individual custard cups, if desired. Set these cups in a pan filled with enough water to reach halfway up the sides of the cups and bake at 400°F for 25 minutes, or until set. This technique is particularly effective for Oatmeal Spoon Bread, making individual servings available for breakfast eaters. For a fancier presentation, the breads may be baked in a see-through souffle dish.

I will give you a few simple recipes for this type of bread. After making them, you should have no trouble varying them. The possibilities are endless: hominy grits can be used in place of the cornmeal; a small quantity of lightly sautéed onions or bell peppers can be added before the eggs; wheat berries that have been cooked until creamy and thick make another wonderful addition. Indeed, if you wished, you could go on and on until you had a small book of spoon breads alone.

❊ Southern Spoon Bread

I spent my high-school and college years in southern Alabama. The first night I "slept over" at a friend's house, I was served spoon bread for supper. I had never had anything quite like it. It was so good that I embarrassed everyone by asking not only for seconds, but for thirds. This recipe is typical of the kind of bread I was served that night.

A good Southern cook will check the size of the eggs before beginning this dish. If the eggs are too small, four should be used instead of three.

Preheat oven to 325°F. Butter a 2-quart baking dish. In a large, heavy saucepan, combine and heat just to the boiling point

2 cups milk
2 tablespoons butter

Remove pan from the heat. Stir into the milk mixture

1 cup yellow cornmeal

Return pan to medium heat and cook, stirring all the while, until thickened. Remove pan from heat. Stir into the thickened mixture, in this order

    1 cup milk
    1 teaspoon salt
    1 teaspoon baking powder
    1 tablespoon sugar
    3 egg yolks, lightly beaten

Stir in one-quarter, then fold in the remainder of

    3 egg whites, stiffly beaten

Spoon the batter into the prepared baking dish. Bake at 325°F for 70 minutes, or until well-browned and set. Serve at once with sweet butter and strawberry preserves. Makes 6 servings.

✳ Buttermilk Spoon Bread

Buttermilk and nutmeg give this spoon bread a subtly different flavor. It is as light as a dandelion seed in a soft summer breeze.

Preheat oven to 325°F. Butter a 2-quart baking dish. In a large, heavy saucepan, combine and heat just to the boiling point

    2 cups water
    ¼ cup butter

Remove pan from heat. Stir into the water mixture

    1 cup white cornmeal

Return pan to medium heat and cook, stirring all the while, until thickened. Remove pan from heat. Stir into the thickened mixture, in this order

    1 cup buttermilk
    ¾ teaspoon salt
    ¼ teaspoon freshly grated nutmeg
    ¼ teaspoon baking soda
    1 teaspoon baking powder
    2 tablespoons sugar
    3 egg yolks, lightly beaten

Stir in one-quarter, then fold in the remainder of

> *3 egg whites, stiffly beaten*

Spoon the batter into the prepared baking dish. Bake at 325°F for 70 minutes, or until well-browned and set. Serve at once with sweet butter and preserves. Makes 6 servings.

✷ Cheddar-Cheese Spoon Bread

Southern cooks use a lot of Tabasco sauce in their cooking. If you have Yankee tastes, you may prefer to leave it out.

Preheat oven to 350°F. Butter a 2-quart baking dish. In a large, heavy saucepan, combine and heat just to the boiling point

> *2 ½ cups milk*
> *3 tablespoons butter*

Remove pan from the heat. Stir into the milk mixture

> *1 cup yellow cornmeal*

Return pan to medium heat and cook, stirring all the while, until thickened. Remove pan from heat. Stir into the thickened mixture, in this order

> *1 teaspoon salt*
> *1 teaspoon baking powder*
> *¼ teaspoon Tabasco sauce, more or less, according to your taste*
> *1 cup grated sharp cheddar cheese*
> *4 egg yolks, lightly beaten*

Stir in one-quarter, then fold in the remainder of

> *4 egg whites, stiffly beaten*

Spoon the batter into the prepared baking dish. Bake at 350°F for 1 hour, or until well-browned and set. Serve at once with sweet butter. Makes 8 servings.

❖ Bacon Spoon Bread

One can make a satisfying lunch or supper with this bread and a plate of cooked turnip greens and black-eyed peas. That's what they used to call the Blue Plate Special at my Dad's lunch counter in the S. H. Kress in Mobile, Alabama. It was what I ordered day after day when I worked for him as a stock clerk during my breaks from school.

Preheat oven to 350°F. In the bottom of a Dutch oven, sauté until crisp and brown

6 slices bacon

Remove bacon, cool, crumble, and set aside. Remove the Dutch oven from the heat and tilt to coat the sides with bacon drippings. Pour off excess drippings and use them to flavor cooked greens. In a large, heavy saucepan, combine and heat just to the boiling point

2 cups milk

Remove pan from the heat. Stir in

1 cup yellow cornmeal

Return pan to medium heat and cook, stirring all the while, until mixture has thickened. Remove pan from heat. Stir into the thickened mixture, in this order

1 cup milk
1 teaspoon salt
1 teaspoon baking powder
crumbled bacon
2 tablespoons grated Parmesan cheese
3 egg yolks, lightly beaten

Stir in one-quarter, then fold in the remainder of

3 egg whites, stiffly beaten

Spoon the batter into the Dutch oven. Bake at 350°F for 1 hour, or until well-browned and set. Serve at once with softened sweet butter. Makes 6 servings.

❖ Oatmeal Spoon Bread

Cooks usually think of cornmeal when they think of spoon breads, but there is no reason that has to be the case. This bread makes a nice breakfast variation. Serve it with bacon and a compote of fruit.

Preheat oven to 350°F. Butter a 1-quart baking dish. Mix together and set aside

> *¼ cup brown sugar*
> *½ teaspoon cinnamon*

In a large, heavy saucepan, combine and heat just to boiling

> *1 cup milk*
> *1 tablespoon butter*

Remove the pan from the heat. Stir into the milk

> *¾ cup old-fashioned rolled oats*

Return the pan to medium heat and cook, stirring all the while, just until the mixture thickens. Remove pan from heat. Stir into the cooked oatmeal, in this order

> *½ cup milk*
> *½ teaspoon salt*
> *½ teaspoon baking powder*
> *1 tablespoon of the reserved brown-sugar mixture*
> *2 egg yolks, lightly beaten*

Stir in one-quarter, then fold in the remainder of

> *2 egg whites, stiffly beaten*

Turn into prepared dish. Bake at 350°F for 35 minutes, or until set and browned on the top. Serve with sweet butter and the remaining brown sugar and cinnamon mixture. Makes 4 servings.

❋ The Magical Breads

Starters, sourdough, and the unleavened loaf

❖ THE MAGICAL BREADS

The early settlers of the West knew how to make their bread without going to the local supermarket for a package of yeast or a can of baking powder: They used sourdough starter.

The "sourdoughs," as these cooks were called, protected their starters with all the resources at their disposal. They sometimes slept with the fermenting pot, knowing that their body warmth would keep the starter in a virile state for daily baking. Today it is much easier to keep and use sourdough starters. Only when the baker does not care to make sourdough breads every day does he need to refrigerate his batter. If kept in use, it may be left to ferment at room temperature.

In the early 1900's, young brides were often given sweet starters made from a yeast mixture of several ingredients, including hops.

Sweet starters, unlike sourdough, had to be kept in a cool storage place to prevent their turning sour. Lucky was the young bride who boasted an icebox, for that made keeping her sweet starter a simple matter. It was less simple for country wives, who had to lower their starter pot into a well to keep it cool. In a modern kitchen, of course, a sweet starter can be made with active dry yeast to first give it life.

The earliest bread was unleavened. The story goes that a baker, probably Egyptian, found out by accident that such bread could rise by itself when he was called away on an urgent matter, left his bread unattended, and returned to find it had risen. He baked the risen loaf and, surprised and pleased with the result, repeated the fermentation. If you are interested in making an unleavened loaf that will rise by itself, follow the recipe included here on page 149.

Sourdough Starters

Once established, a sourdough starter can last a lifetime. Some have been passed down from generation to generation. If something happens to yours, however, do not despair. Simply start another one.

❖ Sourdough Starter #1

In a crockery or glass bowl, combine

2 cups warm water
1 scant tablespoon (or 1 packet) active dry yeast
1 tablespoon sugar
2 cups unbleached all-purpose flour

Beat well. Cover loosely with a clean cloth or plastic wrap. Stir several times a day. In two or three days, the starter will smell sour and be ready to use. Place in a loosely covered crockery or glass container. Refrigerate until needed.

❖ Sourdough Starter #2

Pour into a crockery or glass bowl

2 cups reconstituted nonfat dry milk

Cover with a clean cloth and leave on kitchen counter for 24 hours. Stir in

2 cups unbleached all-purpose flour

Beat well. Cover and leave to ferment, stirring several times a day. After two or three days, it will smell sour and be ready to use. Cover loosely and refrigerate until needed.

❖ Yogurt Starter

Stir together in a crockery or glass bowl

2 cups reconstituted nonfat dry milk
2 tablespoons low-fat plain yogurt
2 cups unbleached all-purpose flour

Beat well. Cover and leave to ferment, stirring several times a day. After two or three days, it will smell sour and be ready to use. Cover loosely and refrigerate until needed.

❄ Potato Starter

Many "sourdoughs" favor this starter. I recommend using Idaho baking potatoes.

In a heavy saucepan, place

> *3 cups water*
> *2 cups peeled and diced potatoes*

Cook, covered, over medium heat until potatoes are completely done and breaking apart, about 20 minutes. Pour mixture through a sieve, rubbing the potatoes through the mesh with a wooden spoon. Let this thick potato water cool down to warm. Add to warm potato water

> *2 tablespoons sugar*
> *2 cups unbleached all-purpose flour*

Stir well to mix. Cover and leave to ferment, stirring several times a day. After two or three days, it will smell sour and be ready to use. Cover loosely and refrigerate until needed.

❄ Bohemian Starter

If you are going to make mostly whole-grain sourdough, you may want to use this starter.

Stir together in a crockery or glass bowl

> *2 cups warm water*
> *2 cups Bohemian Flour (see Pantry Mixes, page 18)*
> *1 tablespoon sugar*

Stir well to mix. Cover and leave to ferment, stirring several times a day. After two or three days, it will smell sour and be ready to use. Cover loosely and refrigerate until needed.

Sourdough Starter Notes

1. To replenish your starter, add equal amounts of water and flour. After stirring, cover with a clean cloth and allow to stand on counter overnight. Refrigerate in the morning. A starter should be used and replenished at least once a week. More often would be better.

2. You can use potato water (water in which peeled potatoes have been boiled) instead of water to replenish your starter.

3. If your starter turns pink or orange, it may contain bacteria. Wash and scald your container.

4. If mold should form on your starter, discard and start over. Mold is more likely to form when the starter consistency is too thick.

5. Always use glass, crockery, or wooden utensils to store and stir your starter. Prolonged contact with metal can alter the character and flavor of sourdough.

6. Do not store starter with a tight-fitting lid, since some expansion may occur. Stoneware crocks or glass apothecary jars with nonscrew lids are ideal.

7. Always let your refrigerated starter return to room temperature before working with it. For the best results, set it out on the counter the night before baking.

8. Never put anything back into your starter except flour and water. Avoid the temptation to add a little of the mixed batter you have on hand, which may include salt, sugar, and fats. Always use lukewarm water, never hot or cold.

9. When making sourdough breads without other leavening, use a very vigorous starter. If necessary, make a new one. You can also use a small amount of active dry yeast to compensate for a sluggish starter. Don't be afraid to experiment.

❋ Shortcut Sourdough Bread

*If you have never made sourdough before, you may want to start with this recipe.
It is fast and easy and has a good, tangy flavor.*

To soften the yeast, in a large mixing bowl combine

> *¼ cup warm water*
> *1 scant tablespoon (or 1 packet) active dry yeast*

Allow yeast to proof. Stir in

> *2 cups sourdough starter*
> *1 tablespoon sugar*
> *1 tablespoon oil*
> *1 teaspoon salt*
> *1 cup unbleached all-purpose flour*

Beat well. To make a stiff dough, gradually add

> *1 ½ to 2 cups unbleached all-purpose flour*

Turn out on a floured surface and knead until smooth and elastic. Cover
and let dough rest for 30 minutes. Shape into an oblong loaf and place in
a well-greased 9 × 5-inch baking pan. Cover and let rise until doubled in
bulk, 45 to 60 minutes. Bake at 375°F for 35 to 40 minutes. Cool on a wire
rack. Makes 1 loaf.

❋ Everyday Sourdough Bread

*This recipe is for the baker who's short on time and who doesn't mind that the
sourdough never develops a strong, sour flavor. It takes only an hour for this sponge
to ferment.*

To soften the yeast, in a large mixing bowl combine

> *2 cups warm water*
> *1 scant tablespoon (or 1 packet) active dry yeast*
> *2 tablespoons sugar*

Allow yeast to proof. Stir in

> 1 cup sourdough starter
> 3 cups unbleached all-purpose flour

Beat well. Cover and let rise 1 hour. Stir down sponge. Stir in

> 2 tablespoons oil
> 2 teaspoons salt

To make a soft dough, gradually add

> 3 to 4 cups unbleached all-purpose flour

Turn out on a floured surface and knead until smooth, adding more flour, if necessary, to prevent sticking. Divide dough into three parts. Shape into oblong loaves and place in well-greased 8½ × 4½ × 2½-inch baking pans. Cover and let rise until doubled in bulk, about 1 hour. Bake at 400°F for 45 to 50 minutes. Cool on wire racks. Makes 3 loaves.

❖ Family-Fare Sourdough

This sourdough sponge must ferment overnight. It makes three loaves in all, and could be doubled for use by a large family or a small restaurant.

The night before baking, in a large bowl combine

> 1 cup sourdough starter
> 1 cup warm water
> 2 teaspoons sugar
> 2 cups unbleached all-purpose flour

Beat well. Cover and let sponge rise overnight. The next morning, to soften yeast, in another bowl combine

> 1 cup warm water
> 1 scant tablespoon (or 1 packet) active dry yeast

Allow yeast to proof. Add to softened yeast mixture

>*2 tablespoons sugar*
>*2 tablespoons oil*
>*1 tablespoon salt*
>*sourdough sponge*

To make a soft dough, gradually add

>*5 to 6 cups unbleached all-purpose flour*

Turn out on a floured surface and knead until smooth, adding more flour, if necessary, to prevent sticking. Place in a greased bowl, turning dough once to grease the top. Cover and let rise until doubled in bulk, about 1½ hours. Knead dough down in bowl. Divide dough into three parts. Shape into oblong loaves and place in well-greased 8½×4½×2½-inch baking pans. Cover and let rise until almost doubled, about 1 hour. Slash tops of loaves with a sharp knife and brush tops with cold water. Bake at 375°F for 40 to 45 minutes. Cool on wire racks. Makes 3 loaves.

❋ Sour Potato Bread

Leftover mashed potatoes are always good in bread dough. I like to make this with potato starter, but any starter will work.

In a large bowl, mix together

>*1 cup warm cooked mashed potatoes*
>*1 cup warm potato water (water in which potatoes were cooked)*
>*1 cup sourdough starter*

Cover and let ferment for 1 hour. To soften yeast, in a small container combine

>*½ cup warm water*
>*1 scant tablespoon (or 1 packet) active dry yeast*

Stir into fermented sourdough mixture

>*softened yeast mixture*
>*2 tablespoons sugar*

2 tablespoons oil

1 tablespoon salt

2 ½ cups unbleached·all-purpose flour

To make a soft dough, gradually add

3 to 3 ½ cups unbleached all-purpose flour

Turn out on a floured surface and knead until smooth. Knead in additional flour, if needed. Place in a greased bowl, turning dough once to grease the top. Cover and let rise until doubled in bulk, about 1 hour. Knead dough down in bowl. Divide dough into three parts. Shape each part into a round ball and place in well-greased round pans. Cover and let rise until almost doubled, 30 to 45 minutes. Dust tops of loaves lightly with flour. Use a kitchen shears to cut a small cross in the top of each loaf. Bake at 375°F for 40 to 45 minutes. Cool on wire racks. Makes 3 loaves.

❖ Sour Bacon-Potato Bread

Substitute bacon drippings for the oil in Sour Potato Bread. Add ½ cup crisply fried crumbled bacon to the batter along with the first cup of flour. Proceed as for Sour Potato Bread.

❖ Raisin Sourdough

You can turn any of your favorite sourdough recipes into a raisin sourdough by fermenting the raisins in the sourdough sponge overnight.

In a large bowl, combine

1 cup sourdough starter

1 cup warm water

2 cups unbleached all-purpose flour

1 cup raisins

Cover and let this sponge stand overnight to ferment. The next morning, to soften yeast, in another large bowl combine

> ½ *cup warm water*
> 1 *scant tablespoon (or 1 packet) active dry yeast*

Stir into softened yeast mixture

> ¼ *cup oil*
> ¼ *cup honey*
> 2 *teaspoons salt*
> 1 *egg*
> *sourdough sponge*

To make a soft dough, gradually add

> 3 *to 4 cups unbleached all-purpose flour*

Turn out on a floured surface and knead until smooth. Place in a greased bowl, turning dough once to grease the top. Cover and let rise until doubled in bulk, 1 to 1½ hours. Knead dough down in bowl. Divide dough in half. Shape into oblong loaves and place in well-greased 9×5-inch baking pans. If any raisins are poking out of the dough, push them back in. Exposed raisins will burn during the baking. I always use black pans from Brick Oven of Chicago for this bread. They have a higher rise than most. If you do not have any large pans like these, you may want to pinch off a piece of the dough for a small, round loaf before dividing the dough in half. Cover and let rise until almost doubled, about 1 hour. Bake in a preheated 400°F oven for 35 to 40 minutes. Cool on wire racks. Makes 2 loaves.

❖ Sour-Wheat Bread

> *The light, sour taste of this textured wheat bread makes it ideal for delicatessen sandwiches.*

To soften yeast, in a large mixing bowl combine

> ¼ *cup warm water*
> 1 *scant tablespoon (or 1 packet) active dry yeast*
> 1 *teaspoon sugar*

Allow yeast to proof. Stir in

> 1 cup sourdough starter
> 1 cup warm water
> 2 cups Wheat-Bread Flour (see Pantry Mixes, page 18)

Beat well. Cover and let rise 1 hour. Stir down sponge. Stir in

> ¼ cup brown sugar
> ¼ cup oil
> 2 teaspoons salt

Stir together and blend into sponge

> ¼ teaspoon baking soda
> 1 cup Wheat-Bread Flour

To make a soft dough, gradually add

> 2 to 3 cups Wheat-Bread Flour

Turn out on a well-floured surface and knead until smooth. Shape into a ball. Cover and let rest 30 minutes. Divide dough in half. Shape into round balls and place in well-greased round pans that have been sprinkled with cornmeal. Cover and let rise until doubled in bulk, about 1 hour. Bake at 375°F for 40 to 45 minutes. Cool on wire racks. Makes 2 loaves.

�֍ Oatmeal Sourdough

> You can make this oatmeal sourdough bread three ways. Slice diagonally for great oven toast.

The night, or day, before baking, to make a sponge, in a large bowl combine

> 1 cup sourdough starter
> 2 cups warm water
> 1 cup old-fashioned rolled oats
> 3 cups unbleached all-purpose flour

Stir well. Cover and let ferment overnight, or as long as 24 hours. When ready to bake, to soften yeast, in another large bowl combine

½ cup warm water
1 scant tablespoon (or 1 packet) active dry yeast

Stir into softened yeast mixture, in this order

¼ cup brown sugar
¼ cup soft butter
1 tablespoon salt
fermented sourdough sponge
2 cups unbleached all-purpose flour

Beat well. To make a soft dough, gradually add

1 to 2 cups unbleached all-purpose flour

Turn out on a floured surface and knead until smooth. Place in a greased bowl, turning dough once to grease the top. Cover and let rise until doubled in bulk, 45 to 60 minutes. Knead dough down in bowl. Divide dough into three parts. Pat or roll each part into an 8-inch square. Starting at one corner of square, roll to a tapered loaf. Place on greased baking sheets, seam side down. Cover and let rise until almost doubled, 30 to 45 minutes. Before baking, brush tops of loaves with

melted butter

Sprinkle loaves with additional

rolled oats

Bake in a preheated 375°F oven for 35 to 40 minutes. Cool on wire racks. Makes 3 loaves.

❖ Raisin-Oatmeal Sourdough

Add 1 cup raisins to ferment with Oatmeal Sourdough sponge. Proceed as for Oatmeal Sourdough.

❖ Cinnamon-Oatmeal Sourdough

After rolling dough out to 8-inch square, brush lightly with

milk or water

Sprinkle with

cinnamon-sugar

Use 2 tablespoons per loaf. Proceed as for Oatmeal Sourdough.

❖ Bohemian Sourdough

In many of my rye recipes, I like to combine white, wheat, and rye flours for a bread with real bite to it. This mix produces an honest peasant type of bread that I call Bohemian.

The night before baking, in a large mixing bowl combine

1 cup Bohemian starter
1 cup warm water
2 cups Bohemian Flour (see Pantry Mixes, page 18)

Cover and let stand overnight. The next morning, in another container combine

¼ cup warm water
1 scant tablespoon (or 1 packet) active dry yeast

Allow yeast to proof. Stir softened yeast mixture into sourdough mixture. Add

2 tablespoons oil
2 tablespoons molasses
2 teaspoons salt
1 tablespoon caraway seeds
1 cup Bohemian Flour

Beat well. To make a stiff dough, gradually add

2 to 3 cups Bohemian Flour

Turn out on a floured surface and knead until smooth. Place in a greased bowl, turning dough once to grease the top. Cover and let rise until doubled in bulk, about 1 hour. Knead dough down in bowl. Divide dough in half. Working with one-half at a time, roll out on a lightly floured surface to a 6×9-inch rectangle. Brush off any flour that may be on the surface of the dough. Starting with the 9-inch side, roll tightly into a long loaf. Place seam side down on a well-greased baking sheet that has been sprinkled with cornmeal. Cover and let rise until almost doubled, 45 to 60 minutes. Brush tops of loaves with a mixture of

1 egg
1 tablespoon water

Using a sharp knife, make several diagonal slashes along the top of each loaf. Bake at 400°F for 30 to 35 minutes. Cool on wire racks. Makes 2 loaves.

❉ Dark Sour-Rye Bread

The first time you make this bread, you will have to look to some other wheat or rye loaf for your crumbs. After the first batch, you can reserve enough for the next baking.

To soften yeast, in a large bowl combine

1 cup warm water
1 scant tablespoon (or 1 packet) active dry yeast
1 teaspoon sugar

Let stand 5 minutes. Stir into softened yeast mixture, in this order

2 cups Bohemian starter
*1 tablespoon powdered Postum
3 tablespoons oil
6 tablespoons dark molasses
2 teaspoons salt

---

*If Postum is not available in your market, substitute instant coffee.

1 cup toasted crumbs from previously baked loaf of Dark Sour-Rye Bread
2 cups Bohemian Flour (see Pantry Mixes, page 18)

Beat well. To make a stiff dough, gradually add

2 to 3 cups Bohemian Flour

Turn out on a floured surface and knead until smooth. Place in a greased bowl, turning dough once to grease the top. Cover and let rise until doubled in bulk, 1½ to 2 hours. Knead dough down in bowl and divide in half. Roll each half into a 9-inch square. Starting with one corner, roll to a tapered cylinder. Place seam side down on well-greased baking sheets. Cover and let rise until almost doubled, 1 to 1½ hours. Before baking, brush tops of loaves with a mixture of

1 teaspoon Postum
1 tablespoon water

Bake at 375°F for 40 to 50 minutes. Cool on wire racks. Makes 2 loaves.

To Toast Bread Crumbs

Spread bread crumbs on an ungreased baking sheet. Bake at 300°F for 5 to 15 minutes, or until well-colored. Stir once or twice during baking. Watch closely so that they do not burn. As there is some shrinkage during toasting, measure after the toasting, not before.

❋ Sourdough French Bread

Everyone who tastes this says it must go with a bowl of seafood gumbo!

The night before baking, in a large bowl combine

1 ½ cups sourdough starter, at room temperature
1 ½ cups warm water
3 cups unbleached all-purpose flour

Beat well. Cover and let stand for 8 to 12 hours. Stir into this sponge

2 teaspoons salt

To make a stiff dough, gradually add

2 to 3 cups unbleached all-purpose flour

Turn out on a floured surface and knead until smooth and elastic. Cover dough with an inverted bowl or a clean cloth while you prepare pans. Grease two double-baguette pans. Divide dough into four parts. Roll each part into a small oval. Starting with a long side, roll each oval into a long loaf. Continue to roll loaf back and forth until it is 2 inches shorter than prepared pan. Place loaves in prepared pans. Glaze generously with a mixture of

1 egg
1 teaspoon water

Slash tops of loaves with kitchen shears. I like to cut across the loaf, spacing cuts 1 inch apart. Place pans on the middle rack of oven. Place a large, flat pan with hot water on the bottom rack of the oven. Close door and let loaves rise until almost doubled in bulk, about 1 hour. Remove pan of water and loaves from oven. Preheat oven to 400°F. Loaves can be glazed again with egg wash or baked as is. If you choose to glaze the loaves a second time, do it carefully so as not to deflate the risen dough. Bake loaves at 400°F for 35 to 40 minutes. Cool on wire racks. Makes 4 loaves.

❖ Basque Sourdough

The Basques started coming to America in the mid-1800s. Their long tradition of raising and tending domestic animals in France and Spain caused them to gravitate to that line of work here. They settled in the West, where they ate only twice a day on the open range.

Before leaving his campsite for the day, a Basque shepherd prepared a batch of sourdough. He baked it in a Dutch oven on a bed of coals. More coals were heaped on top, and the whole thing covered with dirt. When he returned in the evening, the crusty sourdough bread was ready and waiting.*

This recipe has been adapted for kitchen use, but if you are adventurous, you might want to dig a hole in your backyard to bake it as the Basques did.

---

*Don and Myrtle Holm, *The Complete Sourdough Cookbook* (Caldwell, ID: The Caxton Printer, Ltd., 1972) pp. 64, 65, 66.

In a large bowl or flat container, mix together

3 ¼ cups unbleached all-purpose flour
2 tablespoons sugar
1 ½ teaspoons salt
¼ teaspoon baking soda

With your fingers, work in

2 tablespoons lard or shortening

Make a well in the center of the flour mixture and pour into it

2 cups sourdough starter

To make a stiff dough, gradually blend the flour mixture in from the sides. Turn out on a floured surface and knead until smooth and elastic, adding flour if needed. You want a rather firm dough for this bread. Shape dough into a ball and place in a well-greased Dutch oven. Place cover on the oven and let rise until almost doubled in bulk, 1 to 2 hours. Cut the form of a cross in the top of the loaf. Re-cover. Place covered loaf in preheated 450°F oven. Reduce heat to 300°F and bake for 1 to 1½ hours, or until well-browned. Cool on a wire rack. Makes 1 loaf.

❋ Skillet Sourdough

Cast-iron pots and pans were common in early pioneer kitchens. They could be used on the coals of an open fire as well as on the flat top of a wood-burning stove. Later, the more fortunate had a wood-burning range with an oven compartment for the baking of breads and other delicacies. This recipe could have been cooked in such an oven.

Grease a 9-inch cast-iron skillet. In a large, flat bowl, stir together

1 ½ cups unbleached all-purpose flour
½ teaspoon salt
½ teaspoon baking soda
1 tablespoon sugar

Work in with your fingers

4 tablespoons lard or shortening

Make a well in the center of the flour mixture. Pour into that well

¾ cup sourdough starter

Gradually work the flour mixture into the starter. Knead lightly in bowl, adding extra flour only if needed. Press dough into greased skillet in an even, flat shape. Cut dough into eight equal wedges. Brush tops of wedges with

milk or water

Sprinkle liberally with

sugar

Cover and let rest 15 minutes while preheating oven to 400°F. Bake at 400°F for 25 to 30 minutes, or until well-browned. Serve warm. No butter or jam is needed. Makes 8 servings.

❖ Sourdough Corn Bread

This is different from other corn breads you may have tasted. Both the texture and the flavor are uniquely sourdough!

Preheat oven to 425°F. Grease an 8×8-inch baking pan liberally with shortening or butter. In a large mixing bowl, combine

1 cup stone-ground yellow cornmeal
2 tablespoons sugar
¼ cup butter
½ teaspoon salt
1 cup scalded milk

Stir to dissolve butter and sugar. Let cool until just warm. Blend in

> 1 cup sourdough starter
> 1 egg
> 1 teaspoon baking powder

Beat well. Pour into prepared pan. Bake at 425°F for 30 to 35 minutes. Serve warm with butter and preserves. Makes 9 servings.

❋ Sourdough Scones

These are cut into the triangular shape we have come to associate with a scone recipe. They are rich with butter and tangy with sourdough. Try them with sweet butter and bitter marmalade.

Preheat oven to 400°F. Sift into a large bowl

> 2 cups unbleached all-purpose flour
> ½ teaspoon salt
> 1 teaspoon cream of tartar
> 1 teaspoon baking soda
> 1 tablespoon sugar

Using a pastry blender or two table knives, cut into the flour

> 7 tablespoons butter

With a fork, stir into flour mixture

> 1 ¼ cups sourdough starter

Toss on a floured surface until no longer sticky. Divide into four parts. Pat each part into a round shape, ½ inch thick. Cut each round into four equal wedges. Place wedges on a lightly greased or nonstick baking sheet. Bake in preheated 400°F oven for 12 to 15 minutes. Makes 16 scones.

❖ Sourdough Biscuits

If you like biscuits, you will love these. Split the leftovers in half and butter and broil them like English muffins.

Preheat oven to 425°F. Lightly grease a large baking sheet. Sift together into a large bowl

> *3 cups unbleached all-purpose flour*
> *1 tablespoon sugar*
> *1 tablespoon baking powder*
> *1 teaspoon salt*

With a pastry blender or two table knives, cut into dry ingredients

> *1 cup shortening*

With a fork, stir into this mixture

> *2 cups sourdough starter*

Toss on a floured surface until no longer sticky. Knead lightly. Pat or roll out to ½-inch thickness. Section with a floured biscuit cutter or simply cut into squares with a knife. Place on prepared baking sheet. These may be covered and allowed to rest 15 minutes before baking, or baked right away. If you have the time, let them rest. Bake at 425°F for 10 to 15 minutes. Watch these closely as they burn more readily than regular biscuits. Makes about 16 large biscuits.

❖ Bride's Biscuits

Here is a simplified sourdough biscuit recipe for young marrieds or anyone else who wants an easy recipe.

Preheat oven to 450°F. Generously butter an 8×8-inch baking pan. In a medium-sized bowl, mix together with a fork

> *1 ½ cups biscuit mix, such as Bisquick*
> *1 cup sourdough starter*

Knead lightly on a floured surface. Pat or roll out to ½-inch thickness. Cut into nine squares. Place in prepared pan. Brush tops of biscuits with

melted butter

Bake in preheated 450°F oven for 12 to 15 minutes, or until lightly browned. Serve at once. Makes 9 biscuits.

❈ Sourdough Pancakes and Waffles

"Sourdoughs" require that sour flavor in their pancakes as well as in their bread. The taste is addictive. When a restaurant serves sourdough bread with its meals, you can often detect the smell the instant you walk in the door. What a way to whet an appetite!

The night before, in a large mixing bowl combine

1 cup sourdough starter
1 cup milk
1 cup unbleached all-purpose flour

Beat well. Cover and let stand overnight. The next morning, sift together and set aside

1 cup unbleached all-purpose flour
1 tablespoon sugar
½ teaspoon baking soda
½ teaspoon salt
1 teaspoon baking powder

Meanwhile, stir into sponge

2 eggs
¼ cup oil

Stir in the sifted ingredients. *For pancakes:* Bake on a greased griddle at 375°F until deep golden brown. Turn only once. Makes 16 4-inch cakes. *For waffles:* Bake in a preheated hot waffle iron until steaming stops. Makes 4 large waffles.

Sour Buckwheat Cakes

Follow the directions for Sourdough Pancakes and Waffles, substituting buckwheat flour for the second cup of unbleached all-purpose flour. Bake the same way.

❖ Sourdough Doughnuts

Many "sourdoughs" have discovered how to make sourdough doughnuts by trial and error. You can deep-fry small gobs of most any sourdough bread dough for round doughnuts that will disappear before they have a chance to cool.

Sift together and set aside

> 2 cups unbleached all-purpose flour
> ½ teaspoon salt
> 1 teaspoon baking powder
> ½ teaspoon baking soda
> ½ teaspoon nutmeg

In a large bowl, beat

> 1 egg

Stir into egg, in this order

> ½ cup sugar
> ⅓ cup buttermilk
> 2 tablespoons oil
> ½ cup sourdough starter
> sifted dry ingredients

If necessary, add more flour to make a soft dough. Toss on a floured surface until no longer sticky. Roll out to ½-inch thickness and section with a floured doughnut cutter. Place cut doughnuts on waxed paper and cover with a towel. This will prevent their drying out while you work. Fry in 375°F oil until well-browned, turning once. Roll in

> sugar

Serve while still warm. Makes about 10 doughnuts.

❖ Perpetual Sweet-Starter Bread

The starter for this bread should not be soured. It must be used and replenished frequently to keep the yeast active and multiplying. It approximates the kind of bread made around the turn of the century when packaged yeast was not yet readily available to the home cook. Cookbooks written at that time contain recipes for yeast starters made with hops, potatoes, and ginger.

If you bake a lot of bread, using homegrown yeast can stretch your bread dollar, providing a multitude of loaves that require only one tablespoon of the commercial product. A sweet starter is best when used every two or three days. If your starter starts to slow down or turn sour, use it up and start a new one.

In a very large bowl, combine

> *2 cups warm water*
> *2 cups unbleached all-purpose flour*
> *⅔ cup sugar*
> *1 scant tablespoon (or 1 packet) active dry yeast*

Stir well. It is okay to have a few lumps. Cover and let rise until doubled, 1 to 2 hours. *Stir down. Add

> *3 cups warm water*
> *3 cups unbleached all-purpose flour*

Beat well. Cover and let rise until doubled. The time required for this depends upon the age of the starter. Stir down. Remove 3 cups of this batter for your Perpetual Sweet Starter; cover and refrigerate. To remainder, add

> *2 teaspoons salt*
> *2 teaspoons oil*
> ***1 cup unbleached all-purpose flour*

Beat well. To make a stiff dough, gradually add

> *3 to 4 cups unbleached all-purpose flour*

**In order to vary this recipe, you may substitute 1 cup of another flour for the 1 cup of unbleached all-purpose flour called for here. My favorites are stone-ground whole-wheat flour, stone-ground rye flour, dark buckwheat flour, and hi-lysine cornmeal.

Turn out on a floured surface and knead until smooth. Cover and let rest 20 minutes. Knead two or three times to expel air. Divide dough in half. Shape into oblong loaves and place in well-greased 9×5-inch loaf pans. Cover and let rise until doubled. Brush the tops of the risen loaves with

beaten egg (optional)

Slash the tops of the loaves with a sharp knife. This bread will rise quite a bit in the oven and slashing will help prevent a misshapen loaf. Bake at 375°F for 40 to 45 minutes. Cool on wire racks. Makes 2 loaves.

Note: Every baking day bring Perpetual Sweet Starter to room temperature. Start at * and repeat as above.

❊ Salt-Rising Bread

The name salt-rising refers to a part of the process no longer employed by modern bakers: keeping the starter and dough warm by placing it in a bed of heated rock salt. Salt-rising starters produce a close-grained bread that slices well for sandwiches and toast. For this recipe, degerminated cornmeal does not work as well as stone-ground meal which contains the germ.

Make your starter the night before you wish to bake. In a heavy saucepan, scald

1 cup milk

Stir into scalded milk

½ cup white cornmeal
2 tablespoons grated peeled potato
1 tablespoon sugar
1 teaspoon salt

Pour the cornmeal mixture into a clean, scalded quart mason jar. Place the jar in a large bowl. Pour hot tap water into the bowl, at least halfway up the side of the jar. Cover the whole thing with a cloth and let stand overnight in a warm place. An oven with a pilot light is good, as is an electric oven with the oven light lit. If you have neither of these, put the whole thing on a heating pad turned down to low. You are striving for a constant 100°F. When the starter is fermented, to form a sponge, combine in a mixing bowl

2 cups warm water
1 teaspoon (or part of 1 packet) active dry yeast
⅛ teaspoon baking soda
2 ½ cups unbleached all-purpose flour or bread flour

Press the fermented starter through a sieve, pressing back and forth with the edge of a wooden spoon to force as much of the creamy material through the sieve as possible. Add to sponge

sieved fermented starter

Stir well. Place the bowl in a pan of warm water. A roasting pan will do nicely. I have also filled a small sink with warm water and placed the bowl in that. Cover the whole thing with a large towel and let rise until doubled, 45 to 60 minutes. When risen, stir in

2 tablespoons softened butter
1 tablespoon sugar
1 teaspoon salt

To make a stiff dough, gradually add

3 ½ to 4 ½ cups unbleached all-purpose flour or bread flour

Turn out on a floured surface and knead for 5 to 10 minutes. Divide dough in half. Shape each half into a loaf and place in well-greased 9×5-inch baking pans. Cover and let rise until doubled in bulk, 45 to 60 minutes. Bake in a preheated 350°F oven for 50 to 55 minutes, or until lightly browned. Makes 2 loaves.

✶ Unleavened Bread

One day, to approximate the methods of the earliest bakers, I made an unleavened bread; I allowed it to stand, covered, until it rose, and then baked it in the usual way. On my kitchen counter with a room temperature of about 70°F, the rising took about 28 hours. The bread has a chewy texture and a good tangy flavor.

In a pottery bowl, stir together in this order

1 cup warm water
1 teaspoon salt
1 teaspoon sugar
1 teaspoon oil
1 ½ cups Bohemian Flour (see Pantry Mixes, page 18)

Beat well to develop gluten. To make a stiff dough, gradually add

½ to 1 cup Bohemian Flour

Turn out on a floured surface and knead until smooth. Shape into an oblong loaf. Place in a well-greased 8½ × 4½ × 2½-inch baking pan. Cover and let stand on counter for 24 to 36 hours. Bake in a preheated 375°F oven for 40 to 45 minutes. Turn out on a wire rack to cool. Makes 1 loaf.

✳ Breads That Say "Good Morning"

The evanescent waffles and pancakes to start your day

FAMILY-FAVORITE FLAPJACKS
GOLDEN GRIDDLECAKES
FLUFFY FLAPJACKS
SOUR-CREAM PANCAKES
CAKES AND EGGS
COUNTRY CORN CAKES
QUICK BUCKWHEAT CAKES
LIGHT BUCKWHEATS
RAISED GRIDDLECAKES
RAISED CORN CAKES
RAISED BUCKWHEAT CAKES

BUTTERMILK WAFFLES
DAD'S FAVORITE WAFFLES
CRISP CREAM WAFFLES
WHOLE-WHEAT WAFFLES
WALNUT WHEAT WAFFLES
GINGER WHEAT WAFFLES
SESAME WHEAT WAFFLES
BANANA WAFFLES
CRISPY CORN WAFFLES
CLABBERED-CHEESE WAFFLES
GINGERBREAD WAFFLES

❈ BREADS THAT SAY "GOOD MORNING"

Call them what you will—hot cakes, griddlecakes, or flapjacks—pancakes bring to breakfast an old-time goodness. Garnished with sausage or bacon, they are irresistible. Maple syrup, store-bought or homemade, warmed in a pot on the stove, provides the perfect finish.

❈ Family-Favorite Flapjacks

This recipe will take care of two hungry breakfast eaters. Double the quantity, if you need to.

Sift together and set aside

> *1 cup unbleached all-purpose flour*
> *1 teaspoon baking powder*
> *½ teaspoon baking soda*
> *¼ teaspoon salt*

In a large bowl, beat

> *2 eggs*

Blend into beaten eggs

> *2 teaspoons sugar*
> *2 tablespoons oil*
> *1 cup buttermilk*

Add dry ingredients to the buttermilk mixture, stirring only until dry ingredients are moistened. Bake on a lightly greased preheated griddle at 375°F, turning only once. Serve warm with sweet creamery butter and warmed maple syrup. Makes 10 4-inch cakes.

❖ Golden Griddlecakes

These are perfect for pancake addicts, since the ingredients are easy to keep on hand.

Sift together and set aside

> 1 ¼ *cups unbleached all-purpose flour*
> 1 *teaspoon sugar*
> 2 *teaspoons baking powder*
> ½ *teaspoon salt*

In a large bowl, beat

> 1 *egg*

Blend into beaten egg

> 2 *tablespoons oil*
> 1 *cup milk*

Add dry ingredients to the milk mixture, stirring only until smooth. Bake on a lightly greased preheated griddle at 375°F, turning only once. Serve warm with sweet creamery butter and warmed maple syrup. Makes 8 4-inch cakes.

❖ Fluffy Flapjacks

Once, when my parents were gone on a trip, my older brother taught me how to separate eggs. He had lived for a while with our Uncle Durb, who taught him all sorts of culinary tricks, including this one. The pancakes we made that day were not too different from these.

Sift together and set aside

> 1 ½ *cups unbleached all-purpose flour*
> 1 *teaspoon baking powder*
> 1 *teaspoon baking soda*
> ½ *teaspoon salt*

In a large bowl, beat well

3 egg yolks

Blend into beaten egg yolks

1 tablespoon sugar
1/4 cup melted butter, slightly cooled

Divide dry ingredients into thirds and buttermilk in half; add alternately, beginning and ending with the dry ingredients, to egg-yolk mixture

sifted dry ingredients
1 2/3 cups buttermilk

Beat until smooth. Fold in

3 egg whites, beaten until stiff but not dry

Bake on a lightly greased preheated griddle at 375°F, turning only once. This batter also makes excellent waffles. Serve warm with sweet creamery butter and homemade jams and jellies. Makes 16 4-inch cakes.

✤ Sour-Cream Pancakes

These cakes share the luxury of a full cup of sour cream and four eggs. They are outstanding!

Sift together and set aside

1 cup unbleached all-purpose flour
1/4 cup sugar
1 teaspoon baking powder
1/4 teaspoon baking soda
1/2 teaspoon salt

In a large bowl, beat

4 eggs

Blend into beaten eggs

> *1 cup sour cream*
> *¼ cup milk*

Add dry ingredients to the sour-cream mixture, stirring only until dry ingredients are moistened. Batter will be lumpy; it is all right. Bake on a lightly greased preheated griddle at 375°F, turning only once. Serve warm with butter and cinnamon-sugar. Makes 12 4-inch cakes.

❖ Cakes and Eggs

> *I call this another way to eat an egg. The olive oil gives the batter a subtly different flavor. The water contributes to a crisp texture.*

Sift together and set aside

> *2 cups unbleached all-purpose flour*
> *1 tablespoon baking powder*
> *1 teaspoon salt*
> *1 teaspoon sugar*

In a mixing bowl, beat together

> *2 eggs*
> *1 cup milk*
> *1 cup water*
> *1 tablespoon corn oil*
> *1 tablespoon olive oil*

Gently stir into egg mixture

> *sifted dry ingredients*

Preheat griddle to 370°F. When ready to bake pancake, quickly rub a cold stick of butter over the surface of the griddle. Pour about ¾ cup batter gently into the center of the griddle, letting the batter spread out to form a circle. Bake until nicely browned, turning once. While the pancake cooks, fry in another pan in melted butter

> *1 egg*

When the cake is done, place it on a warmed plate, top it with the fried egg, and serve. Offer warmed maple syrup. No butter is necessary. Makes 4 to 5 large cakes.

❖ Country Corn Cakes

A few generations ago, this recipe migrated north from the hills of Kentucky.

Sift together

> 1 cup unbleached all-purpose flour
> 1 tablespoon sugar
> 1 teaspoon baking powder
> 1 teaspoon baking soda
> 1 teaspoon salt

Stir into flour mixture and set aside

> 1 cup yellow cornmeal

In a large bowl, beat

> 3 eggs

Blend into the beaten eggs

> 2 cups buttermilk
> ¼ cup melted butter, slightly cooled

Add dry ingredients to the buttermilk mixture, stirring only until dry ingredients are moistened. Bake on a lightly greased preheated griddle at 375°F, turning only once. Serve warm with sweet creamery butter and warmed maple syrup. Makes 16 4-inch cakes.

❖ Quick Buckwheat Cakes

These quick buckwheat cakes have old-fashioned flavor. The beaten whites lighten what would otherwise be a heavy product.

Sift together and set aside

> 1 cup dark buckwheat flour
> 1 cup unbleached all-purpose flour
> 1 teaspoon salt
> 1 teaspoon baking powder
> 1 teaspoon baking soda
> 1 teaspoon cream of tartar

In a mixing bowl, beat

> 2 egg yolks

Stir into beaten yolks, in this order

> 1 tablespoon molasses
> ¼ cup oil
> 2 cups buttermilk
> sifted dry ingredients

Fold into batter, very gently

> 2 stiffly beaten egg whites

Bake on a lightly greased griddle at 375°F, turning only once. Be sure not to turn these too soon, lest they be heavy. Serve warm with sweet creamery butter and warmed maple syrup. Makes 22 to 24 cakes.

❖ Light Buckwheats

If you do not care for most buckwheat pancake recipes, and yet enjoy them at a place like the Pancake House, it may be that you are objecting to the heaviness of the buckwheat flavor. Commercial mixes have very little buckwheat in them. This is how to make a similar mix in your own kitchen. If you want to make the batter even lighter, you can separate the eggs, folding in the stiffly beaten whites at the end.

Spoon into a measuring cup

> *2 to 3 tablespoons dark buckwheat flour, according to your personal taste*

Fill cup to the rim with

> *unbleached all-purpose flour*

Sift flours with

> *½ teaspoon salt*
> *1 ½ teaspoons baking powder*
> *1 teaspoon sugar*

In a medium-sized bowl, beat

> *2 eggs*

Stir into eggs, in this order

> *¾ cup milk*
> *1 tablespoon melted butter*
> *sifted dry ingredients*

Bake on a lightly greased griddle at 375°F, using ¼ cup batter at a time. Turn only once. Makes 8 cakes.

❖ ABOUT RAISED PANCAKES

Raised pancakes derive from a time when pancakes were served as daily fare. They were mixed from a starter that was replenished daily and stored until ready for the next baking.

If you wish to save pancake starters to make a new batch each day, remove 1 cup of the starter sponge before adding the morning's ingredients. Store, loosely covered, in the refrigerator. Do not use yeast on subsequent days, use your crock of starter instead. Be sure to allow for expansion when storing either batters or starters. A quiet-looking mixture can become active when you are not looking!

Leftover batter may be held over for a second day's baking. Just cover with plastic wrap and store in the refrigerator.

❖ Raised Griddlecakes

Yeast-risen pancakes are very light. Started the night before, these are simple to make.

In a large bowl, combine

> *1 cup warm water*
> *1 scant tablespoon (or 1 packet) active dry yeast*
> *1 tablespoon brown sugar*
> *1 cup unbleached all-purpose flour*

Beat well. Batter may be lumpy—it is okay. Cover and let stand overnight. In the morning, stir in, in this order

> *1 egg*
> *¾ teaspoon salt*
> *1 tablespoon brown sugar*
> *1 cup unbleached all-purpose flour*

Heat together until butter melts

> *3 tablespoons butter*
> *1 tablespoon oil*

Cool slightly. Stir 3 tablespoons of butter-oil mixture into batter. Use the remainder for greasing the griddle. The batter should be slightly thicker than other pancake batters. If too thick, however, you will produce more of an English muffin than a pancake. Thin the batter by stirring in

> *½ cup milk, more or less*

Cover and let rest 15 minutes before baking. Bake on a greased griddle at 375°F, turning only once. Use ¼ cup batter per cake. Serve with butter and either maple syrup or a fruit syrup. Makes 12 cakes.

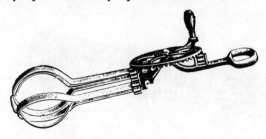

❖ Raised Corn Cakes

You would expect a cornmeal pancake to be heavier than these are. Serve them with syrup for breakfast or with fried pork chops for supper.

In a 3-quart or larger mixing bowl, place

> *1 cup cornmeal*

Stir into the meal

> *2 cups milk, heated just to boiling*

Let cool until just warm. Meanwhile, to soften yeast, in a small container combine

> *¼ cup warm water*
> *1 scant tablespoon (or 1 packet) active dry yeast*
> *1 tablespoon honey*

When milk mixture has cooled down to warm, stir in

> *softened yeast mixture*
> *1 ½ cups unbleached all-purpose flour*

Beat well. Cover and let stand for 6 to 8 hours or overnight. When ready to bake, stir in, in this order

> *1 teaspoon salt*
> *1 tablespoon honey*
> *2 eggs*
> *¼ teaspoon baking soda dissolved in 2 tablespoons warm water*
> *2 tablespoons melted butter*

Cover batter and let rest for 15 minutes. Bake on a preheated greased griddle at 375°F, using ¼ cup batter per cake. Turn only once. Makes 16 cakes.

❖ Raised Buckwheat Cakes

Serve these hearty pancakes with thick slabs of country bacon or fried chunks of leftover country ham. Top them off with gobs of sweet butter and pure maple syrup.

To soften yeast, in a 3-quart or larger bowl combine

> *2 cups warm water*
> *1 scant tablespoon (or 1 packet) active dry yeast*
> *1 tablespoon molasses*

Stir into softened yeast

> *1 teaspoon salt*
> *1 cup dark buckwheat flour*
> *1 ½ cups unbleached all-purpose flour*

Beat until smooth. Cover and let stand overnight. In the morning, stir in, in this order

> *1 tablespoon molasses*
> *1 egg*
> *¼ teaspoon baking soda dissolved in 2 tablespoons warm water*
> *2 tablespoons melted butter*

The batter will be thinner than that for other pancakes; it is okay. Bake on a greased griddle at 375°F, using ¼ cup batter per cake. Turn only once. Makes 16 cakes.

❖ Buttermilk Waffles

Richer than some, these waffles are yummy for breakfast, brunch, or supper.

Sift together into a large bowl

> *1 ¾ cups unbleached all-purpose flour*
> *1 teaspoon sugar*
> *2 teaspoons baking powder*
> *½ teaspoon baking soda*
> *½ teaspoon salt*

In another bowl beat

> *2 eggs*

Blend into beaten eggs

> *1 ¼ cups buttermilk*
> *½ cup melted butter, cooled slightly*

Add buttermilk mixture to the dry ingredients, stirring only until dry ingredients are moistened. Bake in a hot, preheated waffle iron until steaming stops. Serve warm with sweet creamery butter and warmed maple syrup. Makes 3 waffles.

❖ Dad's Favorite Waffles

Sift together into a medium-sized bowl and set aside

> *1 cup unbleached all-purpose flour*
> *1 tablespoon sugar*
> *1 ½ teaspoons baking powder*
> *¼ teaspoon salt*

In another bowl beat

> *1 egg*

Stir into beaten egg

> *1 cup milk*
> *3 tablespoons melted butter, cooled slightly*

Add milk mixture to the dry ingredients, stirring only until dry ingredients are moistened. Bake in a hot, preheated waffle iron until steaming stops. Serve warm with sweet creamery butter and warmed maple syrup. Makes 2 waffles. This recipe may be successfully doubled by using twice the amounts given.

✣ Crisp Cream Waffles

Equal amounts of cream and butter in the batter make these waffles ultrarich—perfect for that special occasion.

Sift together twice and set aside

2 cups unbleached all-purpose flour
½ teaspoon salt
1 tablespoon baking powder
1 tablespoon sugar

Beat together

3 egg yolks
1 cup milk
½ cup whipping cream

Fold into egg-yolk mixture, in this order

sifted dry ingredients
½ cup melted butter, slightly cooled
3 egg whites, stiffly beaten

Bake in a preheated waffle iron until steaming stops. Serve with Whipped Honey Butter (see page 378). Makes 4 large waffles.

✣ Whole-Wheat Waffles

This is a good basic wheat-waffle batter. See the variations below.

Sift together into a large bowl

1 cup unbleached all-purpose flour
1 teaspoon sugar
1 tablespoon baking powder
¾ teaspoon salt

Stir in

¾ cup whole-wheat flour
1 tablespoon wheat germ

In another bowl beat

>   *2 eggs*

Blend into beaten eggs

>   *1 ¼ cups milk*
>   *⅓ cup oil*

Add milk mixture to the dry ingredients, stirring only until dry ingredients are moistened. Bake in a hot, preheated waffle iron until steaming stops. Serve warm with honey-butter. Makes 3 waffles.

❖ Walnut Wheat Waffles

Add ½ teaspoon cinnamon to the dry ingredients when sifting. Add ½ cup finely chopped walnuts to the batter before baking.

❖ Ginger Wheat Waffles

Add ¼ cup very finely chopped candied ginger to the batter before baking.

❖ Sesame Wheat Waffles

Add 1 tablespoon sesame seeds to the dry ingredients after sifting.

❖ Banana Waffles

Expect banana waffles to be a little softer than most. If you have a temperature control on your iron, you may want to set it a little higher than usual.

Sift together and set aside

>   *1 ¾ cups unbleached all-purpose flour*
>   *½ teaspoon salt*
>   *1 tablespoon baking powder*
>   *2 tablespoons brown sugar*

In a mixing bowl, beat

> 2 egg yolks

Stir into egg yolks, in this order

> ¼ cup oil
> ½ cup mashed banana
> 1 ¼ cups milk
> sifted dry ingredients

Fold into batter

> 2 egg whites, stiffly beaten

Bake in a heated waffle iron until steaming stops. Serve with butter and cinnamon-sugar. Makes 3 large waffles.

❖ Crispy Corn Waffles

The combination of cornmeal and buttermilk makes for a great waffle. This recipe will accommodate most families.

Sift together into a large bowl

> 1 cup unbleached all-purpose flour
> 1 cup yellow cornmeal
> 1 tablespoon sugar
> 2 teaspoons baking powder
> 1 teaspoon baking soda
> ½ teaspoon salt

In another bowl beat

> 2 eggs

Blend into beaten eggs

> 2 cups buttermilk
> ⅓ cup oil

Add buttermilk mixture to the dry ingredients, stirring only until moistened. Bake in a hot, preheated waffle iron until steaming stops. Serve warm with sweet creamery butter and warmed sweet sorghum syrup. Makes 4 large waffles.

❊ Clabbered-Cheese Waffles

Clabbered milk is an old-fashioned term for sour milk.

Put into a measuring cup

> *1 tablespoon apple cider vinegar*

Fill the cup with

> *milk*

Let this mixture stand 5 to 10 minutes to clabber. Sift together

> *1 ¼ cups unbleached all-purpose flour*
> *¼ teaspoon salt*
> *¼ teaspoon baking powder*
> *¼ teaspoon baking soda*
> *¼ teaspoon sugar*

In a mixing bowl, beat

> *2 egg yolks*

Stir into egg yolks, in this order

> *2 tablespoons oil*
> *clabbered milk*
> *sifted dry ingredients*

Fold into batter, in this order

> *½ cup grated sharp cheddar cheese*
> *1 tablespoon grated Parmesan cheese*
> *2 egg whites, stiffly beaten*

Bake in a preheated waffle iron until steaming stops. Serve with soft butter and crisply fried crumbled bacon. Makes 2 large waffles.

❖ Gingerbread Waffles

These are just right, not too sweet. They add nice variety to a mixed breakfast buffet.

Sift together and set aside

> 1 ¾ *cups unbleached all-purpose flour*
> ½ *teaspoon salt*
> ½ *teaspoon baking soda*
> 1 *teaspoon baking powder*
> 1 *teaspoon ginger*
> 1 *teaspoon cinnamon*

In a mixing bowl, cream together

> ⅓ *cup shortening*
> ¾ *cup molasses*
> 2 *tablespoons brown sugar*

Add to shortening mixture, one at a time, beating well after each addition

> 2 *egg yolks*

Dividing the dry ingredients into three parts and the buttermilk in half, add alternately, beginning and ending with the dry ingredients

> *sifted dry ingredients*
> ½ *cup buttermilk*

Fold into batter

> 2 *egg whites, stiffly beaten*

Bake in a preheated waffle iron until steaming stops. Serve warm with applesauce or Lemon Curd. These are quite soft. Take care when removing them from the waffle grid. They must be eaten at once. Makes 3 waffles.

❋ The Little Breads

Rolls, biscuits, and muffins for morning, noon, or nighttime

PARKERHOUSE ROLLS
BUTTERMILK BUNS
OLD-FASHIONED WHEAT ROLLS
KAISER ROLLS
GILROY GARLIC ROLLS
COUNTRY CORNMEAL ROLLS
MILK-BAKED ROLLS
FRENCH ROLLS WITH TWO HEELS
POTATO-WATER ROLLS #1
POTATO-WATER ROLLS #2
24-KARAT DINNER ROLLS
SOUTHERN BISCUITS
BUTTER BISCUITS
WHOLE-WHEAT BISCUITS
IRMA'S DROP BISCUITS
FRIED BISCUITS
BEATEN BISCUITS

CREAM BISCUITS
CREAM-CHEESE BISCUITS
SOUR-CREAM BISCUITS
HOMESPUN BISCUITS
CORNMEAL BISCUITS
PEANUT-BUTTER AND JELLY MUFFINS
SWEET STREUSEL MUFFINS
GRAHAM-CRACKER MUFFINS
MUSTARD MUFFINS
MARMALADE MUFFINS
GEORGIA PECAN MUFFINS
CORN MUFFINS
WHOLE-GRAIN CORN MUFFINS
SOUR-CREAM MUFFINS
DATE MUFFINS
WHEAT DATE-NUT MUFFINS

❖ THE LITTLE BREADS

Rolls, biscuits, and muffins! You will want to serve these breads warm, wrapped in a linen towel and placed in a basket or a special bowl. You can serve one kind at a time, or put a mixture on the table.

Hot rolls and cold curled butter can turn an ordinary meal into something special. Serve a soft roll with an old-fashioned supper, a hard, crusty roll with a peasant stew. Perk up a simple salad supper with a highly flavored roll.

❖ Parkerhouse Rolls

Parkerhouse rolls were first served in the old Parkerhouse Hotel in Boston. They can easily be recognized as a small biscuit-shaped roll that is buttered and folded in half before the last rising. Here is my version of that traditional roll.

In a large mixing bowl combine

¼ cup sugar
½ cup shortening
1 ½ teaspoons salt
½ cup boiling water

Stir to dissolve shortening and sugar. Let cool until just warm. Meanwhile, in another container combine

½ cup warm water
1 scant tablespoon (or 1 packet) active dry yeast

Allow yeast to proof. When sugar-shortening mixture has cooled down to warm, stir in

softened yeast mixture
1 egg

Gradually add, mixing well

3 cups unbleached all-purpose flour

Cover and let rise until doubled in bulk, 45 to 60 minutes. Punch dough down. Roll out on a lightly floured surface to a ¼-inch thickness. Section with a floured 3-inch biscuit cutter. Brush with melted butter. Mark a crease with the dull edge of a knife to one side of center of each round. Fold small part over large, pressing to seal. Place on greased baking sheets. Cover and let rise until almost doubled, 30 to 45 minutes. Before baking, sift a light dusting of flour over the tops of the rolls. Bake at 400°F for 12 to 15 minutes. Serve warm. Makes 24 rolls.

❖ Buttermilk Buns

Every now and then I like to go on a buttermilk binge, making every kind of buttermilk bread I can think of. During one of those binges I discovered these tasty buns.

In a large mixing bowl, combine

½ cup sugar
½ cup shortening
2 cups hot buttermilk

Stir to dissolve sugar and shortening. Let cool until just warm. Meanwhile, in another container combine

½ cup warm water
2 scant tablespoons (or 2 packets) active dry yeast

Allow yeast to proof. When buttermilk mixture has cooled down to warm, stir in

softened yeast mixture
3 cups unbleached all-purpose flour or bread flour

Beat well. Cover and let stand for 30 minutes. Stir dough down. To make a soft dough, sift together and gradually add

3 cups unbleached all-purpose flour or bread flour
½ teaspoon baking powder
½ teaspoon baking soda
2 teaspoons salt

Turn out on a floured surface and knead until smooth. Add more flour, if needed. Cover and let rest 30 minutes. Knead lightly. Divide dough into 3 parts. Divide each part into 12 pieces. Shape each piece into a small ball. Arrange balls in 3 well-greased 9-inch cake pans in the following manner: Using 3 pieces each, form a triangle in the center of each pan. Arrange 9 pieces around the perimeter of each triangle. Cover and allow to rise until almost doubled, 30 to 45 minutes. Bake at 375°F for 20 to 25 minutes. Remove buns in one piece from each pan to cool on wire racks. When cool, wrap in foil. If desired, overwrap with a plastic sack to freeze. Reheat in foil wrap. Makes 36 buns.

❖ Old-Fashioned Wheat Rolls

A restaurant in downtown Champaign, Illinois, served rolls similar to these when they first opened. I thought they were so good that I immediately tried to duplicate them.

In a large mixing bowl combine

> ⅓ *cup brown sugar*
> ⅓ *cup shortening*
> 2 *teaspoons salt*
> 1 *cup boiling water*

Stir to dissolve brown sugar and shortening. Let cool until just warm. Meanwhile, in another container combine

> ½ *cup warm water*
> 2 *scant tablespoons (or 2 packets) active dry yeast*
> ¼ *teaspoon ginger*

Allow yeast to proof. When first mixture has cooled down to warm, stir in

> *softened yeast mixture*
> 1 *egg*
> 3 *cups Wheat-Bread Flour (see Pantry Mixes, page 18)*

Beat well. To make a soft dough, gradually add

2 to 3 cups Wheat-Bread Flour

Turn out on a floured surface and knead until smooth. Place in a greased bowl, turning dough once to grease the top. Cover and let rise until doubled in bulk, 45 to 60 minutes. Knead dough down in bowl. Divide dough in half. Divide each half into 12 pieces and shape each piece into a small ball. Place in well-greased muffin cups. Cover and let rise until almost doubled, 30 to 45 minutes. Bake at 400°F for 12 to 15 minutes. Serve at once or cool on wire racks. Makes 24 rolls.

✤ Kaiser Rolls

These crusty German rolls, topped with a generous coating of poppy seeds, can elevate the hamburger from its usual humble status. I like to split them to hold double skinny burgers, one with cheese and the other with barbecue sauce. A fresh dill pickle and one giant batter-fried onion complete the plate.

To form a sponge, in a mixing bowl combine

2 ¼ cups warm water
2 scant tablespoons (or 2 packets) active dry yeast
¼ cup sugar
3 cups bread flour

Beat until smooth. Cover and let stand for 10 minutes. Stir into this sponge

2 teaspoons salt
¼ cup oil

To make a stiff dough, gradually add

2 ½ to 3 cups bread flour

Turn out on a floured surface and knead until smooth and elastic, adding more flour as needed to prevent sticking. Place in a well-greased bowl, turning dough once to grease the top. Cover and let rise until doubled in bulk, 45 to 60 minutes. Punch dough down. Divide dough into 16 equal pieces. Shape each piece into a ball, pulling the sides down and pinching together on the bottom. Place balls of dough on greased baking sheets, about 2 inches apart. Cover and let rest 10 minutes. With floured hands, gently press each ball to flatten slightly. You want to leave them more rounded than an ordinary hamburger bun. Cover again and allow to rise until almost doubled, 20 to 30 minutes. Meanwhile, preheat oven to 400°F. Before baking, brush tops of rolls with a mixture of

1 egg white
1 teaspoon water

Sprinkle generously with

poppy seeds

Using a sharp knife, make 5 slashes, each ¼-inch deep, on each roll, starting from the center out. Bake at 400°F for 15 to 20 minutes, or until well-browned. Cool on wire racks. Makes 16 rolls.

❖ Gilroy Garlic Rolls

These rolls are delicately flavored with garlic, both in the dough and in the filling. They are named in honor of the self-proclaimed garlic capital of the world, Gilroy, California. Each year the citizens of Gilroy host a festival to celebrate their bounteous harvest. Gourmet Alley is the heart of the festival's food showcase, where local chefs produce the famous Garlic Festival Calamari and other culinary wonders. There is also the annual Great Garlic Recipe Contest and Cook-off in which all contestants must use a minimum of three cloves of garlic. If you are interested in attending the festival or competing in the recipe contest, contact the Gilroy Garlic Festival Committee, P.O. Box 2311, Gilroy, California 95020.

To soften yeast, in a large mixing bowl combine

1 cup warm water
1 scant tablespoon (or 1 packet) active dry yeast
1 tablespoon sugar

Let stand 5 minutes. Stir into softened yeast mixture

> *1 tablespoon olive oil*
> *1 teaspoon salt*
> *1 egg*
> *2 cups unbleached all-purpose flour*

Beat well. To make a soft dough, gradually add

> *1 to 1 ¼ cups unbleached all-purpose flour*

Turn out on a floured surface and knead until smooth. Place in a well-buttered bowl, turning dough once to butter the top. Cover and let rise until doubled in bulk, 45 to 60 minutes. Meanwhile, mix together

> *½ cup softened butter*
> *1 clove garlic, put through a garlic press*

Punch down dough. Toss on a lightly floured surface until no longer sticky. Roll dough out to a 9×12-inch rectangle. With a short side facing you, spread bottom two-thirds of rectangle with

> *½ of butter mixture*

Fold top third of dough down over the center third. Fold bottom third of dough up over this. Press edges to seal. Wrap dough in plastic and refrigerate 15 minutes. Roll again to a 9×12-inch rectangle. As before, spread with

> *½ of butter mixture*

Fold as before. Wrap and refrigerate 15 minutes. Roll and fold again, using no butter. Wrap and refrigerate 1 hour. Divide dough in half. Seal cut edges by pinching together. Working with one-half of the dough at a time, roll into a 12-inch circle. Using a sharp knife, cut circle into 12 equal wedge-shaped pieces. Near the wide end of each piece place

> *1 teaspoon Ricotta Filling*

Starting with the wide end, roll each wedge to the point. Place, point side down, on lightly greased or nonstick baking sheets. Cover and let rise until doubled, about 1 hour. Before baking, brush tops of rolls with a mixture of

> *1 egg white*
> *1 teaspoon water*

Bake in preheated 375°F oven for 20 to 25 minutes, or until golden brown. Serve warm. Makes 24 rolls.

Ricotta Filling
In a small bowl, mix together

> ½ cup ricotta cheese
> 2 tablespoons grated Parmesan cheese
> 2 garlic cloves, put through a garlic press
> ½ teaspoon finely chopped fresh Italian parsley
> ½ teaspoon finely chopped fresh oregano
> 1 egg yolk
> pinch of freshly grated pepper
> pinch of freshly grated nutmeg

❖ Country Cornmeal Rolls

In a large mixing bowl combine

> 1 cup yellow cornmeal
> ⅓ cup sugar
> ⅓ cup shortening
> 2 teaspoons salt
> 1 cup boiling water

Stir to dissolve sugar and shortening. Cool until warm. Meanwhile, in another container combine

> ¼ cup warm water
> 1 scant tablespoon (or 1 packet) active dry yeast

Allow yeast to proof. When cornmeal mixture has cooled to warm, stir in

> softened yeast mixture
> 1 cup undiluted evaporated milk
> 2 cups unbleached all-purpose flour or bread flour

Beat well. To make a soft dough, gradually add

> 2 to 3 cups unbleached all-purpose flour or bread flour

Turn out on a floured surface and knead until smooth. Place in a greased bowl, turning dough once to grease the top. Cover and let rise until doubled in bulk, 1 to 1½ hours. Knead dough down in bowl and divide in half. Divide each half into 12 pieces. Shape each piece into a small ball. Place in well-greased muffin cups. Cover and let rise until almost doubled, 45 to 60 minutes. Bake at 400°F for 15 to 20 minutes. Serve at once or cool on wire racks. Makes 24 rolls.

❖ Milk-Baked Rolls

If you like old-fashioned, rich rolls, you will love these. The milk poured around the rolls is absorbed during baking.

In a large bowl beat

> *3 eggs*

Stir into eggs

> *1 tablespoon sugar*
> *2 cups warm milk*
> *1 scant tablespoon (or 1 packet) active dry yeast*
> *4 cups unbleached all-purpose flour*

Beat well. Cover this sponge and let stand for 1 hour. Stir down. Stir into sponge

> *1 teaspoon salt*
> *1 cup softened butter*

To make a soft dough, gradually add

> *2 ¼ to 2 ¾ cups unbleached all-purpose flour*

Cover and let rise again, about 1 hour. Stir down. Toss on a floured surface until no longer sticky. Roll out to ½-inch thickness. Cut into rounds with a 3-inch cutter. Place in three well-buttered 8 × 8-inch Pyrex pans, using 9 rounds per pan. Cover and let rise until doubled in bulk, 45 to 60 minutes. Pour around rolls in pans, using 2 to 3 tablespoons per pan

> *½ cup warm milk*

Bake in a preheated 350°F oven for 20 to 30 minutes, or until browned. Remove from pan and cool on racks. You will have to cut these apart to remove them easily. Serve warm or cold. Makes 27 rolls.

❊ French Rolls With Two Heels

Three companions and I were in Chicago one day for some serious shopping. Having "done" North Michigan Avenue, we stopped at Shucker's restaurant for a late, light fish lunch. As usual, the first thing brought to the table was a loaf of French bread.

Simultaneously, the four of us reached for the two heels, saying in unison, "I'll eat the heel so no one else will have to." Obviously, one loaf of French bread cannot provide four heels, so two of us went without. After that, I decided to design a roll that would look like two heels of French bread that have been joined together. It will surely satisfy the heel-lovers at your table.

To soften yeast, in a large bowl combine

1 cup warm water
1 scant tablespoon (or 1 packet) active dry yeast
1 teaspoon sugar

Let stand 5 minutes. Stir into softened yeast mixture

1 cup warm water
2 teaspoons salt
1 teaspoon oil
3 cups unbleached all-purpose flour

Beat well. To make a soft dough, gradually add

2 to 2 ½ cups unbleached all-purpose flour

Turn out on a floured surface. Knead gently for a full 10 minutes, adding only enough flour to the board to prevent sticking. Place in a greased bowl, turning dough once to grease the top. Cover and let rise until doubled in bulk, about 1 hour. Knead dough down in bowl. Cover and let rise until doubled again, 45 to 60 minutes. Knead dough down in bowl. Divide dough into 16 parts. Roll each part into a ball and place on well-greased baking sheets, leaving ample space (at least 2 inches) between balls of dough. Cover and let rise until doubled, 30 to 45 minutes. Before baking, brush any exposed parts of dough with a mixture of

> *1 egg white*
> *1 teaspoon water*

With a kitchen shears, make one deep slash in the center of each roll, cutting almost halfway through. Bake in a preheated 425°F oven for 20 to 25 minutes, or until well-browned. Makes 16 rolls with two heels.

❖ Potato-Water Rolls #1

> *When I entertain with roast beef or bird, I like to make a casserole called Sinful Potatoes. This dish has an added attraction. It produces hot potato water I can use in rolls.*

In a large bowl combine

> *2 cups hot potato water*
> *2 tablespoons butter*
> *1 tablespoon sugar*
> *1 tablespoon salt*

Stir to dissolve butter and sugar. Let cool until just warm. Meanwhile, to soften yeast, in a small container combine

> *½ cup warm water (can be potato water)*
> *1 scant tablespoon (or 1 packet) active dry yeast*

When first mixture has cooled down to warm, stir in

> *softened yeast mixture*
> *3 cups unbleached all-purpose flour*

Beat well. To make a soft dough, gradually add

> *3 to 3 ½ cups unbleached all-purpose flour*

Turn out on a floured surface and knead until smooth. Place in a greased bowl, turning dough once to grease the top. Cover and let rise until doubled in bulk, 1 to 1½ hours. Knead dough down in bowl. Divide into 24 pieces. Shape each piece into a ball and place on well-greased baking sheets. Cover and let rise until doubled, 45 to 60 minutes. Before baking, sift flour over the tops of the rolls. With a kitchen shears slash the center of each roll. Bake in a preheated 425°F oven for 20 to 25 minutes, or until browned. Cool on wire racks. Makes 24 rolls.

❊ Potato-Water Rolls #2

Cornmeal gives these rolls a pleasant texture. The sponge that stands overnight imparts a touch of sourdough flavor.

In a large bowl combine

> *2 cups warm potato water*
> *2 cups unbleached all-purpose flour*
> *1 teaspoon (about ½ packet) active dry yeast*

Beat well. Cover and let stand on counter for 8 to 12 hours. Stir down sponge. To soften yeast, in a small container combine

> *½ cup warm water*
> *1 teaspoon (about ½ packet) active dry yeast*

Add to the sponge and stir in well

> *softened yeast mixture*
> *¼ cup yellow cornmeal*
> *1 tablespoon oil*
> *1 tablespoon molasses*
> *1 tablespoon salt*

To make a stiff dough, gradually add

> *3 ½ to 4 ½ cups unbleached all-purpose flour*

Turn out on a floured surface and knead until smooth. Place in a well-greased bowl, turning dough once to grease the top. Cover and let rise until doubled in bulk, 1 to 1½ hours. Knead dough down in bowl. Toss on a floured surface until no longer sticky. Divide into 36 equal parts. (Each part will be a little smaller than a golf ball.) Shape each part into a ball and place in a well-greased muffin cup. Cover and let rise until almost doubled, 30 to 45 minutes. Before baking, cut a cross in the top of each roll with a kitchen shears so the rolls resemble a cloverleaf. Bake in preheated 425°F oven for 15 to 20 minutes, or until well-browned. Cool on wire racks. Makes 3 dozen rolls.

❖ 24-Karat Dinner Rolls

Ginger adds just the right touch to these light-as-a-feather, golden-colored buns.

To soften yeast, in a mixing bowl stir together

> 1 cup warm water
> 1 scant tablespoon (or 1 packet) active dry yeast
> 1 teaspoon sugar

Allow yeast to proof. Stir into softened yeast mixture, in this order

> 1 cup cooked and mashed carrots, cooled down to warm
> ¼ cup soft butter
> 2 tablespoons finely chopped crystallized ginger
> 1 ½ teaspoons salt
> 1 egg
> 2 cups unbleached all-purpose flour

Beat well. To make a soft dough, gradually add

> 1 ½ to 2 ½ cups unbleached all-purpose flour

The amount of flour needed can vary, depending on how moist the carrots are. Turn out on a floured surface and knead until smooth. Place in a greased bowl, turning dough once to grease the top. Cover and let rise until doubled in bulk, 45 to 60 minutes. Knead dough down in bowl. Divide into three parts. Divide each part into eight equal pieces. Shape each piece into a round ball and place in well-greased muffin cups. Cover and let rise until almost doubled, 30 to 45 minutes. Bake in a preheated 400°F oven for 20 to 25 minutes, or until lightly browned. Serve warm with sweet butter. Makes 24 rolls.

❖ Southern Biscuits

Southerners are famous for their light biscuits, but anyone can produce them.

Preheat oven to 450°F. Sift together into a large bowl

2 cups unbleached all-purpose flour
2 teaspoons sugar
4 teaspoons baking powder
½ teaspoon salt

Cut into dry ingredients with a pastry blender or two table knives

½ cup shortening

Stir in with a fork just until dough cleans sides of bowl

⅔ cup milk

Knead lightly on a lightly floured surface. Pat or roll out to ½-inch thickness. Cut out with a floured biscuit cutter and place on an ungreased baking sheet. Bake at 450°F for 10 to 12 minutes. Serve warm with honey-butter. Makes 16 biscuits.

❖ Butter Biscuits

Some experts say you should never, never use butter in biscuits, but these are pretty good. Try them and see what you think.

Preheat oven to 450°F. Sift together into a large bowl

2 cups unbleached all-purpose flour
1 tablespoon baking powder
¾ teaspoon salt

Cut into dry ingredients, using a pastry blender or two table knives

6 tablespoons cold butter, cut into 6 pieces

Stir in with a fork just until dough cleans sides of bowl

⅔ cup milk

Knead lightly on a lightly floured surface. Pat or roll out to ½-inch thickness. Cut into squares with a knife and place on an ungreased baking sheet. Bake at 450°F for 10 to 12 minutes. Serve warm with sweet butter and orange marmalade. Makes 12 to 16 biscuits.

✖ Whole-Wheat Biscuits

These biscuits are not quite as rich as some. You can feel virtuous while enjoying them.

Preheat oven to 450°F. Sift together into a large bowl

> *1 cup unbleached all-purpose flour*
> *1 teaspoon sugar*
> *1 tablespoon baking powder*
> *¾ teaspoon salt*

Stir in

> *1 cup whole-wheat flour*
> *1 teaspoon wheat germ*

Cut into dry ingredients

> *¼ cup shortening*

Stir in with a fork just until dough cleans sides of bowl

> *¾ cup milk*

Knead lightly on a lightly floured surface. Pat or roll out to ½-inch thickness. Cut into squares with a knife and place on an ungreased baking sheet. Bake at 450°F for 12 to 15 minutes. Serve with sweet butter and strawberry preserves. Makes 12 to 16 biscuits.

✖ Irma's Drop Biscuits

My friend Irma Zook once said that although stand-up affairs had obviously gained acceptance by the young, she didn't think you had really entertained until you let people put their legs under your table. It was at one of her innovative sit-down suppers that she served these delicious biscuits.

Preheat oven to 350°F. In a 9×12-inch Pyrex dish, combine

¼ cup olive oil
¼ cup melted butter

Swirl dish to coat bottom evenly. In a medium-sized bowl, combine

2 cups biscuit mix, such as Bisquick
¾ cup grated Parmesan cheese

Stir into biscuit mixture with a fork just until dry ingredients are moistened

1 cup whipping cream

Drop by tablespoon into oil and butter in prepared pan. Bake at 350°F for 15 to 20 minutes. Serve warm. Makes 12 to 18 biscuits.

❖ Fried Biscuits

These biscuits go with a down-home meal of fried chicken and cream gravy.

Sift together into a medium-sized bowl

1 cup flour
1 ½ teaspoons baking powder
¼ teaspoon salt

Cut into dry ingredients

2 tablespoons shortening

Stir in with a fork just until dough cleans sides of bowl

½ cup milk

Toss on a lightly floured surface until no longer sticky. Pat or roll out to a 6-inch square. Cut into 36 1-inch squares. Fry in oil heated to 375°F. Fry 6 squares at a time, about 3 minutes to a side, turning only once. Drain on paper toweling in a warm oven. Serve with cream gravy. Makes 36 biscuits.

❖ Beaten Biscuits

Beaten biscuits are another old Southern specialty. You can work out your frustra-tions while making them. Serve them at a traditional Southern dinner featuring Virginia ham. The recipe can be doubled, if necessary.

It is not advisable to reroll the dough, so I cut mine into squares rather than circles.

Sift together into a large bowl

    4 cups unbleached all-purpose flour, sifted twice before measuring the first time
    1 teaspoon salt
    1 teaspoon baking powder
    1 tablespoon sugar

Cut into dry ingredients

    ¼ cup chilled lard

Combine and stir into dry ingredients

    ½ cup cold milk
    ½ cup ice water

On a very lightly floured surface, beat with the side of a rolling pin until the dough blisters. Do not use a roller-bearing pin for this. This will take about 20 minutes, or 300 to 500 smacks. Rhythmically beat and fold the dough during this time. When properly prepared, roll out the dough to ½-inch thickness. Cut into 1½-inch squares. Place squares on a lightly greased baking sheet. Prick deeply with the tines of a fork. Brush tops of biscuits with melted butter. Bake in a preheated 325°F oven for 20 minutes. Do not overbake, as it tends to make these tough. Makes 16 biscuits.

❖ Cream Biscuits

Cream biscuits should really be made with thick, country-fresh cream, spooned rather than poured. If you have access to such a cream, use it in place of the whipping cream and eliminate the butter. It does not need to be beaten.

Preheat oven to 450°F. Sift together

> 2 cups unbleached all-purpose flour
> ½ teaspoon salt
> 1 tablespoon baking powder

Cut in

> 2 tablespoons butter

Fold in

> 1 cup whipping cream, beaten to thicken slightly

Knead lightly on a lightly floured surface. Pat or roll out to a ½-inch thickness. Cut with a 3-inch biscuit cutter and place on a lightly greased baking sheet. Bake in a preheated 450°F oven for 10 to 12 minutes, or until lightly browned. Makes 6 large biscuits.

❋ Cream-Cheese Biscuits

These little tidbits are delightful at teatime.

Preheat oven to 425°F. Sift together twice and set aside

> 1 cup flour
> ¼ teaspoon salt

In a mixing bowl, cream together

> 1 3-ounce package cream cheese
> ½ cup butter
> grated rind of 1 lemon
> 1 tablespoon sugar

Add flour mixture to creamed mixture and blend well. Stir in

> 2 tablespoons finely chopped pecans

Press ball of dough together. Roll out on a lightly floured surface to ¼-inch thickness. Cut with 1½-inch biscuit cutter. Place on an ungreased baking sheet. Bake in preheated 425°F oven for 10 to 12 minutes. Serve warm. Makes 24 biscuits.

❋ Sour-Cream Biscuits

Sour-cream biscuits taste like buttermilk biscuits with a tenderness possible only through the use of sour cream.

Preheat oven to 400°F. Sift together

> 2 cups unbleached all-purpose flour
> ½ teaspoon baking soda
> ½ teaspoon salt
> ½ teaspoon sugar

Cut in

> 2 tablespoons shortening

Fold in

> 1 cup commercial sour cream

You may have to get your hands down into this to knead it together. Roll out on a lightly floured surface to ½-inch thickness. Cut into 2-inch squares. Place on a lightly greased baking sheet. Bake at 400°F for 12 to 15 minutes or until lightly browned. Makes 12 biscuits.

❋ Homespun Biscuits

Some experienced cooks make these without measuring the ingredients. After you get the hang of it, you may be doing that, too. Until then, follow the directions given below. If you wish, you can use self-rising flour and eliminate the called-for baking soda, baking powder, and salt.

Preheat oven to 450°F. Sift together

> 2 cups unbleached all-purpose flour
> 1 teaspoon baking powder
> ½ teaspoon baking soda
> ½ teaspoon salt

Rub in with your fingers

¼ cup lard

Stir in with a wooden spoon, or simply with your hands

1 cup buttermilk

Flour your hands well and pick up about one-twelfth of the dough. Toss it gently between your hands to shape it, more or less, into a flat ball. Place on a lightly greased baking sheet. Repeat until all the dough is used. Bake in preheated 450°F oven for 10 to 12 minutes, or until lightly browned. Makes 12 biscuits.

❖ Cornmeal Biscuits

Make these with a coarsely ground cornmeal for a good, crunchy texture.

Preheat oven to 450°F. Sift together

1 ½ cups unbleached all-purpose flour
1 teaspoon baking powder
½ teaspoon baking soda
½ teaspoon salt
½ teaspoon sugar

Stir into sifted mixture

½ cup cornmeal

Cut in

5 tablespoons shortening

Stir in with a fork, just until dry ingredients are moistened

⅔ cup buttermilk

Toss on a lightly floured surface until no longer sticky. Knead lightly. Roll out to ½-inch thickness. Cut into 2-inch squares. Place on a lightly greased baking sheet. Bake at 450°F for 12 to 15 minutes. Makes 12 biscuits.

❖ Peanut-Butter and Jelly Muffins

These muffins find great success with the very young. They are also popular with senior citizens who unabashedly proclaim their allegiance to peanut butter and jelly.

Preheat oven to 375°F. Grease a 12-cup muffin pan. Sift together and set aside

> *2 cups unbleached all-purpose flour*
> *2 teaspoons baking powder*
> *½ teaspoon salt*

In a mixing bowl, beat

> *2 eggs*

Stir into eggs, in this order

> *¼ cup sugar*
> *1 tablespoon honey*
> *¾ cup creamy peanut butter*
> *1 cup milk*
> *sifted dry ingredients*

Into each muffin cup spoon 1 rounded tablespoonful of batter. Press the back of a spoon into each filled cup, making a small well in the batter of each. Spoon into each well

> *1 teaspoon jelly (crabapple suggested)*

Cover jelly by evenly dividing and spooning remaining batter into muffin cups. Bake in preheated 375°F oven for 20 to 25 minutes, or until golden brown. Serve warm with additional peanut butter and jelly on the side. Makes 12 muffins.

❖ Sweet Streusel Muffins

These are cinnamony sweet, great for breakfast or brunch with steaming hot coffee.

Preheat oven to 375°F. Grease a 12-cup muffin pan. Sift together and set aside

   2 cups unbleached all-purpose flour
   ½ teaspoon salt
   2 teaspoons baking powder

In a mixing bowl, beat

   1 egg

Stir into egg, in this order

   ⅓ cup sugar
   ⅓ cup oil
   1 cup milk
   sifted dry ingredients

Spoon 1 tablespoonful of batter into each muffin cup. Sprinkle over batter in each cup

   1 teaspoon Sweet Streusel Topping

Divide remaining batter evenly and spoon over streusel in muffin cups. Divide remaining streusel evenly and sprinkle over the top of batter. Bake in preheated 375°F oven for 20 to 25 minutes, or until lightly browned. Serve warm. Makes 12 muffins.

Sweet Streusel Topping

This same topping can be doubled to top any quick coffeecake or an impromptu sweetened and baked summer fruit dessert.

In a small bowl, combine

   2 tablespoons unbleached all-purpose flour
   ¼ cup sugar
   ½ teaspoon cinnamon

Rub into flour mixture with your fingers, or cut in with a pastry blender

   2 tablespoons butter

You should have about ½ cup streusel.

❋ Graham-Cracker Muffins

Nice and light, these add a variety to your breadbox.

Preheat oven to 375°F. Grease a 12-cup muffin pan. Sift together

   ½ cup unbleached all-purpose flour
   ¼ teaspoon salt
   2 teaspoons baking powder

Crush about 10 graham crackers with a rolling pin, or process in a blender or food processor, to make

   1 ¼ cups graham-cracker crumbs

Stir crumbs into flour mixture and set aside. In a mixing bowl, cream together

   ¼ cup butter
   ½ cup sugar

Beat into butter mixture, in this order

   1 teaspoon vanilla
   2 egg yolks

Divide dry ingredients into thirds and milk in half and add alternately, beginning and ending with dry ingredients

   reserved flour mixture
   ¾ cup milk

Fold in

   2 egg whites, stiffly beaten

Spoon into prepared muffin cups. Bake at 375°F for 20 to 25 minutes, or until lightly browned. Serve warm with sweet butter. Makes 12 muffins.

✤ Mustard Muffins

If you favor a savory muffin, you will like these. They are warm to the taste, mellowed with some good grated cheese. Be sure to use a strong mustard.

Preheat oven to 350°F. Grease a 12-cup muffin pan. Sift together

> 2 cups unbleached all-purpose flour
> 2 teaspoons baking powder
> 1/2 teaspoon salt or seasoned salt
> 1/8 teaspoon white pepper

Mix into sifted ingredients and set aside

> 1/2 cup (2 ounces) grated extra-sharp cheddar cheese
> 2 tablespoons freshly grated Parmesan cheese

In a mixing bowl, beat

> 1 egg

Stir into egg, in this order

> 1 teaspoon sugar
> 2 tablespoons prepared mustard
> 1/4 cup oil
> 1 cup milk
> reserved dry ingredients with cheese

Spoon into prepared muffin cups. Bake in preheated 350°F oven for 25 to 30 minutes, or until golden brown. Serve warm. Makes 12 muffins.

Mustard-Muffin Variations

Before spooning batter into muffin cups, you may add up to 1/2 cup of meat leftovers to these muffins. Crumbled crisply fried bacon, crumbled cooked spicy pork sausage, or crumbled and cooked sweet and spicy Italian sausage are all possibilities. Be sure to drain meat well before adding it to the batter or it may make the muffins soggy.

❊ Marmalade Muffins

Marmalade makes a surprise filling for these lightly spiced muffins. Use your homemade marmalade or a good quality commercial brand.

Preheat oven to 375°F. Grease a 12-cup muffin pan. Sift together and set aside

> *2 cups unbleached all-purpose flour*
> *1 teaspoon baking powder*
> *¼ teaspoon baking soda*
> *¼ teaspoon salt*
> *¼ teaspoon ginger*

In a mixing bowl, beat

> *1 egg*

Stir into egg, in this order

> *¼ cup sugar*
> *¼ cup oil*
> *1 cup buttermilk*
> *sifted dry ingredients*

Spoon about 1 heaping tablespoonful of batter into each muffin cup. Press the back of a spoon into each filled cup, making a small well in the batter of each. Spoon into each well

> *1 teaspoon marmalade*

Cover marmalade by evenly dividing and spooning remaining batter into muffin cups. Bake in preheated 375°F oven for 25 to 30 minutes, or until golden brown. Serve warm. Makes 12 muffins.

❊ Georgia Pecan Muffins

Molly Culbert, who is an old buddy of mine, stocks pecans among the food items in her flower shop. Yes, flower shop. She calls her shop Flowers and Gifts by Molly Culbert, and the pecans sneak in under the gift part. Molly's pecans come from

Connor's Farms, Dalton, Georgia, in the Vidalia onion region of that state. Mrs. Connor is the one who brings us marvelous Vidalia Onion Relish and other delights. If you're driving through central Illinois and come close to the intersection of Illinois Routes 1 and 9, turn east three blocks north of the intersection and go for a couple of blocks until you find Molly's shop on the north side of Main Street. It is filled with a wonderment of things besides flowers and pecans and is well worth a visit. If you don't ever expect to get to Molly's ask at your local gourmet shop for Connor's pecans and try them in these muffins.

Preheat oven to 375°F. Grease a 12-cup muffin pan. Sift together and set aside

> *1 ¾ cups unbleached all-purpose flour*
> *½ teaspoon salt*
> *2 teaspoons baking powder*
> *¼ teaspoon cinnamon*
> *⅛ teaspoon nutmeg*

In a mixing bowl, beat

> *2 eggs*

Stir into eggs, in this order

> *⅓ cup sugar*
> *¼ cup melted butter, slightly cooled*
> *¾ cup milk*
> *reserved dry ingredients*
> *¾ cup chopped fresh Georgia pecans*

Spoon into prepared muffin cups. Sprinkle tops of muffins lightly with

> *sugar*

Bake in preheated 375°F oven for 20 to 25 minutes, or until lightly browned. Serve warm with sweet butter. Makes 12 muffins.

❖ Corn Muffins

These sweet corn muffins are good for that basket of mixed breads.

Preheat oven to 425°F. Grease a 12-cup muffin pan. Sift together into a large bowl

> 1 cup unbleached all-purpose flour
> ¼ cup sugar
> 4 teaspoons baking powder
> ½ teaspoon salt

Stir in

> 1 cup yellow cornmeal

In another bowl, beat

> 2 eggs

Stir into beaten eggs

> 1 cup milk
> ¼ cup melted butter, cooled slightly

Add milk mixture to the dry ingredients, stirring only until the dry ingredients are moistened. Spoon into prepared muffin cups. Bake at 425°F for 20 to 25 minutes. Serve warm. Makes 12 muffins.

❖ Whole-Grain Corn Muffins

Substitute 1 cup whole-wheat flour for the unbleached all-purpose flour. Increase salt to ¾ teaspoon. Proceed as for Corn Muffins.

�֍ Sour-Cream Muffins

I've adapted this recipe from the Hoopeston Cookbook, *published in 1930. It was originally credited to Mrs. S. W. Boughton.*

Preheat oven to 400°F. Grease a 12-cup muffin pan. Sift together into a large bowl and set aside

> 1 ½ *cups unbleached all-purpose flour*
> 1 *teaspoon baking powder*
> ½ *teaspoon baking soda*
> ½ *teaspoon salt*

In another bowl, beat

> 1 *egg*

Blend into beaten egg

> ½ *cup sugar*
> 1 *cup commercial sour cream*

Add sour-cream mixture to the dry ingredients, stirring only until dry ingredients are moistened. Spoon into prepared muffin cups. Combine and sprinkle over tops of muffins, using 1 teaspoon per muffin

> 2 *tablespoons finely chopped pecans*
> 2 *tablespoons cinnamon-sugar*

Bake at 400°F for 20 to 25 minutes. Serve warm. Makes 12 muffins.

✖ Date Muffins

Use these old-fashioned muffins to accompany a fresh fruit salad for a light luncheon menu.

Preheat oven to 375°F. Grease a 12-cup muffin pan. Sift together and set aside

> 1 ¾ *cups unbleached all-purpose flour*
> 2 *teaspoons baking powder*
> ½ *teaspoon salt*

In a large bowl, cream

> ¼ *cup butter*
> ⅓ *cup sugar*

Add to creamed mixture and beat until light

> *1 egg*
> *1 teaspoon vanilla*

Dividing dry ingredients into thirds and milk in half, add alternately to egg mixture, beginning and ending with the dry ingredients

> *sifted dry ingredients*
> ¾ *cup milk*

Gently stir in

> *1 cup finely chopped dates*

Spoon into prepared muffin cups and sprinkle tops lightly with sugar. Bake at 375°F for 25 to 30 minutes. Serve warm. Makes 12 muffins.

❖ Wheat Date-Nut Muffins

Substitute 1¼ cups unbleached all-purpose flour and ½ cup whole-wheat flour for the 1¾ cups unbleached all-purpose flour. Stir in ½ cup chopped pecans along with the chopped dates. Proceed as for Date Muffins.

❊ Stove-top Breads

*Steamed, simmered, and fried breads for
variety's sake*

CORN TORTILLAS
FLOUR TORTILLAS
ENGLISH MUFFINS
CRUMPETS
BROOKLYN BAGELS
EGG BAGELS
CORNER TAVERN PRETZELS
BOSTON BROWN BREAD

BOSTON BLOND BREAD
MY FAVORITE DUMPLINGS
CHEESE DUMPLINGS
DOWN-HOME DUMPLINGS
LITTLE BUTTER DUMPLINGS
RICE FRITTERS
BEER BATTER FRITTERS
RUM-RAISIN FRUIT FRITTERS

❄ STOVE-TOP BREADS

When it's too warm to bake, or if you just want to make something different, try some stove-top bread. Breads cooked on top of the stove can be fried, steamed, or simmered. Some are simmered and then baked.

Tortillas are a southwestern specialty fried on a dry or very lightly greased skillet. English muffins and crumpets are baked on a lightly greased griddle. Their batters are similar, though crumpet batter is somewhat wetter. Bagels and pretzels are simmered before baking. You will be surprised at how easy it is to make them.

❄ Corn Tortillas

Ordinary cornmeal cannot be used to make tortillas. The job requires instant corn masa mix. The two types I am familiar with are Quaker masa harina instant masa mix and MaSeCa instant corn masa mix. They both work quite well. I slightly prefer the flavor of MaSeCa. If you live in a community where fresh tortillas are made regularly, you may be able to obtain freshly prepared masa, which, of course, is best of all. Here are directions for using a mix.

In a mixing bowl, stir together

> *2 cups MaSeCa instant corn masa mix*
> *½ teaspoon salt (optional)*

Stir into masa mixture

> *1⅛ to 1¼ cups lukewarm water*

Stir until all the flour is moistened and the mixture sticks together. The dough should be soft but not sticky. If needed, add more water, 1 teaspoon at a time, until consistency is corrected. Divide the dough into 12 equal pieces. Roll each piece into a ball and place on waxed paper. Cover them all with a damp cloth to prevent their drying out. Work with one piece at a time. Flatten the ball slightly between your hands and place on a piece of waxed paper. Cover with a second piece of waxed paper and with a rolling pin roll to a 6-inch round. You can also use a flat object, such as a large, round cake tin, to press down on the dough, thereby flattening it. Remove the top piece of waxed paper. Flop the exposed side down on a heated, very lightly greased skillet.

Quickly and carefully remove the remaining waxed paper. Cook on the first side just until the edges begin to curl. Turn the tortilla over. Cook on the second side a little longer than the first and turn again. Cook for a very short time and remove to a plate that has been covered with a kitchen towel. Cover the warm tortilla with a second towel and continue to cook additional tortillas. Stack them on top of one another, keeping the towel on top of the stack. This will help them retain their heat and flexibility. Use for tacos or enchiladas. Makes 12 tortillas.

❖ Flour Tortillas

A fresh, warm flour tortilla is heavenly. Spread it with butter, roll it up, and eat.

In a mixing bowl, stir together well

> *2 cups unbleached all-purpose flour*
> *1 teaspoon salt*
> *1 teaspoon baking powder*

Rub into flour mixture with your fingers

> *¼ cup butter, cut into small pieces*

Mix in to form a soft dough that is not sticky

> *½ cup, more or less, very warm tap water*

Cover dough in bowl and let rest 5 minutes. Divide dough into 12 equal pieces. Roll each piece into a ball, toss lightly in flour, and return to the bowl. Cover and let rest for 15 to 30 minutes. Working with one ball at a time, roll out until very thin. The circle should be about 6 inches in diameter. Turn the dough over repeatedly while rolling, dusting with flour only when necessary to prevent sticking. Brush off any flour that may remain on the surface of the tortilla. Cook on a dry, medium-hot, heavy skillet until blistered. Flip over and cook the other side, just until very lightly browned. Cool on a plate covered with a paper towel or serve at once. When tortillas are completely cooled, they may be stacked and stored in a plastic bag in the refrigerator or freezer. Before serving, reheat on a medium-hot, dry skillet. Makes 12 flour tortillas.

Note: If you have never made tortillas before, you will probably be slow in rolling them out. Beware of overheating your skillet if you do not have a new tortilla ready to go on every time a cooked one comes off! If they appear to be cooking too rapidly, lower the heat.

✣ English Muffins

If you do not have a 3 ¾-inch muffin cutter, you can section these in squares. Corn flour is perfect for dusting the muffins, giving them a good color and just the right floured look. If you wish, substitute a not too coarsely ground cornmeal. English Muffins can also be baked in a 425°F oven. They should be turned after 6 minutes and baked about 6 minutes longer. It's traditional to toast them before an open wood fire. A broiler is less romantic, but more often used in our modern world.

In a mixing bowl, combine

> *1 cup scalded milk*
> *2 tablespoons butter*
> *1 tablespoon sugar*
> *1 ½ teaspoons salt*

Stir to dissolve butter and sugar. Let cool until just warm. Meanwhile, to soften yeast, in a small container combine

> *½ cup warm water*
> *1 scant tablespoon (or 1 packet) active dry yeast*

When milk mixture has cooled down to warm, stir in, in this order

> *softened yeast mixture*
> *1 egg*
> *2 cups unbleached all-purpose flour*

Beat well. To make a soft dough, gradually add

> *1 ½ cups unbleached all-purpose flour*

Stir well. Scrape dough down in bowl. Cover and let rise until doubled in bulk, 45 to 60 minutes. Stir dough down. Turn out on a floured surface and toss until no longer sticky. This is a very sticky dough, so be generous with your flour. Roll to ¼-inch thickness. Section with an English Muffin cutter into 3¾-inch rounds. Transfer to a baking sheet covered with sifted corn flour. Sift additional corn flour on top of the muffins. Cover with waxed paper and allow to rise until almost doubled, 30 to 45 minutes. Bake the muffins slowly on an ungreased griddle. Transfer them to the griddle carefully, using a large spatula and your floured fingers. They will be quite soft. Start with a hot griddle, lowering the temperature as the muffins cook, if needed, so as not to burn them. Turn them gently. They will bake about 8 minutes or more per side and can be turned more than once. If turned too soon the first time, they may deflate. Cool on wire racks. Makes 12 muffins.

To serve: Pull apart with the tines of two forks. Toast them, butter, and serve.

Crumpets

Crumpets can be described as wet English Muffins. They aren't wet after they are cooked, but before, and are full of holes that were just made for soaking up butter. They are best eaten soon after they are made. If you do not have muffin rings, use salvaged tunafish cans which have had both ends removed.

In a mixing bowl, combine

2 cups scalded milk
1 tablespoon butter
1 teaspoon sugar
1 teaspoon salt

Let cool until just warm. Meanwhile, to soften yeast, in a small bowl combine

½ cup warm water
1 scant tablespoon (or 1 packet) active dry yeast

When milk mixture has cooled down to warm, stir in, in this order

> *softened yeast mixture*
> *3 cups unbleached all-purpose flour*

Beat well. Cover and let rise until batter doubles in bulk, 30 to 45 minutes. Stir batter down. Stir into batter

> *¼ teaspoon baking soda dissolved in 2 tablespoons warm water*

Cover and allow batter to rest 15 to 20 minutes. Grease 3¾-inch muffin rings. Place greased muffin rings on a lightly greased hot griddle. Fill the rings with ½ cup batter and bake the crumpets slowly until they are well-risen and lightly browned on one side. When ready to turn, they should present a mass of tiny holes. If not, there is not enough liquid in the batter. This is your chance to add more. Turn them and bake on the other side. Then remove rings and cool until they can be handled. Clean and grease the rings for the next batch. Lower the heat if the crumpets appear to be cooking too quickly. Transfer baked crumpets to a wire rack. Continue to bake the remainder. To serve, split the crumpets and toast until crisp and golden brown. Serve with gobs of butter and good home-made jelly. Makes 10 crumpets.

Note: If you prefer thin crumpets to be served immediately, use only ⅓ cup batter per crumpet. Do not split or toast. Makes 15 crumpets.

❖ Brooklyn Bagels

Theoretically, a bagel can be produced from any yeast-risen dough. One merely needs to form it into doughnut shapes, simmer it on the stove top in sweetened or salted water, and finish it off in the oven. But how does one make a really good bagel? One that has a thick crust and a good chewy interior? To find the answer, I researched some baking manuals intended for commercial use. I learned what the deli-baker already knows. The ingredients missing in most recipes are: malt, to give bagels their distinctive flavor; and a high-gluten flour mixture, to give the bagels backbone.

These commercial recipes call for weighing the ingredients to produce 20 dozen or more bagels at once. Being more cook than chemist, I did not easily convert that to home-batch proportions. After some experimentation, however, I devised what I think will work well for your bagel operation.

In a large bowl, mix together

> *1 ½ cups unbleached all-purpose flour*
> *½ cup Arrowhead Mills Vital Wheat Gluten*
> *1 ½ teaspoons salt*

To soften yeast, in a small bowl combine

> *¼ cup warm water*
> *1 scant tablespoon (or 1 packet) active dry yeast*

To dissolve malt extract, in another bowl combine

> *1 cup hot water*
> *1 tablespoon Eden barley malt extract (liquid)*

Let malt mixture cool down to warm. Make a well in the center of the flour mixture. Pour into the well, in this order

> *softened yeast mixture*
> *malt water*

Stir together until smooth. Beat this dough vigorously to develop the gluten. To make a very stiff dough, gradually add

> *½ to 1 cup unbleached all-purpose flour*

Turn out on a floured surface and knead for a full 10 minutes. Divide dough into 12 equal pieces. Shape each piece into a ball. Cover balls of dough with a cloth and work with one at a time. Place the ball on a very lightly floured surface. Flatten slightly. Poke the center of the ball with a forefinger, going all the way through. Now use the fingers of both hands to gently open up the ring. (Those of you who are potters will know exactly what I am talking about.) Try to keep the doughnut-shaped roll you are forming symmetrical. The hole should be about one-third of the bagel's diameter. Place shaped rings on an oiled baking sheet. Cover and let rise for 15 to 20 minutes. They should not quite double in size. Meanwhile, ready the boiling liquid. In a large pot, heat

> *2 quarts water*

Stir into water

> *3 tablespoons barley malt extract*

Heat to boiling. Reduce heat and keep regulated to a healthy simmer. Preheat oven to 475°F. One at a time, slip risen bagels into simmering water. Bagels should float. If they sink, do not worry. They will soon rise to the surface. After about 30 seconds, turn them over. They should remain in the water about 1 minute in all. You may simmer several at a time, but do not crowd them in the pot. Remove with a skimmer and place 1 inch apart on a well-oiled baking sheet. Brush bagels with a mixture of

1 egg
1 tablespoon water

If desired, sprinkle with

coarse salt
OR
poppy seeds

Bake at 475°F for 10 to 12 minutes, or until well-browned. Cool slightly on wire racks. Serve warm. Cool, wrap individually, and freeze any that are not to be eaten right away. To serve frozen bagels: Defrost in their wrapping, unwrap, reheat and serve. They are traditionally served with lox (smoked salmon) and cream cheese, affectionately known as "loxunbagels." They may also be eaten plain, or cut in half and toasted, and served with butter and preserves. Makes 12 bagels.

❖ Egg Bagels

Egg bagels are more delicate than water (Brooklyn) bagels.

To soften yeast, in a mixing bowl combine

1 cup warm potato water (water in which peeled potatoes have been boiled)
1 scant tablespoon (or 1 packet) active dry yeast
1 ½ teaspoons sugar

Let stand 3 minutes. Stir in

1 ½ teaspoons salt
1 egg
2 tablespoons oil
2 cups unbleached all-purpose flour

Beat well to develop gluten. To make a stiff dough, gradually add

¾ to 1 ¼ cups unbleached all-purpose flour

Turn out on a floured surface and knead until smooth. Place dough in a greased bowl, turning dough once to grease the top. Cover and let rise until doubled, 45 to 60 minutes. Punch dough down. Pat or roll out on a lightly floured surface to ½-inch thickness. Cut with a floured doughnut cutter. Place on an oiled baking sheet. Cover and let rise for 20 to 25 minutes. They should not quite double in size. Meanwhile ready the boiling liquid. (You may use malted water as described in Brooklyn Bagels, if you wish.) In a large pot, heat to boiling

2 quarts water
3 tablespoons sugar

Reduce heat and keep regulated to a healthy simmer. Preheat oven to 425°F. Place baking rack in upper third of oven. One at a time, slip risen bagels into simmering water. After 30 seconds, turn them over. Simmer 30 seconds on the second side. You may simmer several at a time, but do not crowd them into the pot. Remove with a skimmer and place on a well-oiled baking sheet, 1 inch apart. Brush bagels with a mixture of

1 egg
1 tablespoon water

Sprinkle with

poppy seeds
OR
sesame seeds

Bake at 425°F for 12 to 15 minutes, or until well-browned. Cool slightly on wire racks. Serve warm. Makes 12 bagels.

❖ Corner Tavern Pretzels

Pretzels are not unlike a bagel in composition. Their thinness allows them to have more surface exposed, which gives them a higher ratio of chewy crust.

To dissolve barley malt extract, stir together in a mixing bowl

> *1 cup hot water*
> *1 teaspoon barley malt extract*

Let cool until just warm. Stir into malt water, in this order

> *1 scant tablespoon (or 1 packet) active dry yeast*
> *¾ teaspoon salt*
> *1 tablespoon soft butter*
> *½ cup Arrowhead Mills Vital Wheat Gluten*
> *1 cup unbleached all-purpose flour*

Beat this vigorously to develop the gluten. To make a stiff dough, gradually add

> *½ to ¾ cup unbleached all-purpose flour*

Turn out on a floured surface and knead until smooth and elastic. Place in a dry bowl. Cover and let rise for 30 minutes. Turn out and press into a flat circle to expel air. Cut into eight equal wedge-shaped pieces. Using the palms and fingers of both hands, roll each piece back and forth on a dry board to form a 20-inch rope with tapered ends. Dough will be quite elastic. Do not rush it. If you have trouble rolling it out, cover and let it relax for a couple of minutes.

Curve the rolled strip of dough to form a broad horseshoe with the open end toward you. Twist the ends around each other and lay them to rest on top of the loop you have just formed. Press ends firmly to seal.

Place the formed pretzels on a lightly greased baking sheet and allow to rise uncovered for about 30 minutes. In the meantime, preheat oven to 425°F. Place oven rack in upper third of oven. In a stainless steel or enameled pot, bring to a boil

> *1 quart water*
> *4 tablespoons baking soda*

Reduce heat to maintain a healthy simmer. Turn pretzels upside down and slip, one at a time, into simmering water. You may simmer more than one at a time, but do not crowd them in the pot. After 30 seconds, turn them over gently. Simmer 30 seconds on the second side. Remove them from the water with a skimmer and place back on the greased baking sheet. Sprinkle over the pretzels

coarse salt

Bake them at 425°F for 15 minutes, or until well-browned. Transfer to racks to cool slightly. Serve warm with a chilled mug of beer. These are best eaten fresh. Makes 8 large pretzels.

❖ Boston Brown Bread

Early colonists in New England combined native corn with European rye to supplement their meager supply of wheat. Boston cooks devised the method of steaming the bread. Served with the now famous Boston baked beans, there is nothing like it.

The bread can be steamed in two 1-pound coffee cans. Alternatively, any sort of metal or stonewear mold that will stand up to steaming, can be used as long as the batter does not exceed three-fourths of the capacity of the mold. The traditional shape for the bread is cylindrical, but other shapes are possible. The mold must be tightly covered before steaming. Some molds have their own covers. You can always fashion one from foil securely held with string or a stout rubber band.

The easiest steamer to use is a pasta pot with a perforated insert. Lacking that, a rack can be placed in the bottom of a large stock pot. You will want your containers of dough to be suspended above the bottom of a pan large enough to accommodate them easily. Warming the molasses makes it easier to pour and mix with the buttermilk. If you have a 2-quart bowl with a handle and spout, it will make transferring the dough a breeze.

Several hours, or the night before you are ready to make your bread, combine in a stainless-steel or glass bowl

1 cup dark raisins
2 tablespoons dark rum

When ready to proceed, place a jar of molasses in a container of hot tap water to warm. Generously grease two 1-pound coffee cans. Line the bottom of the cans with circles of waxed paper. To mix well, stir together in a large bowl

    1 cup rye flour
    1 cup yellow cornmeal
    1 cup graham flour
    1 teaspoon salt
    2 teaspoons baking soda

In another bowl, stir together

    2 cups buttermilk
    1 cup slightly warmed molasses
    the plumped raisins

Add the buttermilk mixture to the dry ingredients. Mix well. Spoon or pour into prepared cans. Cover cans with lids or foil. Place on rack in steamer pot. Fill pot with boiling water to halfway up containers. Cover pot. Over low to medium heat simmer for 1½ to 2 hours, or until a wooden pick inserted in the center comes out clean. Toward the end of the steaming time, preheat oven to 350°F. When bread tests done, remove lids and place containers in oven for about 3 minutes to dry bread slightly. Remove from cans and cool on wire racks. Remove waxed paper. Bread is best served warm. Leftovers may be served cold, spread with softened cream cheese. Or sliced and toasted and served with sweet butter. Makes 2 loaves.

❖ Boston Blond Bread

The last time I made Boston Brown Bread, I asked myself: "What would happen if the ingredients were traded for their lighter-colored cousins?" I tried it and the results are most pleasing.

Several hours, or the night before you are ready to make your bread, combine in a stainless-steel or glass bowl

    1 cup golden raisins
    2 tablespoons light rum

When ready to proceed, place a jar of honey in a container of hot tap water to warm. Generously grease two 1-pound coffee cans. Line the bottom of

the cans with circles of waxed paper. To mix well, stir together in a large
bowl

> 1 cup rye flour
> 1 cup white corn meal
> 1 cup unbleached all-purpose flour
> 1 teaspoon salt
> 2 teaspoons baking soda

In another bowl, stir together

> 2 cups buttermilk
> 1 cup slightly warmed honey
> the plumped raisins

Add the buttermilk mixture to the dry ingredients. Mix well. Spoon or
pour into prepared cans. Cover cans with lids or foil. Place containers of
dough on rack in steamer pot. Fill pot with boiling water to halfway up
containers. Cover pot. Over low to medium heat simmer for 1½ to 2 hours,
or until a wooden pick inserted in the center comes out clean. Toward the
end of the steaming time, preheat oven to 350°F. When bread tests done,
remove lids and place containers in oven for about 3 minutes to dry bread
slightly. Remove from cans and cool on wire racks. Remove waxed paper.
Makes 2 loaves.

❖ My Favorite Dumplings

*Simmered on the top of a pot of stewed chicken, these dumplings are heritage cookery
at its best. If the lid is lifted several times during the steaming, the dumplings are
likely to be tough. Trust the recipe and do not look under the lid while they are
cooking. Your dumplings should double in size and be light and airy. Serve them
to company for an old-fashioned American meal.*

Sift into a bowl

> ⅞ cup unbleached all-purpose flour (1 cup minus 2 tablespoons)
> 2 teaspoons baking powder
> ¼ teaspoon salt

Resift dry ingredients twice. In a small container, beat together

> 1 egg
> ¼ cup milk
> 2 tablespoons finely chopped fresh parsley

Slowly and gently stir egg mixture into dry ingredients. Drop batter by tablespoonfuls into simmering stock. The stock should be kept at a simmer and not allowed to boil, or the dumplings will cook too quickly and become heavy. It helps to dip the spoon into the stock each time before dipping it into the batter. The dumplings should not quite touch each other. Cover and simmer 5 minutes, no peeking allowed. Turn dumplings and simmer 5 minutes longer. Serve at once. Makes 8 dumplings.

❖ Cheese Dumplings

These dumplings are the perfect topping for a homemade garden tomato soup.

Sift together

> 1 cup unbleached all-purpose flour
> 2 teaspoons baking powder
> ½ teaspoon salt

Stir into sifted ingredients

> ¼ cup grated cheddar cheese
> 1 tablespoon grated Parmesan cheese

In a small container, beat

> 1 egg

Stir into egg, in this order

> 6 tablespoons milk
> 1 tablespoon finely chopped chives

Slowly and gently stir egg mixture into dry ingredients. Drop batter by tablespoonfuls into simmering tomato broth. Do not crowd. Cover and simmer 5 minutes. Turn dumplings. Cover and simmer 5 minutes longer. Serve at once. Makes 10 to 12 dumplings.

❋ Down-Home Dumplings

Some Southerners call these dumplings "slickers." They are as light and airy as any Yankee dumpling.

Sift together into a bowl

>2 cups unbleached all-purpose flour
>2 teaspoons baking powder
>½ teaspoon salt

Cut into the flour mixture with a pastry blender or two knives

>¼ cup butter

Stir in with a fork just until the dry ingredients are moistened

>¾ cup cooled chicken broth

Turn out on a lightly floured surface and knead gently three or four times. Pat or roll out to ½-inch thickness. Cut into 1-inch squares. Toss cut pieces in flour to coat all sides. Drop, one at a time, into a pot of boiling chicken broth. Do not crowd. You may have to cook these in several batches. Reduce heat to medium-low and cover pot. Cook for 8 minutes, or until done all the way through. Serve at once, but warn diners that they may be quite hot. Makes 6 to 8 servings.

❋ Little Butter Dumplings

These little dumplings liven up a vegetarian stew.

Cream together

>2 tablespoons soft butter
>¼ teaspoon salt

Add, one at a time, beating well after each

>2 eggs (be sure these are at room temperature)

Gently stir in

> *½ cup unbleached all-purpose flour*

Drop by teaspoonfuls into simmering broth. Cover and simmer 8 minutes. Serve with soup or stew in a warmed bowl. Makes 16 little dumplings.

❖ Rice Fritters

Small cakes of fried leftover rice, with some good maple syrup, have always been one of my favorite breakfasts. Add a little cheese and herbs and you have a great seasoned fritter for dinner. (Either brown or white rice may be used.)

In a large bowl, mix together

> *1 cup cold cooked rice*
> *¼ cup dried bread crumbs*
> *2 tablespoons unbleached all-purpose flour*
> *⅛ teaspoon salt*

Blend into rice mixture

> *1 egg*

Divide mixture into six portions. Shape each portion into a small patty. It helps to wet your hands before handling the dough. Fry patties in a heavy skillet over medium to high heat in

> *1 to 2 tablespoons melted butter*

Add more butter, if needed. Remove from skillet when well-browned on both sides and serve immediately. Makes 6 fritters.

To Make Seasoned Rice Fritters

Add to the rice mixture before adding egg

> *¼ cup shredded sharp cheddar cheese*
> *2 teaspoons chopped fresh parsley*
> *pinch freshly ground pepper*

Proceed as before.

❖ Beer Batter Fritters

This is not the most complicated beer batter, but I think it is the best. Whenever I make it, I try it out with something new. In the past, I've used summer squash, eggplant, mushrooms, young succulent green beans, and even seedless grapes. I've dipped edible flowers, such as just-opened elderberry blossoms, in the batter and fried them. (Elderberry blossoms also make a perfect garnish for an elegant dinner plate.)

If you catch your own fresh fish, fillet some and fry it in the batter. That really is the best!

In a small bowl, mix together

> *1 ½ cups unbleached all-purpose flour*
> *1 teaspoon salt*
> *1 teaspoon Hungarian paprika*

With a wire whisk, blend in

> *1 ½ cups (one 12-ounce can) beer*

In another bowl, place

> *½ cup unbleached all-purpose flour*

Cut the food to be fried into bite-sized pieces. Roll them in the flour to coat them all over. Then dip them into the beer batter. Let the excess batter drip off and slip them into oil heated to 375°F. Fry until lightly browned on all sides. Remove with a slotted spoon and drain on paper towels. Let cool just until cool enough to eat. If the batter thickens while you use it, it can be thinned with additional beer. This should make enough batter for 6 hungry eaters.

❖ Rum-Raisin Fruit Fritters

Many fruits can be used in fruit fritters. My favorites are rum-soaked raisins.

In a small container combine

> *1 cup raisins*
> *¼ cup Dark Meyers's Rum*

Allow raisins to stand for at least an hour, stirring occasionally. Sift together and set aside

   ½ cup plus 2 tablespoons unbleached all-purpose flour
   ½ teaspoon baking powder
   ⅛ teaspoon salt
   1 tablespoon sugar

Drain the raisins, reserving any remaining rum. In a mixing bowl, beat together

   1 egg
   ¼ cup milk
   1 tablespoon reserved rum
   1 tablespoon oil

Gently stir into the egg mixture

   sifted dry ingredients
   drained raisins

Drop by rounded teaspoonfuls into oil heated to 370°F. Fry until browned on both sides, turning once. Drain on paper towels. Roll in sugar. Makes 24 fritters.

❋ With a Sweet Touch

Doughnuts, coffee cakes, and rolls; something sweet for the break you deserve

SWEET-ROLL DOUGH

THE ALL-AMERICAN CINNAMON ROLL

PHILADELPHIA STICKIEST BUNS

GRAND MARNIER SUGAR ROLLS

CINNAMON SAUCISSON

HOT CROSS BUNS

SOUR-CREAM DANISH

SWEET GINGER COFFEE CAKE

SOUR-CREAM COFFEE CAKE

DOUGHNUT PUFFS

DROP DOUGHNUTS

BUTTERMILK DOUGHNUTS

SOUR-CREAM DOUGHNUTS

BEIGNETS

GLAZED DOUGHNUTS

FAMILY-FAVORITE FRIED BREAD

❉ WITH A SWEET TOUCH

Everyone gets a craving now and then for a little something sweet. When that occurs, it is much better to have something homemade than something from the supermarket shelf. The sweet breads from my oven are unabashedly rich. I make no apologies for using refined sugar, sweet creamery butter, or any other ingredient that makes them so good. If we are going to indulge ourselves in something sweet, I figure it should be the very best we can make.

You may chide me for my preferences. But honey does not appear to me to be superior to granulated sugar. One tablespoon of corn oil has the same body-fat potential as does one tablespoon of butter. Making a doughnut heavy with whole-wheat flour seems to me a futile exercise in whole-grain idolatry.

I'm reminded of a college classmate who went to a doctor for her weight problem. She was told that she could eat anything as long as it was between two slices of whole-wheat bread. She promptly placed her daily candy bar between those two slices and ate the whole thing.

Sweets are sweets and fats are fats. Use an ingredient only if it will enhance. Bon Appétit!

❉ ABOUT SWEET ROLLS

Sweet rolls are best when made with a richer dough than for bread. That dough should not, however, be so rich that it will not rise well, nor should it have a yeasty, uncooked taste after baking. I think the following recipe for sweet-roll dough is just right. I suggest you use it for the All-American Cinnamon Roll; Philadelphia Stickiest Buns; and, my favorite, Grand Marnier Sugar Rolls.

✳ Sweet-Roll Dough

In a large bowl, combine

1 cup scalded milk
2 tablespoons butter
¼ cup sugar
¾ teaspoon salt

Stir to dissolve butter and sugar. Let cool until just warm. Meanwhile, to soften yeast, in another container combine

¼ cup warm water
1 scant tablespoon (or 1 packet) active dry yeast
1 teaspoon sugar

When milk mixture has cooled to warm, stir in

softened yeast mixture
1 egg
2 cups unbleached all-purpose flour

Beat well. To make a soft dough, gradually add

1 ½ to 1 ¾ cups unbleached all-purpose flour

Turn out on a floured surface and knead until smooth. Place in a buttered bowl, turning dough once to butter the top. Cover and let rise until doubled in bulk, 45 to 60 minutes. Punch dough down. Shape and bake as directed in the following recipes for sweet rolls and coffee cakes.

✳ The All-American Cinnamon Roll

T. J. Cinnamon's of Kansas City, Missouri, has started a cinnamon-roll craze that may sweep the country. * I'm sure the fad will die down, but the roll will remain as good as ever!

---

*Mimi Sheraton, "The Sweet Smell of Success," Time, April 21, 1986, p. 79.

Use one batch of Sweet-Roll Dough. Butter two 9-inch round cake pans. After the first rising of the dough, punch dough down. Roll out on a lightly floured surface to a 10×18-inch rectangle. Dot the surface of the dough with

> *3 tablespoons cold butter, cut into small slivers*
> *1 cup raisins*

Press these into the dough. Mix together, then set aside 2 tablespoons of the mixture, and sprinkle dough with the remainder of

> *1 cup brown sugar*
> *1 tablespoon cinnamon*

Press this gently into the dough. Starting with one long side, roll dough up firmly. Cut roll in half across the middle. Starting from the middle out, cut each half into 1¼-inch slices. You should have 14 slices in all. Place one of the end slices in the center of each pan, cut side up. Surround each with 6 of the remaining slices. Cover and let rise until doubled, 45 to 60 minutes. Bake in a preheated 350°F oven for 25 to 30 minutes, or until well-browned. Invert rolls onto a wire rack and then reinvert them so that they are right side up on a serving plate. After they have cooled a bit, drizzle with a mixture of

> *1 cup sieved powdered sugar*
> *1 teaspoon vanilla extract*
> *2 to 3 tablespoons hot milk*

Using 1 tablespoonful for each pan, sprinkle with the reserved cinnamon-sugar mixture. Serve warm. Makes 14 cinnamon rolls.

✻ Philadelphia Stickiest Buns

Sticky buns are—well, sticky! They invite you to lick your fingers. Real fans say, "The stickier, the better!" and these are the stickiest.

Use one batch of Sweet-Roll Dough. In a heavy saucepan melt

> *¼ cup butter*

Add to butter and heat over low heat, stirring just until mixture is smooth

> *¾ cup brown sugar*
> *½ cup dark corn syrup*

Divide between two 9-inch round cake pans, spreading the mixture evenly over the bottoms. Divide between the two and sprinkle over the sticky mixture

> *¾ cup chopped pecans*

After the first rising of the dough, punch dough down. Roll out on a lightly floured surface to a 10×18-inch rectangle. Sprinkle evenly with

> *¾ cup raisins*

Press raisins into the dough. Sprinkle over all a mixture of

> *¾ cup brown sugar*
> *2 teaspoons cinnamon*

Press this gently into the dough. Starting with a long side, roll dough tightly. Cut roll in half across the middle. Starting from the middle out, cut each half into 1¼-inch slices. You should have 14 slices in all. Place one of the end slices in the center of each pan, cut side down. Surround each with 6 of the remaining slices. Cover and let rise until doubled, 45 to 60 minutes. Bake in a preheated 350°F oven for 25 to 30 minutes, or until well-browned. Cover each pan of baked buns with an inverted plate and turn over quickly. Remove pans. Let them cool a bit and serve them warm. Makes 14 sticky buns.

❖ Grand Marnier Sugar Rolls

Several hours or the night before baking, to plump currants, combine in a small bowl

> *½ cup currants*
> *1 tablespoon Grand Marnier*

Use one batch of Sweet-Roll Dough. Butter two 9-inch round cake pans. After the first rising of the dough, punch dough down. Roll out on a lightly floured surface to a 10×18-inch rectangle. Spread the plumped currants over the surface of the dough. Combine and sprinkle over the currants

> ¾ cup sugar
> grated rind of 1 orange
> ½ cup chopped walnuts

Press this gently into the dough. Starting with one long side, roll up firmly. Cut roll in half across the middle. Starting from the middle out, cut each half into 1¼-inch slices. You should have 14 slices in all. Place one of the end slices in the center of each pan, cut side up. Surround each with 6 of the remaining slices. Divide between the two pans and drizzle over the cut surfaces of the rolls

> 4 tablespoons melted butter

Cover and let dough rise until doubled, 45 to 60 minutes. Bake in a preheated 350°F oven for 25 to 30 minutes, or until well-browned. Invert rolls onto a wire rack and then reinvert them so that they are right side up on a serving plate. After they have cooled a bit, drizzle with a mixture of

> 1 cup sieved powdered sugar
> 2 to 3 tablespoons Grand Marnier

Serve warm. Makes 14 sugar rolls.

❖ Cinnamon Saucisson

When this comes out of the oven it reminds me of linked sausage in an old-time butcher shop. It is a terrific coffee cake for nibblers.

Use 1 batch Sweet-Roll Dough. Lightly butter a 14- or 15-inch pizza pan. Mix together and have ready

> ½ cup sugar
> ½ cup brown sugar
> 2 teaspoons cinnamon
> ½ cup chopped pecans

In a second container, have ready

½ cup melted butter

After the first rising, punch dough down. Tear off a small portion of the dough. Roll it into a rope, about ½ inch thick. Pinch the rope into pieces about 6 inches long. It doesn't matter if the pieces are not all exactly the same size. One at a time, dip pieces in melted butter and then roll them in the sugar mixture. Form the first piece of dough into a coil in the center of the buttered pan. Continue circling this coil with subsequent strips to form a spiral shape. Continue in this fashion until all of the dough is used. Cover lightly and let rise until almost doubled, 30 to 45 minutes. Before baking, sprinkle the top of the cake with any of the sugar mixture that may be left over. Bake in a preheated 350°F oven for 25 to 30 minutes, or until well-browned. Cool slightly. Drizzle with a combination of

¾ cup sieved confectioner's sugar
1 to 2 tablespoons warm coffee

Serve warm. Makes 1 large coffee cake.

❖ Hot Cross Buns

Culinary historians disagree about the origin of Hot Cross Buns. Some say that they evolved from ancient pagan rites of spring. Others firmly believe that their roots are Christian. In any case, Hot Cross Buns, sometimes called Good Friday Buns, are delightful little breads that should not be reserved only for the Easter season.

They must be adequately spiced or they will seem ordinary. Because the batter is so rich, the currants must be kneaded in after the first rising. This gives the dough a chance to develop, and keeps the buns light. The cross can be made several ways. It can be cut into the tops of the buns before baking. Alternately, crosses can be formed with dough strips or icing as suggested here.

Stir together and set aside

> 1 cup unbleached all-purpose flour
> ¼ cup graham flour
> ¼ cup brown sugar
> 1 teaspoon salt
> 1 teaspoon cinnamon
> ½ teaspoon nutmeg
> ¼ teaspoon ginger

To soften the yeast, in a mixing bowl combine

> 1 cup warm milk
> 1 scant tablespoon (or 1 packet) active dry yeast

Stir into softened yeast mixture, in this order

> spiced flour mixture
> 1 egg
> 1 egg yolk
> ¼ cup butter, softened

To make a soft dough, gradually add

> 1 ¾ to 2 cups unbleached all-purpose flour

Scrape dough down in bowl. Cover and let rise until doubled in bulk, 45 to 60 minutes. Punch or stir dough down. Stir or knead in

> ¾ cup dried currants

Turn out on a lightly floured surface and toss until no longer sticky. Pat or roll out to a ½-inch thickness. Cut into rounds with a floured water glass. Place rounds on a lightly greased and lightly floured baking sheet, spacing them 1 inch apart. Cover and let rise until doubled, 30 to 45 minutes. Before baking, brush the tops of the buns with a mixture of

> 1 egg white
> 1 teaspoon water
> 1 teaspoon sugar

Bake in a preheated 375°F oven for 15 to 18 minutes, or until lightly browned. Do not overbake or buns will dry out. Transfer to racks to cool.

While still slightly warm, spoon onto each bun two intersecting lines, forming a cross, with a mixture of

> ¾ cup sieved confectioner's sugar
> 1 tablespoon lemon juice
> 1 tablespoon melted butter

Serve warm or cold. Makes 12 buns.

❖ Sour-Cream Danish

> *Rich with butter and sour cream, this easily mixed dough produces a very tender pastry. Plan on two or three per person. The rolls are small.*

To soften yeast, combine in a mixing bowl

> ¾ cup warm water
> 1 scant tablespoon (or 1 packet) active dry yeast

Stir into softened yeast mixture

> ¼ cup sugar
> 1 egg
> 1 cup (1 8-ounce carton) commercial sour cream
> 1 ½ teaspoons salt
> 1 cup unbleached all-purpose flour

Beat until smooth and set aside. In another large, flat bowl, place

> 3 cups unbleached all-purpose flour

Cut into flour with a pastry blender until butter particles are the size of peas

> 1 cup cold butter

Make a well in the center of the flour-butter mixture. Pour yeast batter into the well. Using a large, flexible spatula, fold in wet ingredients until all dry ingredients are moistened. Do not rush or overwork the dough. Transfer mixed dough to a buttered bowl. Gently press a buttered piece of plastic over the top of the dough. Cover bowl tightly with a second piece of plastic. Chill dough for at least 4 hours, or up to 4 days.

When ready to bake, lightly butter a baking sheet. Working with one-quarter of the dough at a time, roll out into a 12-inch square. At the beginning of the rolling process, check often to see if the rolling surface and the dough need a dusting of flour to prevent sticking. Spread on the rolled-out dough with a pastry brush

1 tablespoon melted butter, slightly cooled

Fold dough in half, making a 6×12-inch rectangle. Press gently to expel any trapped air. Roll rectangle gently to enlarge it to an 8×12-inch size. Measure and cut this into 12 equal 1×8-inch strips. Work with one strip at a time. Holding it between your hands, twist it five or six times. Hold one end of the strip down on the baking sheet and twist the other end around it to form a pinwheel. Tuck the last end under. When all are formed, cover and let rise until doubled in bulk, 45 minutes to 1½ hours, depending on how long the dough has been chilled. Using floured fingers, gently make a small depression in the center of each risen roll. Spoon into each depression

½ to 1 teaspoon apricot or plum jam

Brush parts of rolls not covered with jam with a mixture of

1 egg
1 teaspoon water

Bake in a preheated 375°F oven for 15 to 20 minutes, or until well-browned. Cool on wire racks. While still warm, drizzle with a mixture of

½ cup sieved confectioner's sugar
1 tablespoon lemon juice

Serve warm. One-quarter of the dough makes 12 Danish. Repeat the shaping and baking directions to make 48 Danish in all.

❖ Sweet Ginger Coffee Cake

This coffee cake is as light as a newly blown balloon. The little bits of crystallized ginger in the frosting add a zing that will awaken your tastebuds.

Preheat oven to 350°F. Grease and flour a fluted tube or bundt pan. Sift together and set aside

1 ¾ cups unbleached all-purpose flour
½ teaspoon salt
2 teaspoons baking powder
2 teaspoons ginger

In a mixing bowl, cream

½ cup butter

Gradually blend into butter

1 cup sugar

Add, one at a time, beating well after each addition

2 eggs

Divide the sifted ingredients into three parts and the milk into two, add alternately, beginning and ending with the dry ingredients

the sifted dry ingredients
½ cup milk

Spoon batter into prepared pan. Bake in preheated 350°F oven for 40 to 45 minutes, or until a wooden pick inserted in the center comes out clean. Turn out to cool on a wire rack. While still slightly warm, pour over the coffee cake a mixture of

1 cup sieved confectioner's sugar
1 tablespoon finely chopped crystallized ginger
2 tablespoons lemon juice
1 tablespoon melted butter

Serve warm or cold. Makes 1 large coffee cake.

❖ Sour-Cream Coffee Cake

Preheat oven to 350°F. Grease an 8 × 8-inch pan. Sift together and set aside

> 1 ½ cups unbleached all-purpose flour
> 2 teaspoons baking powder
> ½ teaspoon baking soda
> ½ teaspoon salt

In a large bowl, cream

> 3 tablespoons butter
> ¾ cup sugar

Beat into creamed mixture

> 1 egg
> ½ teaspoon vanilla

Divide dry ingredients into thirds and sour cream in half; add alternately to the egg mixture, beginning and ending with the dry ingredients

> sifted dry ingredients
> 1 cup commercial sour cream

Pour into prepared pan. Combine with a pastry blender and sprinkle over the top

> ½ cup sugar
> 1 teaspoon cinnamon
> 2 tablespoons unbleached all-purpose flour
> 2 tablespoons butter

Bake at 350°F for 35 to 40 minutes, or until a wooden pick inserted in the center comes out clean. Serve warm. Makes 9 servings.

❖ Doughnut Puffs

This is basically the same paste as that used for cream puffs. The paste is flavored with a little nutmeg and deep-fried for puffy doughnuts. The French would call these Beignets Soufflés.

Be sure to have your eggs at room temperature. Sift together and set aside

1 cup unbleached all-purpose flour
1/4 teaspoon freshly ground nutmeg
1 tablespoon sugar

In a heavy saucepan, combine

1 cup water
1/2 cup butter
1/4 teaspoon salt

Over high heat, bring mixture to a full boil. Add the dry ingredients all at once and remove from heat, stirring constantly all the while. Stir vigorously until the mixture leaves the sides of the pan and forms a ball around the spoon. Add, one at a time, beating until smooth and glossy after each addition

4 eggs

Drop the mixture by rounded teaspoonfuls into oil heated to 375°F and fry until well-browned on all sides. Drain on paper towels. Sprinkle with powdered sugar. Serve at once; these will not keep. Makes 36 puffs.

✣ Drop Doughnuts

With this recipe you can easily whip up doughnuts for breakfast or a sweet treat any time.

Sift into a large bowl

1 1/2 cups unbleached all-purpose flour
1 tablespoon baking powder
1/4 cup sugar
1/2 teaspoon salt

In a small container, beat together

1 egg
1/2 cup milk
1 tablespoon oil

Stir egg mixture into dry ingredients, mixing until smooth. Drop batter by rounded teaspoonfuls into oil heated to 375°F. Fry until golden brown, turning once. Drain on paper towels. Roll in granulated sugar. Serve warm. Makes 24 doughnuts.

❖ Buttermilk Doughnuts

You will want a soft dough for these doughnuts. If too much flour is used, they will not be as tender. They may be served plain or sugared.

Stir the flour well before measuring. Spoon it lightly into the cup to measure. Sift together and set aside

> *4 cups unbleached all-purpose flour*
> *1 teaspoon salt*
> *1 teaspoon baking soda*
> *1 teaspoon baking powder*
> *½ teaspoon nutmeg*

In a large bowl, beat

> *2 eggs*

Add, in this order, stirring well after each addition

> *1 cup sugar*
> *¼ cup melted shortening, cooled down to warm*
> *1 cup buttermilk*

Begin by folding in, finish by stirring

> *sifted dry ingredients*

Work with one-third of the dough at a time. Toss on a floured surface until no longer sticky. Gently roll to ¼-inch thickness. Section with a floured doughnut cutter, laying cut doughnuts on waxed paper. Fry in oil heated to 375°F until well-browned, turning once. Drain on paper towels. Roll in

> *sugar (optional)*

Serve warm or cold. Makes 24 doughnuts.

❖ Sour-Cream Doughnuts

For a tender little mouthful, handle these gently while rolling.

Sift together and set aside

> 2 ½ *cups unbleached all-purpose flour*
> ½ *teaspoon salt*
> ½ *teaspoon baking soda*
> ½ *teaspoon baking powder*
> ¼ *cup sugar*

In a large bowl, beat

> 1 *egg*

Stir into egg

> 1 *cup sour cream*

Add gradually—you may not need it all

> *sifted dry ingredients*

Toss on a floured surface until no longer sticky. Roll to ⅜-inch thickness. Cut with a 1½-inch biscuit cutter. Cut a ½-inch slit in the center of each circle. Gently pull the slit open to make miniature doughnuts. Fry in oil heated to 375°F until well-browned, turning once. Drain on paper towels. Roll in cinnamon-sugar. Serve warm or cold. Makes 36 doughnuts.

❖ Beignets

Beignets, or creole doughnuts, often seem elusive to the home baker. No matter how you refine the recipe, homemade beignets never seem to have quite the same romance as those served in the French Quarter of New Orleans. Serve them, of course, with chickory-laced coffee. Have a pitcher of hot milk to dilute the coffee and a bowl of powdered sugar for extra sweetening.

To soften yeast, in a small container combine

> ¼ *cup warm water*
> 1 ½ *teaspoons (or part of 1 packet) active dry yeast*

Allow yeast to proof. Meanwhile, to dissolve butter and sugar, stir together in a large bowl

> *2 tablespoons butter, cut into several pieces*
> *¼ cup sugar*
> *1 teaspoon salt*
> *¼ cup boiling water*

If the butter does not dissolve completely, it is all right. Allow butter mixture to cool down to warm. Stir in, in this order

> *1 egg*
> *softened yeast mixture*
> *1 cup evaporated milk*
> *2 cups unbleached all-purpose flour*

Beat well. To make a soft dough, gradually add

> *1 ½ to 1 ¾ cups unbleached all-purpose flour*

Toss on a floured surface until no longer sticky. Knead very lightly. Try not to incorporate additional flour, as you want to keep a soft dough. Place in a greased bowl, turning dough once to grease the top. Cover with waxed paper, then a china plate. Refrigerate dough for 8 to 12 hours. Divide dough in half—it is easier to work with one-half of dough at a time. Roll chilled dough on a lightly floured surface to ¼-inch thickness. The beignets will puff quite a bit when cooking, so you do not want to roll them any thicker than ¼ inch. Cut into 2½-inch squares. Lay cut squares on waxed paper and cover with a towel to prevent drying out. Let rest 10 minutes. Heat oil to 375°F. Fry dough until puffy and brown. You will want to turn beignets several times. If you wait too long to turn them the first time, they will become lopsided, making it impossible to cook the second side. Drain on paper towels. Sieve powdered sugar over them generously and serve warm. Makes about 30 beignets.

❄ Glazed Doughnuts

You may remember these old-time yeasty doughnuts from your childhood, when they were always made with lard. If you cannot find pure fresh pork lard, use shortening instead.

In a large bowl, combine

1 ½ cups scalded milk
½ cup sugar
¼ cup lard
1 teaspoon salt

Stir to dissolve sugar and lard. Let cool until just warm. Meanwhile, to soften yeast, in a small container combine

¼ cup warm water
1 scant tablespoon (or 1 packet) active dry yeast

When milk mixture has cooled down to warm, stir in, in this order

softened yeast mixture
2 eggs
½ teaspoon freshly grated nutmeg
3 cups unbleached all-purpose flour

Beat well. Add and beat well

1 cup unbleached all-purpose flour

Fold in, ¼ cup at a time, until you have a soft dough

1 to 1 ½ cups unbleached all-purpose flour

Stir until smooth. Scrape dough down in bowl. Cover and let rise until doubled in bulk, 1 to 1½ hours. Stir dough down. Turn dough out on a floured surface and toss until no longer sticky. Gently roll to ⅜-inch thickness. Section with a floured doughnut cutter and transfer cut doughnuts to floured wax paper. Cover and let rise 20 minutes. In oil heated to 375°F, fry until golden brown, turning once. Drain on paper towels. While still warm, spread with glaze. Use Lemon Glaze for one dozen and Mocha Glaze for the other dozen. Makes 24 doughnuts.

Lemon Glaze

Mix together in a small bowl, in this order

> *¼ cup melted butter*
> *grated rind of 1 lemon*
> *2 cups powdered sugar*

Add, 1 tablespoonful at a time, until of spreading consistency

> *up to 6 tablespoons freshly squeezed lemon juice*

Makes enough glaze for 12 doughnuts.

Mocha Glaze

Melt together in the top of a double boiler

> *4 ounces semisweet chocolate*
> *¼ cup butter*

Remove pan from double boiler. Blend in, in this order

> *1 teaspoon vanilla extract*
> *2 cups powdered sugar*

Stir in, 1 tablespoonful at a time, until glaze is of spreading consistency

> *up to 6 tablespoons hot coffee*

Makes enough glaze for 12 doughnuts.

❖ Family-Favorite Fried Bread

> *This recipe is so easy I can make it while the football game is on television and never lose track of the score.*

To soften the yeast, in a large mixing bowl combine

> *1 cup warm water*
> *1 scant tablespoon (or 1 packet) active dry yeast*

Stir into softened yeast mixture

> *3 tablespoons sugar*
> *3 tablespoons oil*
> *½ teaspoon salt*
> *¼ teaspoon nutmeg*
> *1 ½ cups unbleached all-purpose flour or bread flour*

Beat well. To make a soft dough, gradually add

> *1 to 1 ½ cups unbleached all-purpose flour or bread flour*

Cover and let rise in bowl until doubled in bulk, 45 to 60 minutes. Stir dough down. Toss on a lightly floured surface just until no longer sticky. With floured hands, pinch off pieces of dough and roll into small balls. Place balls on waxed paper. Cover with another piece of waxed paper and allow to rest 15 to 20 minutes. Fry in 375°F hot oil until golden brown. Drain on absorbent paper. Roll while still warm in

> *cinnamon-sugar*

Serve immediately with steaming mugs of coffee. Makes about 48 pieces.

❋ Presentation Breads

For special occasions with family and friends

✻ PRESENTATION BREADS

The lowliest loaf of homemade bread is fit fare for company. There is no homemade bread I would be ashamed to serve to a guest. There are, however, breads that are special because they require more care and time to prepare, or have a fancier appearance. These warrant a special presentation.

Most of the loaves included here should be seen in their entirety before being sliced. You will want to think about how they should be served to greatest effect. This rarely takes much effort, and seeing your breads attractively presented provides the best inspiration for baking I can think of. Use the breads that follow to fuel your creative presentations.

✻ ABOUT CROISSANTS

You do not have to be a master baker to master these buttery, flaky croissants. After you have grown more confident, feel free to layer other simple doughts with a butter, or butter and cheese mixture, to form flaky rolls of many kinds. Keep these tips in mind:

1. Croissant-making is not advised on a warm, muggy day, unless you have an air-conditioned kitchen.

2. Even in a cool atmosphere, the dough may need to be repeatedly chilled to keep it from becoming oily and hard to handle.

3. The dough must remain pliable. A short mixing or kneading prevents the gluten from developing. A small amount of cake flour also helps toward that end.

4. Refrigerating the dough between rolling and folding helps to keep the butter chilled and also to prevent the dough from rising. There should be as little rising as possible during the time the layers are formed.

5. If the dough sticks, sprinkle a little flour to correct the problem. Do not be afraid to lift the dough to check. Remember, the dough scraper is, in this instance, the baker's best friend.

6. If butter breaks through, dust the dough with flour, cover, and refrigerate for 15 to 20 minutes.

7. Above all, relax. Remember that you, not the dough, are in charge. Your first croissants may not look professional, but they are sure to be delicious.

❖ Classic Croissants

Although "croissant" is a French word meaning crescent, the buttery, flaky roll did not begin in France. It was born in Hungary in 1686. Bakers, working late at night and deep below the surface streets of Budapest, heard the Turks tunneling into their city. They spread the alarm which led to the defeat of the advancing army. As a reward for their patriotic vigilance, the bakers were awarded the privilege of producing a commemorative pastry. It was shaped like a crescent, the emblem of Turkey. The French subsequently adopted this pastry and they, as well as many other Europeans, habitually eat fresh, warm croissants for breakfast.

Tear off and have ready two 12-inch squares of waxed paper.

To soften yeast, in a mixing bowl combine

> *1 ½ teaspoons (or part of 1 packet) active dry yeast*
> *1 ¼ cups warm milk*
> *1 tablespoon sugar*

Let stand 3 minutes. Stir into softened yeast mixture, in this order

> *1 ¼ teaspoons salt*
> *½ cup cake flour*
> *2 ½ cups unbleached all-purpose flour*

Beat just until a rough, sticky dough forms. Cover and set aside while preparing butter mixture. Spread on a cold work surface

> *1 ¼ cups (2 ½ sticks) cold butter, cut into about 20 pieces*

Sprinkle butter with

> *3 tablespoons unbleached all-purpose flour*

Work butter and flour together by alternately mashing it with the heel of your hand and gathering it back up with the aid of a dough scraper. Work quickly. As soon as the mixture is smooth and workable, shape it into a small rectangle. Place the rectangle between the sheets of waxed paper. Roll and pat it out to a 6×8-inch rectangle. Straighten the sides of this rectangle. Place on a baking sheet and refrigerate the butter mixture.

Clean the work surface and sprinkle it generously with flour. Turn the dough out on it and toss until no longer sticky. Pat or roll out to a 10× 14-inch rectangle.

Unwrap butter mixture and place it on the bottom half of the dough, leaving a 1-inch border on three sides. Fold top half over butter, and seal edges. Give the dough a quarter turn so sealed edge is to your right.

Roll to 10×16-inch rectangle, moving the dough away from you.

Fold bottom third of dough up over the middle, fold top third down to cover this. Turn again so that the flap is to your right. Repeat rolling and folding one more time. Dust dough with flour; wrap in plastic. Place on a baking sheet and refrigerate for 30 minutes to chill. (You have now completed two turns.)

Roll and fold as before. Dust, wrap, and chill for 45 minutes.

Roll and fold for the fourth and last time. Dust, wrap, and chill for at least 1 hour, or for as long as overnight.

When ready to shape: Roll to just slightly larger than a 10×20-inch rectangle. Trim the edges to make the rectangle exactly 10×20 inches. This will remove any folded edges that might prevent the rising of the shaped rolls. Mark the 20-inch side into quarters and the 10-inch side in half. Cut straight lines across the dough at these points, dividing it into eight 5-inch squares. Cut each square in half diagonally, making 16 triangles in all.

Work with one triangle at a time. Gently stretch the triangle by pulling the points apart. Starting with the short side, gently roll up dough, leaving the last point slightly tucked under. Place croissants on a baking sheet, leaving 2 inches between each one. Curve outside points toward one another.

When all are formed, brush with a mixture of

1 egg
1 tablespoon milk

Do not cover. Allow to rise until quite light, 1½ to 2 hours. Repeat glazing with egg mixture two more times, at 30-minute intervals. Preheat oven to 425°F. Place oven rack in upper third of oven. Bake at 425°F for 8 minutes. Reduce heat to 375°F and bake for 10 minutes longer, or until well-browned. Cool slightly on wire racks. Serve warm with sweet butter and homemade preserves. Makes 16 croissants.

❖ Large Croissants

There is a trend toward larger croissants. Here's how to shape croissants that are large enough for a whole-meal sandwich.

Follow the recipe for Classic Croissants. When ready to shape: Roll to slightly larger than a 15-inch square. Trim as before. Cut the square into four equal 7½-inch squares. Cut each square in half diagonally, making eight triangles in all. Shape and glaze as described above. Bake in a preheated 425°F oven for 10 minutes. Reduce heat to 375°F and bake for 12 minutes longer, or until well-browned. Cool slightly on wire racks. Serve warm. Makes 8 large croissants.

❖ C. J.'s Croissants

C. J.'s Croissants come from Candy Underhill, the owner and operator of C. J.'s Kitchen in Danville, Illinois. Candy artfully combines an interior-design service and a gourmet cookware shop, where she teaches gourmet cooking classes on a regular basis.

To soften yeast, in a mixing bowl combine

1 ¼ cups milk heated to warm (115°F)
1 scant tablespoon (or 1 packet) active dry yeast
1 tablespoon sugar

Add, 1 cup at a time, mixing well with a fork

2 cups unbleached all-purpose flour

Stir into batter with the fork

1 teaspoon salt

Add, ¼ cup at a time, stirring well with the fork

½ cup unbleached all-purpose flour

Turn out on a well-floured surface and toss until no longer sticky. Knead gently until smooth, working in only as much flour as needed to prevent sticking. Place in a well-buttered bowl, turning dough once to butter the top. Cover and let rise for 1 hour. Punch dough down. Cover and let rise in the refrigerator for an hour. Gently press the dough down to expel air, leaving it in a relaxed state. Turn dough out onto a floured surface and roll to a 10 × 15-inch rectangle. Spread the surface of the dough with

½ cup softened butter

With the long side facing you, fold the right third over the center. Fold the left third over all. Roll out again to slightly less than a 10 × 15-inch rectangle. Each time you roll the dough from here on out, it will be a rectangle that is slightly smaller in size than before. Spread the surface of the dough with

½ cup softened butter

Fold dough into thirds as before. Roll out again to a rectangle and fold into thirds. Roll out for the fourth time and fold into thirds. Place folded dough in a plastic bag and allow it to rest in the refrigerator for at least 2 hours, or as long as overnight. When ready to shape croissants, cut dough in half. Work with one-half at a time. Roll out each half into a 12-inch circle. Using a pizza cutter, cut dough into 12 equal wedges. Roll each wedge to the point and place, point side down, on ungreased baking sheets. When all are shaped, brush the tops of the croissants with a mixture of

1 egg yolk
1 teaspoon cream

Let rise uncovered for 1 hour. Bake in a preheated 375°F oven for 20 to 30 minutes, or until well-browned. Cool on wire racks. Makes 24 croissants.

�֎ ABOUT BRIOCHE

The rich egg dough used for brioche is delicious when fresh. It does stale quickly, however. What you do not plan to eat within 24 hours should be wrapped and frozen for later use. Leftovers can be used for an extravagant French toast or bread pudding.

Many novice bakers feel that brioche is beyond their ability. This need not be the case. Start with the recipe below.

�֎ Braided Brioche

This brioche can also be baked as an oblong loaf.

In a mixing bowl, combine

> *½ cup butter, cut into 8 pieces*
> *2 tablespoons sugar*
> *1 teaspoon salt*
> *½ cup scalded milk*

Stir to dissolve butter and sugar. Let cool until just warm. Meanwhile, to soften yeast, in a small container combine

> *¼ cup warm water*
> *1 scant tablespoon (or 1 packet) active dry yeast*
> *1 tablespoon sugar*

When milk mixture has cooled down to warm, stir in, in this order

> *softened yeast mixture*
> *2 eggs*
> *1 egg yolk*
> *2 cups unbleached all-purpose flour*

Beat well. To make a stiff batter, gradually add

> *1 to 1 ½ cups unbleached all-purpose flour*

Batter should be thick, but not too thick to stir in all the added flour. Scrape dough down in bowl. Cover and refrigerate for several hours or overnight. When ready to use, punch dough down. Divide into three parts. Roll each part into a 15-inch rope. Place in a lightly greased or nonstick baking pan and braid ropes together. Pinch ends together and tuck slightly under. If you wish to make this in loaf form, simply form each part into a ball and drop the balls in a row into a buttered 9×5-inch baking pan. Cover lightly and let rise until more than doubled, 1 to 1½ hours. Before baking, brush top of loaf with a mixture of

> *1 egg white*
> *1 teaspoon water*
> *½ teaspoon sugar*

Take care not to brush the wash into the seams of the braid. Bake in a preheated 375°F oven for 35 to 40 minutes or until well-browned. The 9 ×5-inch loaf may take a little longer. Cool on a rack. Makes 1 loaf.

❖ Water-Risen Brioche

> *Water-risen yeast dough insures the lightness of this large brioche. The tubular loaf is impressive and most suitable for a buffet service.*

Read through the recipe and assemble all ingredients and utensils before beginning. In a small bowl, combine

> *½ cup warm water*
> *2 scant tablespoons (or 2 packets) active dry yeast*
> *¾ cup unbleached all-purpose flour*

Beat well. To make a soft dough, gradually add

> *2 to 4 tablespoons unbleached all-purpose flour*

Knead in bowl until smooth, adding additional flour if needed. Fill a 3- or 4-quart bowl two-thirds full of warm water (about 85°F). Shape dough into a ball. Cut a cross in the top of the ball and drop it into the warm water. Leave it until it rises to the top of the bowl. This will give you about 10 minutes to mix the remainder of the bread dough. If the yeast-risen dough is ready before you are, pour off the water. The dough should not sit in the water longer than 10 or 15 minutes and should have risen to the top of the water in that time. In a large bowl, beat

> *6 eggs*

Stir into eggs

> *2 tablespoons sugar*
> *2 teaspoons salt*

Add, one cup at a time, beating well after each

> *3 cups unbleached all-purpose flour*

Add, 2 tablespoons at a time, blending well after each addition

> *1 cup softened butter*

Add and blend into egg dough

> *water-risen ball of dough*

Scrape dough down in bowl. Cover and let rise until doubled in bulk, 1 to 1½ hours. Stir dough down. Spoon into a well-buttered 10-inch tube pan. Use a spatula to smooth the top of the dough. Cover and let rise almost to the top of the pan, 1 to 1½ hours. Bake in a preheated 375°F oven for 40 to 45 minutes, or until well-browned. Be sure to bake through completely. If top browns too deeply before interior is done, cover with a tent of foil. Turn out to cool on a wire rack. Makes 1 large loaf.

❖ Petite Brioche

This will make enough dough for twelve 3-inch brioches. The dough is delicate and although the top knots are not always tall, the texture of the bread is outstanding. Chilling the dough during the second rise makes it easier to shape. Serve this classic with a fresh fruit compote on your finest china. Strong coffee should be laced with hot milk for café au lait.

To soften yeast, in a small container combine

> *¼ cup warm water*
> *1 scant tablespoon (or 1 packet) active dry yeast*

In a mixing bowl, beat

   3 eggs

Stir into eggs, in this order

   softened yeast mixture
   ¾ teaspoon salt
   ⅓ cup sugar

To make a stiff dough, gradually add

   2 to 2 ½ cups unbleached all-purpose flour

Grasp your wooden spoon down low on the handle, near the bowl of the spoon, and use it as an extension of your hand. Rhythmically kneading the dough and turning the bowl, work in, 1 tablespoon at a time

   8 tablespoons soft butter

When all of the butter has been blended in, scrape dough down in bowl. Butter a piece of plastic and place it loosely over the dough, butter side down. Cover the whole thing tightly with another piece of plastic. Refrigerate for 6 to 8 hours, or overnight. When ready to shape, butter twelve 3-inch brioche tins. Punch dough down. Divide dough into four parts. Set one part aside. Divide each of the remaining three parts into four pieces. With lightly floured hands, shape each piece into a ball and drop into buttered tins. Divide remaining part into twelve equal pieces. Shape each of these into a small ball. With one finger, make an indentation in the center of each larger ball and position a small ball in that hole. When all are formed, cover lightly and let rise until slightly more than doubled, 1 to 1½ hours. Preheat oven to 375°F. Before baking, brush brioches gently with a mixture of

   1 egg yolk
   1 tablespoon milk

Take care not to brush glaze into the joint between the large and small balls of dough. Bake brioche at 375°F for 18 to 20 minutes, or until well-browned. Turn out to cool slightly on wire racks. Serve warm. Makes 12 brioches.

❖ Pain au Chocolat

French schoolboys are said to love their chocolate, especially in these rolls.

Use the dough for Petite Brioche. After the refrigerator rising period, punch dough down. Divide it in half and work with one-half at a time. Toss on a floured surface until no longer sticky. Gently roll out into a 9-inch circle. Dough should be about ¼ inch thick. Cut the circle into six equal wedges. On the wide end of each wedge place a tablespoonful of chopped semisweet chocolate, or semisweet chocolate morsels. Starting with the wide end, roll to the point. Place, point down, on a lightly greased baking sheet. Tuck pointed ends under slightly, sealing well. Cover lightly and allow to rise until doubled in bulk, about 1 hour. Bake in preheated 375°F oven for 18 to 20 minutes, or until well-browned. Cool slightly on wire racks. Eat while still warm enough that the chocolate is somewhat soft. May be reheated. Makes 12 chocolate-filled rolls.

❖ The Mother-Earth Loaf

This bread takes some time and muscle, but is well worth the effort. The crust is thick and chewy; the interior has a tender, porous texture. Italian bakers make a bread like this daily from a sponge called "The Mother." When they bake "The Mother" itself, it is called "The Mother Loaf." Carol Field, in her book The Italian Baker, *tells us that bakers in the southern part of Italy call their sponge "The Father." I use a small amount of whole-grain flour, adding an earthiness to the flavor and to the name.*

Serve this bread with a thick peasant soup or a simple main-dish pasta, and a full-bodied dry red California Charbono. Let diners tear off chunks to eat rather than slice the loaf. It is best eaten the day it is made.

In a large bowl, combine

> *1 ¾ cups warm water*
> *1 scant tablespoon (or 1 packet) active dry yeast*
> *¼ cup stone-ground whole-wheat flour*

Stir to soften yeast. Let stand 10 minutes. Stir into yeast mixture

1 teaspoon salt
2 cups unbleached all-purpose flour or bread flour

Beat this batter steadily and rhythmically for 10 minutes. Stir in

1 cup unbleached all-purpose flour or bread flour

Beat for 5 more minutes. Stir in, ¼ cup at a time, beating well after each addition

¾ cup unbleached all-purpose flour or bread flour

After all the flour has been added and beaten in, scrape down the sides of the bowl with a spatula. Stir again. Scrape again. Cover with plastic wrap and let stand for 1 hour or more, until the dough has doubled in size. Meanwhile, grease a 14-inch pizza pan and sprinkle liberally with cornmeal. Do not punch, knead, or stir down the dough. Gently transfer dough to prepared pan, using a spatula.

Sift flour over the top of the dough. Place in a cold oven on the center shelf. Place a flat pan of hot water on a shelf below, or on the bottom of the oven. Close oven door and let rise until dough has doubled, 45 to 60 minutes. Remove pan of water from the oven. Turn oven on and set temperature at 400°F. Bake at that temperature for 40 to 45 minutes, or until loaf is well-browned. Cool on a wire rack. Makes 1 large, flat loaf.

❖ Monkey Bread

This rich and light pull-apart loaf makes a simple meal festive.

To dissolve butter and sugar, in a large mixing bowl combine

1 cup scalded milk
¼ cup butter
2 tablespoons sugar
1 teaspoon salt

Let cool until just warm. Meanwhile, to soften yeast, in a small container combine

1 scant tablespoon (or 1 packet) active dry yeast
¼ cup warm water
1 teaspoon sugar

When milk mixture has cooled down to warm, stir in, in this order.

softened yeast mixture
2 eggs
3 cups unbleached all-purpose flour

Beat well. To make a soft dough, gradually add

1 ½ to 1 ¾ cups unbleached all-purpose flour

Turn out on a floured surface. Knead until smooth. Place in a buttered bowl. Butter top of dough lightly. Cover and let rise until doubled in bulk, 45 to 60 minutes. Knead dough down in bowl. Turn dough out on a lightly floured surface. Roll to ⅜-inch thickness. Cut into 2×3-inch rectangles. Dip pieces in

½ cup melted butter, cooled slightly

Hold pieces of dipped dough over melted butter to let excess drip off. Drop pieces in a haphazard fashion into a well-buttered 10-inch tube pan with at least a 3-quart capacity. Cover and let rise until doubled, 45 to 60 minutes. Bake in preheated 375°F oven for 35 to 40 minutes, or until well-browned. Turn out on a large plate and serve while warm. Let diners break off their own already buttered bread. Makes 1 loaf.

❖ ABOUT POPOVERS

Popovers utilize a very thin batter and are raised by steam. As the popover rises, the protein in the eggs and the gluten in the flour form a crust that keeps the popover from falling. Popovers can be made with either all-purpose flour or bread flour. I prefer to use bread flour as I find it provides a better gluten structure.

You can use a muffin pan to bake popovers, but the best are baked in a pan especially made for that purpose. The cups in a popover pan are deeper and narrower than those in a muffin pan, and will produce a more spectacular shape. The best popover pan is made of heavy black metal. The recipes that follow were developed with such a pan. If you use a muffin pan or a popover pan that is not black, you will want to raise the temperatures to 450°F and 375°F respectively. Some bakers do not preheat the oven for popovers. Preheating the oven, however, produces a popover with a firmer interior.

Popover pans should be evenly greased before batter is poured into them. Either shortening or lard will work. Do not use oil. The batter should be well beaten until smooth, but no more than that. The pans do not require heating before use.

If you open the oven door before the minimum baking time has elapsed, your popovers may collapse. After they come out of the oven, they should be removed from their pans and served without any standing time. If they must be kept, they should be punctured on the side with a fork to let some of the trapped steam escape. Otherwise, they may turn soggy.

✻ Perfect Popovers

Preheat oven to 425°F (450°F if pans are not black). Grease a 6-cup popover pan. In a medium-sized mixing bowl, preferably one with a pouring spout, stir together

> 1 cup bread flour
> ¾ teaspoon salt

Add and blend in with a wire whisk

> 1 cup milk

Continue beating until mixture is smooth. Add, one at a time, blending well after each addition

> 3 eggs

Pour batter evenly into prepared popover cups. Cups should be about half full. Do not scrape bowl. Place popover pan in preheated 425°F oven. Bake for 20 minutes. Reduce temperature to 350°F (375°F if pans are not black) and bake 15 to 20 minutes longer. Remove popovers from pans and serve at once. Makes 6 perfect popovers.

❖ Parmesan Popovers

Add 4 tablespoons grated Parmesan cheese to the dry ingredients and follow the directions for Perfect Popovers.

❖ Whole-Grain Popovers

Substitute ¼ cup stone-ground whole-wheat flour for ¼ cup of the bread flour. Add 1 teaspoon dark molasses to the mixture before adding the eggs. Follow the directions for Perfect Popovers.

❖ Sally Lunn

This rich batter bread is a descendent of the little English tea buns which were in vogue during American colonial times. Some say it is named after little Sally Lunn, who hawked her tea buns daily up and down the streets of Bath, England, in the eighteenth century. Others say it is a perversion of the French Soleil et Lune *(sun and moon), which describes the golden crowns and white bases of the smaller buns.*

There are many versions. The ingredients of my favorite include a small amount of lemon rind, which I think adds freshness to the flavor.

To dissolve butter and sugar, in a large bowl combine

> *¾ cup scalded milk*
> *½ cup butter*
> *5 tablespoons sugar*
> *1 teaspoon salt*

Let cool to just warm. Meanwhile, in a small bowl, to soften yeast combine

> *¼ cup warm water*
> *1 scant tablespoon (or 1 packet) active dry yeast*
> *1 teaspoon sugar*

When milk mixture has cooled down to warm, stir in, in this order

> softened yeast mixture
> 3 eggs
> finely grated rind of ½ lemon
> 3 cups unbleached all-purpose flour

Beat well. To make a stiff batter, gradually add

> 1 cup unbleached all-purpose flour, more or less

Scrape bowl down. Cover with buttered plastic and let rise until doubled in bulk, 45 to 60 minutes. Stir dough down. Spoon into a well-buttered 9-inch fluted tube pan. Smooth top of batter with a spatula. Cover again with buttered plastic and let rise until batter reaches top of pan. Bake in a preheated 375°F oven for 40 to 45 minutes, or until dark golden brown. Turn out to cool slightly on a wire rack. Serve warm, thinly sliced, with homemade vanilla ice cream or a soft stove-top custard and lightly sugared fresh berries. Leftover slices may be toasted and served with sweet butter. Makes 1 large loaf.

❈ Babas Au Rhum

> *Although the baba is thought of as a French dessert bread, it was first baked to satisfy the appetite of a Polish king. The king named it after Ali Baba, the hero of his favorite folk tale.* *

In a small bowl, blend together

> ¼ cup scalded milk
> ¼ cup soft butter

Set this milk mixture aside to cool to lukewarm. To soften yeast, in another small container combine

> ¼ cup warm water
> 1 scant tablespoon (or 1 packet) active dry yeast

Woman's Day Encyclopedia of Cookery, Vol. 1 (New York: Fawcett, 1966), p. 131.

In a mixing bowl, beat

1 egg
2 egg yolks

Gradually beat into eggs

¼ cup sugar

Stir into the egg mixture, in this order

milk mixture
softened yeast mixture
½ teaspoon salt
grated rind of ½ lemon
¼ cup dried currants
1 ¾ cups unbleached all-purpose flour

Beat until smooth. Cover and let rise until doubled in bulk, 1 to 1½ hours. Stir batter down. Butter individual molds or custard cups and place them on a baking sheet. The molds should have a capacity of about 1 cup. I have used ovenproof coffee cups. Butter them very well, as this batter has a tendency to stick. Spoon batter into molds, using about ⅜ cup batter per mold. Cover and let rise until the batter doubles, 30 to 45 minutes. Bake in a preheated 350°F oven for 15 to 20 minutes, or until a wooden pick inserted in the center comes out clean. Turn out to cool, upside down, on a wire rack that has been positioned over a large plate. As they cool, spoon over them

Hot Rum Syrup

Spoon 1 tablespoon of the syrup over each baba. Repeat four times, or until all the syrup is used. Serve either warm or cold on a dessert plate. Offer unsweetened whipped cream. Makes 6 babas.

Hot Rum Syrup

In a heavy saucepan, stir together over medium heat until sugar is dissolved

1 cup water
¾ cup sugar

Increase heat so that mixture boils rapidly for 5 minutes. Remove from heat and stir in

> 1 teaspoon lemon juice
> 1/4 cup rum

❖ Savarin

Make the batter for Babas, but omit the currants. After the first rising, spoon the batter into a well-buttered 5-cup ring mold. Be sure to butter the mold well, as this batter has a tendency to stick. Cover and let rise to the top of the pan. Bake in a preheated 350°F oven for 25 to 30 minutes, or until a wooden pick inserted in the center of the dough comes out clean. Cool on a wire rack. Savarin may be doused with Rum Syrup and served in the same manner as Babas. Alternatively, fill the ring with fresh seasonal fruits that have been marinated in brandy or a liqueur. To serve, place a slice of the savarin and several spoonfuls of the fruit in each dessert dish. Offer Custard Cream.

Custard Cream
In the top of a double boiler, beat together

> 3 egg yolks
> 1/4 cup sugar
> pinch salt (optional)

Combine and then stir into the egg-yolk mixture

> 1 cup cold milk
> 1 1/2 teaspoons cornstarch

Place over simmering water and cook, stirring constantly, until the mixture thickens. The custard should be almost ready to boil, but should not be allowed to do so. Remove from heat and stir in

> 1/4 to 1/2 teaspoon vanilla extract, according to taste

Cool before using—the custard should cool at room temperature for at least ½ hour. Stir gently several times during that ½ hour. It should then be covered and refrigerated.

❖ Little Gingerbreads with Lemon Sauce

My mother's gingerbread was always my favorite. She'd make it in a sheet pan and serve it warm, after supper, with her freshly made lemon sauce. I like to make mine in individual molds for a slightly fancier service. They are the perfect end to an old-fashioned American supper.

Preheat oven to 350°F. Grease nine 1-cup molds. I use ovenproof coffee cups. Sift together and set aside

> *2 ½ cups unbleached all-purpose flour*
> *1 teaspoon baking powder*
> *1 teaspoon baking soda*
> *½ teaspoon salt*
> *2 teaspoons ginger*
> *1 teaspoon cinnamon*
> *¼ teaspoon cloves*
> *¼ teaspoon nutmeg*

In a mixing bowl, beat

> *2 eggs*

Stir into eggs, in this order

> *¾ cup brown sugar*
> *¾ cup molasses*
> *½ cup melted butter, slightly cooled*
> *sifted dry ingredients*

Add gradually, stirring all the while

> *1 cup boiling water*

Spoon batter into prepared cups. Bake in preheated 350°F oven for 30 to 35 minutes, or until the gingerbread begins to pull away from the sides of the molds. Turn out of molds to cool on a wire rack. Serve either warm or cold with

Lemon Sauce

Makes 9 gingerbread.

Note: These may be baked in standard-sized muffin cups, using about ¼ cup batter for each. They will not be as tender as the larger gingerbreads. Bake at 350°F for 20 to 25 minutes. Makes 24 gingerbread.

Lemon Sauce

In a heavy saucepan, stir together

¾ cup sugar
1 tablespoon cornstarch
1 cup cold water

Place over medium heat and cook, stirring constantly, until thickened. Remove from heat. Stir into thickened mixture, in this order

grated rind of 1 lemon
¼ cup lemon juice
3 tablespoons soft butter

Serve warm.

❋ For the Snack Attack

Bread sticks, crackers, and flat breads

CRACKLING FLAT BREAD
PIZZA DOUGH
NEAPOLITAN PIZZA
PESTO PIZZA
BACON-CHEESE FLAT BREAD
THE PERSONAL PIZZA
PITA
LAVASH
BUTTERY BREAD STICKS
BAGUETTE BREAD STICKS
GRISSINI

RYE BREAD STICKS
RYE WAFERS
SESAME-WHEAT BREAD STICKS
SESAME-WHEAT WAFERS
HOMEMADE SALTINE CRACKERS
BUTTER-AND-EGG CRACKERS
BUTTERMILK CRACKERS
HOMEMADE HONEY GRAHAMS
GINGERBREAD MEN
CRISP GINGER CRACKERS

❖ FOR THE SNACK ATTACK

Little crackers, crisp breadsticks, and flat breads are often neglected by the home baker. But they are not difficult to make and their appearance will always bring applause.

For brief snacks or for the appetizer course of a large meal, crackers and bread sticks team beautifully with flavored butters, dips, and cheeses. They can also accompany a soup or a salad. Flat breads, particularly the filled ones, can almost replace a full meal when something lighter is desired. Pita pockets enclose a multitude of fillings.

❖ Crackling Flat Bread

I make this bread with the cracklings from rendered lard. If you don't have cracklings, you can substitute thick bacon that has been fried and chopped. The onions used in this recipe are the dried ones found in the market next to the spices.

To soften yeast, in a mixing bowl combine

1 cup warm water
1 teaspoon sugar
1 scant tablespoon (or 1 packet) active dry yeast

Stir into softened yeast mixture

1 teaspoon salt
2 tablespoons dried minced onions
¼ cup stone-ground whole-wheat flour
1 cup unbleached all-purpose flour or bread flour

Beat well. To make a stiff dough, gradually add

1 to 1 ½ cups unbleached all-purpose flour or bread flour

Knead into the dough in the bowl

1 cup crisp cracklings, finely chopped

Cover bowl and let rise until doubled in bulk, 45 to 60 minutes. Press dough down in the bowl to expel air. On a lightly floured surface, roll dough the size of your largest baking sheet or pizza pan. Either grease the pan or use one that is nonstick. Transfer rolled dough to pan and pat to conform to the shape of the pan. Cover and let rise until almost doubled, 30 to 45 minutes. Use your fingers to form small depressions all over the surface of the dough. Brush the surface with a mixture of

> 1 egg
> 1 tablespoon water

Sprinkle with

> coarse salt
> coarsely ground pepper

Bake in a preheated 400°F oven for 15 to 20 minutes, or until well-browned. Cool slightly on a wire rack. Serve warm with cold mugs of beer. Let diners break off what they want to eat. Makes 1 large, flat loaf.

❖ Pizza Dough

> *Use this dough for the pizza recipes that follow and for Bacon-Cheese Flat Bread.*

To soften yeast, in a large bowl combine

> 1 ¼ cups warm water
> 1 scant tablespoon (or 1 packet) active dry yeast
> 1 teaspoon sugar

Let stand 5 minutes. Stir in, in this order

> 1 teaspoon salt
> 2 tablespoons olive oil
> 1 cup bread flour
> 1 cup unbleached all-purpose flour

Beat well. To make a stiff dough, gradually add

> ¾ to 1 cup unbleached all-purpose flour

Turn out on a lightly floured surface and knead until smooth. Place in a bowl oiled with ½ teaspoon olive oil, turning dough once to oil the top. Cover and let rise until doubled, 30 to 45 minutes. Flatten dough to expel air. Do not knead. You want this dough to be relaxed. Stretch and pat out dough to fit across the bottom and up the sides of an oiled or nonstick 10 ×15-inch jelly-roll pan. Make the sides a little thicker than the bottom. Fill and bake as directed below.

✣ Neapolitan Pizza

Pizza has become whatever we want it to be at the moment, including a vehicle for a week's worth of leftovers. In 1985, fearing the demise of the traditional pizza, 20 Neapolitan pizzeria owners formed the Real Neapolitan Pizza Association, dedicated to preserving the traditional ingredients and methods of preparing pizza. * This recipe should meet with their approval.

Use your fingers to spread a thin coating of olive oil over the top of the dough. Spread with about ⅛-inch thickness of

Tomato Sauce (see recipe below)

Sprinkle over the tomato sauce

2 cups shredded mozzarella cheese

Sprinkle over all

¼ cup grated Parmesan cheese
dried oregano, rubbed between your fingers, the amount guided by your taste
buds

If you are not sure, go lightly. You can add more the next time. Bake in a preheated 450°F oven for 15 to 20 minutes, or until the crust is browned and the cheese is melted and well-browned. Cut into small pieces with a kitchen shears to serve for appetizers. This can also serve for a pickup meal with a platter of fresh raw vegetables and a glass of hearty Chianti. Makes 12 servings.

---

*William Ecenbarger, "Pizza: Slice of Americana Now Bigger than Burgers," *Chicago Tribune,* Jan. 8, 1986, Sect. 2, p. 3.

❖ Pesto Pizza

In a heavy skillet, heat

>   2 tablespoons olive oil
>   2 tablespoons butter
>   2 garlic cloves, pressed

Sauté in this mixture

>   2 cups sliced or chopped zucchini
>   or
>   2 cups sliced or chopped onions
>   or
>   a combination of both

Spread top of dough with about ⅛-inch thickness, more or less, of

>   Pesto Sauce (see recipe below)

Spread sautéed vegetables over Pesto Sauce. Top with

>   2 cups shredded mozzarella cheese

Bake in a preheated 450°F oven for 15 to 20 minutes, or until crust is well-browned and cheese is melted and beginning to brown. Serve as described under Neapolitan Pizza. Makes 12 servings.

❖ Bacon-Cheese Flat Bread

>   Drink a cold glass of beer with this specialty.

Sprinkle over the dough

>   2 cups shredded extra-sharp cheddar cheese

In a small bowl, beat together

>   2 eggs
>   ⅓ cup milk
>   ½ teaspoon salt
>   ¼ teaspoon dry mustard

Pour this over the cheese. Sprinkle over all

1 cup crumbled crisp-fried bacon

Bake in a preheated 400°F oven for 20 to 25 minutes, or until crust is well-browned and custard is set. Cut into small rectangles and serve as before. Makes 12 servings.

❖ The Personal Pizza

After the first rising, divide the dough into 12 equal portions. Roll each to a thin, free-form, flat shape. Crimp the edges to form a rim. Have one container of pesto and one of tomato sauce with a variety of toppings available: Italian sausage, cherry tomatoes, canned artichoke hearts, chopped cooked ham, mushrooms, and peppers, etc. Let diners build their own pizza. Place them all on a large heavy-weight oiled baking sheet and bake in a preheated 500°F oven for 5 to 7 minutes. If your oven will not heat to 500°F, baking may take a little longer. Serve with red or white California jug wine. Makes 12 servings.

Tomato Sauce

This makes a good basic tomato sauce. Use it on Pizza or add some freshly sautéed garden vegetables and spoon it onto your favorite cooked pasta.

In a large stainless-steel pot, heat

2 tablespoons olive oil
2 tablespoons butter

In the heated oil, sauté

4 garlic cloves, minced
1 onion, chopped

When onion is translucent, add

6 pounds Roma tomatoes, stem and blossom ends removed, quartered

Cook over medium heat, stirring occasionally, until tomatoes are quite soft. Press the mixture through a sieve and return sieved mixture to heat. Stir in, in this order

> ½ cup dry white wine
> 2 tablespoons finely chopped fresh basil leaves (about ½ cup leaves before chopping)
> ½ teaspoon dried oregano
> ½ teaspoon dried hot red pepper flakes, crushed between your fingers
> ½ teaspoon salt, or to taste

Simmer, stirring occasionally, until reduced to half. Stir a little of the hot sauce into the contents of

> 1 6-ounce can tomato paste

Stir tomato-paste mixture into sauce. Cook, stirring, for a little while longer, until sauce and paste have achieved a mellow marriage. Sauce may be cooled and stored in the refrigerator for up to a week.

Pesto Sauce

I make my Pesto in a food processor.

Use the metal blade throughout. Cut into chunks and then process until finely grated

> 5 ounces Parmesan cheese

Remove to a side bowl. With machine running to mince, drop through feedtube

> 4 large garlic cloves

Add to workbowl and process until finely chopped

> 4 cups washed and dried basil leaves

Add grated Parmesan cheese and pulse on/off to mix. With machine running, add through the feedtube until mixture is smooth and creamy

> 1 cup olive oil, more or less

Transfer pesto to a glass jar. Run a knife down the edges of the jar to eliminate any air pockets. Cover top of pesto with a thin film of olive oil to prevent oxidation. Cover tightly and store in refrigerator for up to a week; in the freezer for up to 6 months. Frozen pesto should be thawed in the refrigerator for 24 hours before use.

✵ Pita

Stuff pita pockets with your favorite sandwich filling, or cut them into strips for buttered, toasted snacks. Be sure to use bread flour. Unbleached flour will not puff as readily.

To soften yeast, in a mixing bowl combine

    1 cup warm water
    1 scant tablespoon (or 1 packet) active dry yeast

Stir into the softened yeast mixture

    1 teaspoon salt
    1 teaspoon olive oil
    ¼ cup stone-ground whole-wheat flour
    1 cup bread flour

Beat well to develop the gluten. To make a stiff dough, gradually add

    1 cup bread flour, more or less

Turn out on a floured surface and knead until smooth and elastic. Place in a bowl oiled with

    ½ teaspoon olive oil

Turn dough once to oil the top. Cover and let rise until doubled in bulk, 45 to 60 minutes. Punch dough down. Divide into eight equal parts. Shape each part into a ball by pulling down on the sides and tucking them under. Place them on a floured baking sheet. Dust tops with flour and cover them. Let rest 10 minutes. Work with one at a time. On a lightly floured surface, gently flatten each ball with the palm of your hand, and then roll out to a 5- or 6-inch circle. They should be about ⅛ inch thick. Place rolled pita on large, floured baking sheets, four to a sheet. Dust their tops, cover, and let rest 15 to 20 minutes. Meanwhile, preheat oven to 500°F. Place one oven rack in the lowest position in the oven and a second one in the highest position. When ready to bake, place one sheet of pita on the lowest rack of the oven. Quickly close the oven door. After 4 minutes, quickly transfer this first sheet of pita to the top rack and place the second sheet on the bottom rack. After 4 minutes, remove the top sheet of pita and move the second sheet to the top rack. Bake the second sheet 4 additional minutes. As the pita come out of the oven, lay them on a clean towel. Cover with a second towel; cool the pita between the towels. This will keep them soft and chewy. After they are cooled, they may be wrapped in plastic and refrigerated or frozen for later use. If you wish to use them warm as they come out of the oven, they need not be cooled completely. Makes 8 pita.

❉ Lavash

Large rounds of lavash, or Armenian cracker bread, are meant to be broken apart at the table.

In a mixing bowl, combine

1 ½ cups warm water
1 scant tablespoon (or 1 packet) active dry yeast
1 teaspoon salt
2 cups Wheat-Bread Flour (see Pantry Mixes, page 18)

Beat well. To make a stiff dough, gradually add

1 ¼ to 1 ½ cups Wheat-Bread Flour

Turn out on a floured surface and knead until smooth. Place in a well-greased bowl, turning dough once to grease the top. Cover and let rise until doubled in bulk, 45 to 60 minutes. Punch dough down. Cover and let rise again, 30 to 45 minutes. Meanwhile, preheat oven to 400°F. *Place a baking stone in the oven while the oven is preheating. Using about one-eighth of the dough at a time, roll to paper thinness, forming circles 10 to 12 inches in diameter. These must be very thin if you want them to be crisp after

---

*If you do not have a baking stone and a baker's peel, you can bake the shaped cracker on a lightly greased baking sheet.

baking. Use additional flour, if needed, to prevent sticking. When shaped, sprinkle *each* circle with

> *1 tablespoon toasted sesame seeds*

Press the seeds gently into the dough. Transfer dough to a floured baker's peel (wooden paddle). Use the baker's peel to transfer the dough to the heated baking stone. Use a series of small, quick jerks to dislodge the dough from the peel. Bake at 400°F for 6 to 8 minutes, or until bread is blistered and browned. Cool on a wire rack. While the first cracker is baking, you can be shaping and readying the next. Makes 8 large crackers.

To Toast Sesame Seeds

In a heavy iron skillet, place

> *½ cup sesame seeds*

Toast over low to medium heat, stirring frequently, until seeds are golden.

❖ ABOUT BREAD STICKS

Bread sticks can be made from any number of yeast-bread doughs. One needs merely to take small portions of the dough after the first rising, roll them to pencil thinness, and then bake them with or without a final rising. The dough recovers somewhat while you are working with it, and the first-shaped sticks will have risen more than the last. They are a good first bread project for children, who delight in the rolling process.

A simple dough, such as that used for French bread, is more suitable for bread sticks than a richer one. The dough for one loaf, containing 2½ to 3 cups flour, will make 16 to 30 bread sticks, depending on their length. After rolling, they may be brushed with an egg glaze or water, sprinkled with coarse salt or seeds, and baked until well browned at temperatures ranging from 325°F to 400°F.

Finished bread sticks should be cooled on wire racks and displayed in a tall, skinny container. They cannot be successfully wrapped for room-temperature storage, as wrapping will soften them. They can, however, be wrapped and frozen for later use. Defrosted sticks can be recrisped for a short time in a moderate oven.

❖ Buttery Bread Sticks

These flaky bread sticks do wonders for soups or salads. They do not keep well, so it is best to make them the day they are to be eaten.

To soften yeast, in a mixing bowl combine

> 1 cup warm milk
> 1 teaspoon sugar
> 1 teaspoon (or part of 1 packet) active dry yeast

Let stand 5 minutes. Stir in, in this order

> 1 egg yolk
> 1 tablespoon soft butter
> 1 ½ cups unbleached all-purpose flour

Beat well. Add and stir in until all flour is incorporated

> 1 cup unbleached all-purpose flour

Scrape dough down in bowl. Cover and let rise until doubled in bulk, 30 to 45 minutes. Meanwhile, in a small bowl, knead together

> ¼ cup butter
> ¼ cup grated Parmesan cheese

Transfer kneaded butter mixture onto a piece of waxed paper. Cover with a second piece of waxed paper and roll out to a 3×7-inch rectangle. Place in refrigerator to chill. When dough has risen, stir it down. Toss on a lightly floured surface till no longer sticky. Press or roll out to an 8×12-inch rectangle. With long side of dough and short side of butter mixture facing you, place butter mixture in center of rolled-out dough. Fold right third of dough over center. Fold left third of dough over center, forming a 4× 8-inch package. Firmly seal edges. Turn package of dough one-quarter turn to the right. Roll again into an 8×12-inch rectangle and fold in thirds as before. Wrap package of folded dough in plastic wrap and refrigerate 15 minutes to firm butter mixture. Roll firmed dough into 14 × 16-inch rectangle. Cut in half down the length of the dough to form two 7 × 16-inch rectangles. Cut across each of these at 2-inch intervals to form 2 × 7-inch strips, making 16 strips in all. Starting with a long side, roll each strip into a cylinder. Place seam side down on lightly buttered baking sheets. When all have been formed, brush tops of cylinders with a mixture of

1 egg white
1 tablespoon water
½ teaspoon salt

Do not cover. Allow to rise for 20 minutes. Preheat oven to 375°F. Before baking, brush cylinders a second time with egg-white glaze. Bake at 375°F for 20 minutes, or until golden brown. Cool on wire racks. Makes 16 bread sticks.

❖ Baguette Bread Sticks

These are a hybrid, sort of a cross between baguettes and bread sticks. They are baked till crispy on the outside and somewhat dry on the inside. Serve them at an informal wine tasting with several types of hard and semi-soft cheese. Limit the wines to one type and region, such as the medium to dry white wines from Napa Valley.

To soften yeast, in a mixing bowl combine

1 ½ cups warm water
1 scant tablespoon (or 1 packet) active dry yeast
1 teaspoon sugar

Let stand 5 minutes. Stir in

1 ½ teaspoons salt
3 tablespoons olive oil
2 cups bread flour

Beat well. To form a stiff dough, gradually add

1 to 1 ½ cups bread flour

Turn out on a floured surface and knead until smooth. Place in a bowl oiled with ½ teaspoon olive oil, turning dough once to oil the top. Cover and let rise until doubled in bulk, 45 to 60 minutes. Punch down dough. Shape into a ball. Flatten ball into a circle 9 inches in diameter. Divide circle into eight equal wedge-shaped pieces. Work with one piece at a time. Press out into a 6-inch-long oval. Starting with a long side, roll tightly into a cylinder. Rolling back and forth over the surface with the palms of your hands, roll out to a 12-inch cylinder. Place on a lightly greased baking sheet that has been sprinkled with cornmeal. Cover cylinders and let rise until almost doubled in bulk, 30 to 45 minutes. Preheat oven to 450°F. Before baking baguette bread sticks, brush with a mixture of

> 1 egg white
> 1 tablespoon water

Using a very sharp knife, make three slanted cuts down the length of each stick. Bake at 450°F for 12 to 15 minutes, or until well-browned. Turn oven off. Let sticks remain in oven for an additional 5 minutes to dry interiors of sticks. Cool on wire racks. Makes 8 bread sticks.

❖ Grissini

Grissini are little Italian bread sticks. Barley malt extract and stone-ground whole-wheat flour give them their authentic flavor. They are so much better than what you find wrapped in those impossible-to-open plastic wrappers in the bread baskets of most restaurants!

To dissolve barley malt extract, in a mixing bowl combine

> 1 cup hot water
> 1 teaspoon barley malt extract

Cool until warm. To soften yeast, add

> 1 teaspoon (about ½ packet) active dry yeast

Allow yeast to proof. Stir into softened yeast mixture

> 1 teaspoon salt
> 1 tablespoon olive oil
> ¼ cup stone-ground whole-wheat flour
> 1 ½ cups unbleached all-purpose flour

Beat well to develop the gluten. To make a stiff dough, gradually add

½ to 1 cup unbleached all-purpose flour

Turn out on a lightly floured surface and knead until smooth and elastic. Place in a bowl oiled with ½ teaspoon olive oil, turning dough once to oil the top. Cover and let rise until doubled in bulk, 45 to 60 minutes. Flatten dough to expel air. Do not knead; you want this dough to stay relaxed. Brush excess flour to the side and turn dough out on kneading surface. With your hands, shape into a 6×8-inch rectangle. Sprinkle over the surface of the rectangle

⅓ cup sesame seeds

Press seeds into the dough. Cut rectangle in half to form two 4×6-inch rectangles. Now make perpendicular cuts to divide each small rectangle into eight ¾×4-inch strips, making 16 strips in all. Working with one piece at a time, pick up and stretch until 10 to 12 inches long, twisting slightly as you stretch. Place on a lightly oiled baking sheet. Bake in a preheated 400°F oven for about 20 minutes, or until well-browned. Cool on a wire rack. Makes 16 grissini.

✵ Rye Bread Sticks

Stand these bread sticks up in a pottery mug at your next party and watch them disappear.

To soften yeast, in a medium-sized bowl combine

1 cup warm water
1 tablespoon sugar
1 scant tablespoon (or 1 packet) active dry yeast

Allow yeast to proof. Stir in

1 egg yolk
3 tablespoons soft or melted butter
1 teaspoon salt
1 tablespoon caraway seed
1 ½ cups Bohemian Flour (see Pantry Mixes, page 18)

Beat well. To make a stiff dough, gradually add

1 to 2 cups Bohemian Flour

Turn out on a floured surface and knead until smooth. Place in a buttered bowl, turning once to butter the top. Cover and let rise until doubled, 45 to 60 minutes. Punch dough down and divide into thirds. Divide each third into eight pieces. Roll each piece on a lightly floured surface to an 8-inch stick. Place sticks at least ¾ inch apart on greased baking sheets. Cover and let rise until almost doubled, about 30 minutes. Before baking, brush sticks with a mixture of

1 egg white
1 teaspoon salt

Bake sticks in a preheated 400°F oven for 15 to 18 minutes, or until golden brown. Cool on wire racks. Makes 24 bread sticks.

❖ Rye Wafers

Use the dough for Rye Bread Sticks. After the first rising, preheat oven to 400°F. Divide dough into thirds. Work with one-third of dough at a time. Keep remaining dough covered with plastic to prevent drying out. On a lightly floured surface, roll to the thickness of cardboard. Section with a pastry cutter or knife into 2-inch squares. Place squares ½ inch apart on nonstick baking sheets. Brush tops of squares with

melted butter

Bake immediately in a preheated 400°F oven for 10 to 12 minutes, or until golden brown. Cool on wire racks. Try to schedule the rolling out of the second and third pieces of dough so that they are ready to go in the oven when the previous ones come out. Cool on wire racks. Makes 90 wafers.

❋ Sesame-Wheat Bread Sticks

These bread sticks will keep you coming back for more. Great for the snack attack any time!

To soften yeast, in a medium-sized bowl combine

1 cup warm water
1 teaspoon brown sugar
1 scant tablespoon (or 1 packet) active dry yeast

Allow yeast to proof. Stir in

1 teaspoon salt
1 tablespoon oil
1 ½ cups Wheat-Bread Flour (see Pantry Mixes, page 18)
2 tablespoons Toasted Sesame Seeds (see directions below)

Beat well. To make a stiff dough, gradually add

½ to 1 cup Wheat-Bread Flour

Turn out on a floured surface and knead until smooth. Place in an oiled bowl, turning dough once to oil the top. Cover and let rise until doubled, 45 to 60 minutes. Punch dough down and divide into thirds. Divide each third into 8 pieces. Roll each piece on a lightly oiled surface to an 8-inch stick. Roll oiled sticks on a surface coated with sesame seeds, pressing seeds into surface of sticks. Be generous with your seeds—the more that adhere to these sticks, the better they are. Place sticks on ungreased baking sheets at least ¾ inch apart. Cover and let rise until almost doubled, about 30 minutes. Bake sticks in a preheated 400°F oven for 15 to 18 minutes, or until golden brown. Cool on wire racks. Makes 24 bread sticks.

❋ Sesame-Wheat Wafers

Use the dough for Sesame-Wheat Bread Sticks. After the first rising, preheat oven to 400°F. Divide dough into thirds. Work with one-third of dough at a time. Keep remaining dough covered with plastic to prevent drying out. On a lightly floured surface, roll to the thickness of cardboard.

Section with a pastry cutter or knife into 2-inch squares. Place squares ½ inch apart on nonstick or lightly oiled baking sheets. Brush tops of squares with

melted butter

Bake immediately in a preheated 400°F oven for 10 to 12 minutes, or until golden brown. Cool on wire racks. Try to schedule the rolling out of the second and third pieces of dough so that they are ready to go in the oven when the previous ones come out. Cool on wire racks. Makes 90 wafers.

To Toast Sesame Seeds

Spread sesame seeds in a thin layer in a dry skillet. Heat over medium heat, stirring frequently, until lightly browned.

✖ ABOUT CRACKERS

Crackers can be made from both leavened and unleavened doughs. When making yeast breads or biscuits, often part of the dough can be thinly rolled and cut into small shapes for impromptu crackers.

Cracker dough (except those which are yeast-based) should not be overworked, as the development of gluten will toughen the cracker. Easily mixed quick doughs should just come together into a cohesive ball that may be rolled without excessive sticking. If dough consistency needs correction, liquid or flour should be added in small amounts until the texture is improved. The secret of making good crackers is to roll them very thin.

✖ Homemade Saltine Crackers

This is just a basic, go-with-everything cracker. One of my favorite "secret" snacks is a spoonful of chocolate ice cream on a saltine cracker. The crispness and saltiness of the cracker prove a good foil for the smooth richness of the ice cream.

Preheat oven to 425°F. In a bowl, mix together

    2 cups unbleached all-purpose flour
    1 teaspoon sugar
    ½ teaspoon salt

With your fingers rub into the flour mixture

    3 tablespoons shortening

Stir in with a fork just until the dough begins to form a ball and clean the sides of the bowl

    ⅔ cup cold milk

Roll out the dough on a lightly floured surface to slightly less than ⅛ inch. You may want to turn the dough over a couple of times early in the rolling process, much as you would with a pie dough. Sprinkle the top of the dough with

    coarse salt

Gently press the salt into the dough. Cut into squares or rounds and place on an ungreased baking sheet. I prefer to use a small biscuit cutter that measures 1¾ inches. Prick the crackers in 3 or 4 places with the tines of a fork. Bake in preheated 425°F oven for 6 to 8 minutes, or until the edges of the crackers begin to color. Remove pan from oven and turn crackers over. Return to oven to bake another 5 minutes, or until edges are brown. Cool, right side up, on wire racks. Makes 60 small, round saltines.

❖ Butter-and-Egg Crackers

These crackers are richer than most.

Preheat oven to 425°F. Sift into a mixing bowl

    2 cups unbleached all-purpose flour
    1 teaspoon salt
    1 teaspoon baking powder
    1 tablespoon sugar

Cut into small pieces and add to flour mixture

¼ cup cold butter

Work butter into flour mixture with your fingers. Beat together and add to flour-butter mixture, stirring with a fork

1 egg
6 tablespoons milk or light cream

If necessary to make the dough come together, add milk 1 teaspoon at a time. When dough comes together, toss on a lightly floured surface till no longer sticky. Roll to slightly less than ⅛-inch thickness. Cut with a 3-inch round cutter. Place rounds on lightly buttered or nonstick baking sheets. Scraps may be rerolled if care is taken not to work too much flour into the dough. Prick tops of rounds with tines of a fork in a pattern that pleases you. Bake in preheated 425°F oven for 6 minutes. Remove from oven, turn crackers over, return to bake an additional 5 minutes, or until well-browned. You may have to remove some earlier than others. Cool on wire racks. Makes 30 large, round crackers.

✤ Buttermilk Crackers

These combine the tangy flavor of a buttermilk biscuit with the crispness of a cracker.

Preheat oven to 425°F. Sift together into a bowl

2 cups unbleached all-purpose flour
1 tablespoon sugar
¾ teaspoon salt
¼ teaspoon baking soda

Work in with your fingers

2 tablespoons lard or shortening

Add and stir with a fork

¾ cup buttermilk

Toss on a lightly floured surface until no longer sticky. Working with one-half of the dough at a time, roll to slightly less than ⅛-inch thickness.

Cut into 2-inch squares. Place on an ungreased baking sheet. Brush the tops of the crackers lightly with

melted butter

Bake at 425°F for 10 to 12 minutes, or until crisp and well-browned. Cool on wire racks. Makes about 40 small crackers.

❖ Homemade Honey Grahams

One of the best meals I ever had consisted mainly of honey grahams. I would like to tell you about it.

My family was living in Hilo, Hawaii, when Pearl Harbor was bombed. No one could be sure that enemy planes would not return to spread their destruction a second time, so my father decided to send us to be near relatives in California.

After waiting for a place on board ship for quite some time, we finally booked passage in March of 1942. Our ship was the largest of a convoy of seven and it showed evidence of prior elegance. Despite its size, it progressed very slowly as we tacked our way across the Pacific.

No one knew where we would be docking. Only that it would be either San Francisco or San Diego. On the last day of the voyage we ran out of food. There were not even the powdered eggs that had been routinely scrambled every morning for breakfast.

That didn't really worry us, though, for by dawn we could see land. It didn't take long to make out San Francisco with its hills and bridges.

But then things came to a standstill. The rest of the convoy cruised to the docking area. Our ship, because of its size, had to wait for low tide to clear the Golden Gate Bridge.

Cheers went up from all on board when we finally sailed beneath its ochered golden glory. Then the news began to circulate that our ship would now have to wait for high tide to dock. Everything grew very still. My sister and I waited silently at the rail, by now feeling very hungry.

Darkness fell and still we waited. The city lights began to come up and we worked up some enthusiasm for how bright the San Francisco brownout seemed, compared with the darkness of Honolulu. Finally the gangplanks were lowered. We gathered our group and our parcels and made our way down together. We were bone-tired from the long wait.

At the bottom were smiling uniformed women from the Red Cross. They held trays filled with steaming mugs of hot chocolate and graham crackers spread thinly with peanut butter.

I took a mug of chocolate and a cracker. I have never had anything in my life that tasted more delicious than that cracker! Before I began to eat, I asked if I could have another. I was told I could have all I wanted. For me, the war was over.

Preheat oven to 350°F. In a large bowl, cream together

> *2 tablespoons shortening*
> *2 tablespoons butter*
> *1 tablespoon smooth peanut butter*

Blend into the creamed mixture, in this order

> *5 tablespoons brown sugar*
> *¼ cup honey*
> *¾ teaspoon salt*
> *1 egg*
> *½ teaspoon baking soda dissolved in 2 teaspoons water*

Add

> *2 cups graham flour*

Mix thoroughly. If dough is still sticky, add more flour, a spoonful at a time, until the dough holds together. Dust a surface with additional graham flour. On this surface roll the dough to ⅛-inch thickness. This is easier to do if you work with one-half of the dough at a time. Cut into 2½-inch squares and place on ungreased baking sheets. Bake at 350°F for 8 minutes. Turn crackers over. Bake an additional 7 minutes. Cool on wire racks. Allow to cool completely before serving. Makes 32 crackers.

�֎ Gingerbread Men

These are a tradition at our house. Every year, some time after Thanksgiving, we make Gingerbread Men. Since they keep so well, there is no hurry to eat them. One a day keeps the holiday blahs away.

Cream together

> 1 cup shortening
> ¾ cup sugar

Stir in, in this order, beating well after each addition

> 1 teaspoon lemon juice
> 1 egg yolk
> 1 cup molasses
> ½ cup buttermilk or sour milk

Sift together and stir into first mixture

> 1 cup unbleached all-purpose flour
> 1 teaspoon baking soda
> ½ teaspoon salt
> 1 teaspoon cloves
> 1 teaspoon allspice
> 1 teaspoon ginger

Add gradually, until dough is no longer sticky when touched with a finger

> about 3 cups unbleached all-purpose flour

Cover the dough and chill for about 2 hours to make it firm for handling. Working with one-third of the dough at a time, roll out on a lightly floured surface to ¼-inch thickness. Cut with a floured Gingerbread Man cookie cutter. Place at least ½ inch apart on ungreased baking sheets. Decorate the men with

> plump raisins (optional)

Bake in a preheated 375°F oven for about 10 minutes, or until browned on the edges. Yield depends on the size of the cookie cutter you use. Makes 12 6-inch-tall men. Scraps can be rerolled to make 2 or 3 more men, or can be used for Crisp Ginger Crackers.

❋ Crisp Ginger Crackers

If the dough for Gingerbread Men is thinly rolled, it can be made into crisp crackers. I sometimes make about a dozen Gingerbread Men and use the rerolls for these crackers.

Use the dough for Gingerbread Men. Roll to a thickness of ⅛ inch. Cut into 2-inch squares or diamonds. Bake on lightly greased or nonstick baking sheets at 375°F for 5 to 7 minutes, or until brown around the edges. One batch of dough makes 150 crackers.

✲ The Quickest Loaves of All

Quick breads for teatime or anytime

- Orange Tea Bread
- Lemon-Zucchini Loaf
- Coconut-Cake Bread
- Banana Bread
- Granny Smith Apple Bread
- Rhubarb-Nut Bread
- Blueberry-Lemon Loaf
- Brandied Apple Bread
- Graham-Cracker Bread
- Pumpkin Bread
- Sweet Whole-Wheat Bread
- Sweet Prune 'n Wheat Bread
- Sweet-and-Spicy Nut Loaf
- Spicy Green-Tomato Bread
- Golden Carrot Bread
- Caraway-Cheese Beer Bread
- Irish Soda Bread
- Irish Currant Loaf

❋ THE QUICKEST LOAVES OF ALL

Quick breads, easy to mix and plop into a pan, have always been popular. They taste good sliced cold, and often mellow with age. They are perfect contributions to potluck suppers.

Fruits find their way into most quick breads, adding to their moistness. Nuts add crunch and richness. Spices perk up the batters. Some of these breads are made with vegetables from a summer garden. Some resemble cake and some are more like yeast bread.

Here are a few recipes to add to your collection for sharing and giving.

❋ Orange Tea Bread

This is the kind of tea bread that used to be served at ladies' clubs and afternoon socials. The classic tea service always included several tea breads spread with butter and cream cheese. These were accompanied by a small footed silver bowl filled with mixed nuts. A companion bowl held softly colored mints. At one end of the table sat the guest of honor, who poured coffee. This enabled her to see and visit with everyone. At the other end of the table a good friend poured the tea. Sugar cubes, a thinly sliced lemon, and a pitcher of country cream rounded out the service.

Preheat oven to 350°F. Grease and flour an 8½ × 4½ × 2½-inch baking pan. Sift together and set aside

> 1 ½ cups unbleached all-purpose flour
> 1 teaspoon baking powder
> ¼ teaspoon baking soda
> ½ teaspoon salt
> ¼ teaspoon cloves

In another bowl, beat

> 1 egg

Stir into beaten egg

> 1 tablespoon freshly grated orange rind
> ½ cup sugar
> ¼ cup melted butter, cooled slightly

Combine with enough milk to measure a total of ¾ cup

juice of 1 orange with pulp

Stir this into egg mixture. Add liquid mixture to dry ingredients, stirring only until moistened. Stir in

½ cup chopped pecans

Turn into prepared pan. Bake at 350°F for 1 hour, or until a wooden pick inserted in the center comes out clean. Turn out to cool on a wire rack. Wrap in foil to store. Makes 1 loaf.

✳️ Lemon-Zucchini Loaf

You will find the combination of lemon and ginger in this moist zucchini bread refreshing.

Preheat oven to 350°F. Grease and flour a 9×5-inch baking pan. Sift together and set aside

1 ¾ cups unbleached all-purpose flour
2 teaspoons baking powder
½ teaspoon baking soda
½ teaspoon salt
1 teaspoon ginger

In a medium-sized bowl beat

2 eggs

Beat into eggs, in this order

1 cup sugar
½ cup oil
2 tablespoons lemon juice

Stir into egg mixture, in this order

> zest of 1 lemon, cut into thin strips*
> 1 ½ cups grated unpeeled zucchini
> reserved flour mixture
> ½ cup coarsely chopped pecans or walnuts
> ½ cup golden raisins

Turn into prepared pan. Bake in preheated 350°F oven for 65 to 70 minutes, or until a wooden pick inserted in the center comes out clean. Cool in pan 10 minutes, then turn out on a wire rack to cool completely. Makes 1 loaf.

❖ Coconut-Cake Bread

> *This tender cakelike bread draws raves every time it is served.*

Preheat oven to 350°F. Grease and flour a 9×5-inch baking pan. Sift together and set aside

> 2 cups unbleached all-purpose flour
> ½ teaspoon salt
> 2 teaspoons baking powder

In a mixing bowl, beat together

> ½ cup soft butter
> 1 teaspoon vanilla extract

Beat into butter mixture

> 1 cup sugar

Add, one at a time, beating well after each addition

> 2 eggs

Add alternately with the dry ingredients, beginning and ending with the dry ingredients

> ¾ cup milk

---

*If you remove the zest from the lemon with a tool called a lemon zester, the thin yellow peel will be in the size of the strips desired.

❄ Rhubarb-Nut Bread

This is a sweet bread but the tart taste of rhubarb balances the overall flavor.

Preheat oven to 350°F. Grease and flour a 9×5-inch baking pan. Sift together and set aside

> 1 ¾ cups unbleached all-purpose flour
> ½ teaspoon salt
> 1 teaspoon baking soda
> 1 teaspoon cinnamon
> ¼ teaspoon cloves

In a medium-sized bowl, beat together

> 1 egg
> ¾ cup brown sugar
> ¼ cup oil

Stir into the egg mixture

> 1 ¼ cup Stewed Rhubarb (see recipe below)

Add flour mixture and stir just until dry ingredients are moistened. Fold in

> 1 cup coarsely chopped walnuts

Turn into prepared pan. Bake at 350°F for 1 hour, or until a wooden pick inserted in the center comes out clean. Cool in pan 10 minutes, then turn out on a wire rack to cool. Wrap in foil to store. Makes 1 loaf.

Stewed Rhubarb

Simmer in a saucepan just until rhubarb is tender. Do not cook until completely soft

> 4 cups finely chopped fresh rhubarb
> ¼ cup water

Stir into cooked rhubarb

> 1 cup sugar

Add more water only if needed to prevent sticking or burning.

❖ Blueberry-Lemon Loaf

This batter contains a delicious blend of tart and sweet flavors.

Preheat oven to 350°F. Grease and flour an 8½ × 4½ × 2½-inch baking pan.
Sift together and set aside

> 1 ½ cups unbleached all-purpose flour
> ½ teaspoon salt
> ¾ teaspoon baking soda

In a medium-sized mixing bowl, cream

> 6 tablespoons butter

Cream into butter, 1 tablespoon at a time

> 12 tablespoons sugar

Beat into butter mixture, one at a time, beating well after each addition

> 2 eggs

Stir in

> zest from 1 lemon, cut into thin strips*

In a measuring cup, mix together

> 1 teaspoon fresh lemon juice
> enough milk to bring lemon-milk mixture to ½ cup

To the creamed butter mixture add reserved flour mixture alternately with
the lemon-milk mixture, beginning and ending with the dry ingredients.
Blend well after each addition. Spoon one-third of the batter into the
prepared pan. Fold into remaining batter

> 1 cup fresh blueberries

Spoon batter with blueberries into pan. The blueberries have a tendency
to sink to the bottom when the loaf is baking—this tactic will help you

---

*If you remove the zest from the lemon with a tool called a lemon zester, the thin
yellow peel will be in the size of the strips desired.

achieve a better distribution. Bake in preheated 350°F oven for 50 minutes, or until a wooden pick inserted in the center comes out clean. Cool in pan 5 minutes, then turn out on a wire rack to cool completely. Makes 1 loaf.

❊ Brandied Apple Bread

Sometimes when I am out of brandy, I use whiskey in this bread. It works just as well.

Preheat oven to 350°F. Grease and flour a 9×5-inch baking pan. Sift together and set aside

> 1 ¾ *cups unbleached all-purpose flour*
> 1 *teaspoon baking powder*
> ½ *teaspoon baking soda*
> ½ *teaspoon salt*

Cream in a large bowl

> ½ *cup butter*
> 1 *cup brown sugar*

Add to creamed mixture one at a time, beating well after each addition

> 2 *eggs*

Stir into the egg mixture, in this order

> ¼ *cup brandy*
> 1 *cup freshly grated unpeeled tart apples*
> *sifted dry ingredients*
> ½ *cup chopped raisins*
> ½ *cup chopped walnuts*

Turn into prepared pan. Bake at 350°F for 1 hour, or until a wooden pick inserted in the center comes out clean. Turn out to cool on a wire rack. Wrap in foil to store. Makes 1 loaf.

✣ Graham-Cracker Bread

This bread is even better the second day. Slice it thin for bread-and-butter sandwiches and serve it at teatime.

Preheat oven to 350°F. Grease and flour a 9×5-inch baking pan. Sift together into a large bowl and set aside

1 cup unbleached all-purpose flour
1 teaspoon baking soda
½ teaspoon salt
1 teaspoon cinnamon

Stir into sifted flour

1 cup graham-cracker crumbs

In another bowl beat

2 eggs

Blend into beaten eggs, in this order

½ cup brown sugar
1 cup commercial sour cream

Stir the sour-cream mixture into the dry ingredients, stirring only until dry ingredients are moistened. Pour into prepared pan. Bake at 350°F for 1 hour, or until a wooden pick inserted in the center comes out clean. Turn out to cool on a wire rack. When cold, slice and serve with sweet butter. Wrap in foil to store. Makes 1 loaf.

✣ Pumpkin Bread

Some of my friends take a pumpkin from the field and cook it themselves. Starting from scratch has its virtues, but I generally make pumpkin bread with canned pumpkin. This is one case when I prefer to let someone else do the work.

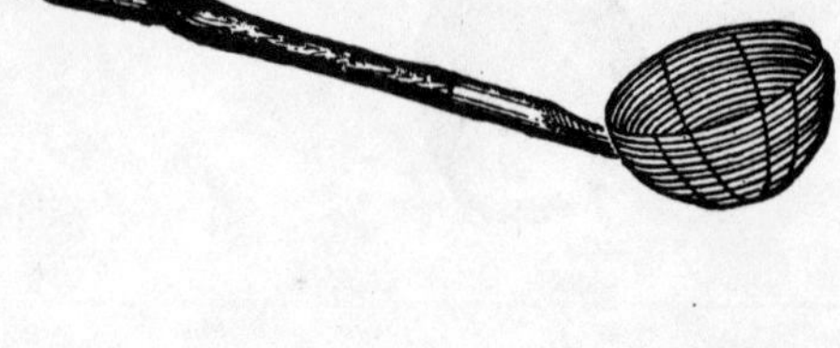

Preheat oven to 350°F. Grease and flour a 9×5-inch baking pan. Sift together into a large bowl and set aside

1 ¾ *cups unbleached all-purpose flour*
¾ *cup sugar*
1 *teaspoon baking powder*
1 *teaspoon baking soda*
1 *teaspoon salt*
½ *teaspoon cinnamon*
¼ *teaspoon cloves*
¼ *teaspoon nutmeg*
¼ *teaspoon ginger*

Beat together in another bowl, in this order

⅓ *cup oil*
⅓ *cup molasses*
2 *eggs*
1 *cup canned pumpkin*

Blend pumpkin mixture into dry ingredients. Pour into prepared pan. Bake at 350°F for 1 hour, or until a wooden pick inserted in the center comes out clean. Cool in pan 5 minutes. Turn out to cool completely on a wire rack. Wrap in foil to store. Makes 1 loaf.

❖ Sweet Whole-Wheat Bread

People are surprised that a quick bread made totally with whole-wheat flour can be this good. Try it. I think you will agree.

Preheat oven to 350°F. Grease and flour a 9×5-inch baking pan. Sift together into a large bowl and set aside

2 ¾ *cups whole-wheat flour*
1 ½ *teaspoons baking soda*
¾ *teaspoon salt*
1 *teaspoon cinnamon*
¼ *teaspoon nutmeg*
¼ *teaspoon ginger*

In another bowl, blend together in this order

1 egg
½ cup sugar
¼ cup oil
¼ cup molasses
1 ½ cups buttermilk

Stir the buttermilk mixture into the dry ingredients, stirring only until dry ingredients are moistened. Pour into prepared pan. Bake at 350°F for 1 hour, or until a wooden pick inserted in the center comes out clean. Cool in pan 5 minutes. Turn out to cool completely on a wire rack. When cold, slice and serve with sweet butter. Wrap in foil to store. Makes 1 loaf.

❖ Sweet Prune 'n Wheat Bread

Stir into the buttermilk mixture, before adding it to the dry ingredients

1 cup finely chopped cooked pitted prunes

Proceed as for Sweet Whole-Wheat Bread.

❖ Sweet-and-Spicy Nut Loaf

This cakelike bread should convince you to break for tea. If not, use it for dessert.

Preheat oven to 350°F. Grease and flour a 9×5-inch baking pan. Sift together and set aside

1 ¾ cups unbleached all-purpose flour
½ teaspoon salt
2 ½ teaspoons baking powder
1 teaspoon cinnamon
½ teaspoon cloves
¼ teaspoon nutmeg

In a large bowl, cream together

½ cup soft butter
1 cup sugar

Add, one at a time, beating well after each addition

2 eggs

Dividing dry ingredients into thirds and milk in half, add alternately to butter mixture, beginning and ending with dry ingredients

sifted dry ingredients
½ cup milk

Fold in

1 cup ~~chopped pecans~~ MASHED BANANAS

Turn into prepared pan. Bake at 350°F for 1 hour, or until a wooden pick inserted in the center of the loaf comes out clean. Cool in pan 5 minutes. Turn out to cool completely on a wire rack. Slice thin and spread with soft sweet butter to serve. Makes 1 loaf.

❊ Spicy Green-Tomato Bread

This bread is good to make early in the summer when the tomato plants are covered with unripened fruit, and again in the fall, just before frost.

Preheat oven to 350°F. Grease and flour a 9×5-inch baking pan. Sift together and set aside

2 cups unbleached all-purpose flour
1 teaspoon baking powder
1 teaspoon baking soda
½ teaspoon salt
1 teaspoon cinnamon
¼ teaspoon cloves
¼ teaspoon allspice
¼ teaspoon nutmeg

In a medium-sized bowl, beat

2 eggs

Beat into eggs, in this order

1 cup brown sugar
½ cup oil
1 teaspoon vanilla extract

Stir into egg mixture, in this order

1 ½ cups shredded and drained green tomatoes
reserved flour mixture
½ cup coarsely chopped walnuts
½ cup dark raisins

Turn into prepared pan. Bake in preheated 350°F oven for 65 minutes, or until a wooden pick inserted in the center comes out clean. Cool in pan 5 minutes, then turn out on a wire rack to cool completely. Makes 1 loaf.

❖ Golden Carrot Bread

Make this bread in the summer when the carrot crop is abundant. It freezes well.

Preheat oven to 350°F. Grease and flour a 9×5-inch baking pan. Sift together and set aside

1 ½ cups unbleached all-purpose flour
1 teaspoon baking powder
½ teaspoon baking soda
½ teaspoon salt
½ teaspoon ginger

Beat together in a large bowl, in this order

⅓ cup oil
¾ cup sugar
2 eggs
1 teaspoon freshly grated lemon peel

Stir into beaten mixture, in this order

sifted dry ingredients
2 cups grated raw carrots, firmly packed
1 cup golden seedless raisins

Pour into prepared pan. Bake at 350°F for 1 hour, or until a wooden pick inserted in the center comes out clean. Cool in pan 5 minutes. Turn out to cool completely on a wire rack. Wrap in foil to store. Makes 1 loaf.

❖ Caraway-Cheese Beer Bread

This savory bread goes well with a simple soup or salad. Leftovers, if there are any, can be sliced thin and oven-toasted for a quick cocktail tidbit.

Preheat oven to 350°F. Grease and flour a 9-inch fluted tube pan. Sift together and set aside

> *3 ½ cups unbleached all-purpose flour*
> *¾ teaspoon salt*
> *½ teaspoon baking soda*
> *1 teaspoon baking powder*

Stir into sifted ingredients

> *1 tablespoon caraway seed*
> *½ teaspoon cracked pepper*

In another bowl, beat together

> *1 egg*
> *1 tablespoon sugar*
> *1 tablespoon oil*

Stir into egg mixture

> *1 ½ cups (1 12-ounce can) beer*

Add the flour mixture and stir just until the dry ingredients are moistened. Fold in

> *1 cup shredded extra-sharp cheddar cheese*

Turn into prepared pan. Bake at 350°F for 1 hour, or until a wooden pick inserted in the center comes out clean. Cool in pan 5 minutes, then turn out on a wire rack to cool completely. Serve warm or cold. Makes 1 9-inch round loaf.

✷ Irish Soda Bread

I always bake my soda breads in a Dutch oven. A covered stonewear baker, such as La Cloche from Sassafras, however, will work just as well.

Preheat oven to 450°F. In a large, flat bowl, stir together well

 4 cups unbleached all-purpose flour
 1 teaspoon salt
 1 teaspoon baking soda
 1 teaspoon sugar

Rub into the flour mixture with your fingers

 ¼ cup shortening

Stir into the flour mixture

 1 tablespoon caraway seeds (optional)

Make a hollow in the center of the flour mixture and pour into it

 1 ⅔ cups buttermilk

Stir lightly with a fork until the dough comes together. Turn out onto a lightly floured surface and knead seven or eight times until the dough is smooth. Shape into a ball and place, smooth side up, in the well-greased bottom of a Dutch oven. Cut a cross in the top of the loaf. Cover Dutch oven and place in oven preheated to 450°F. Bake for 5 minutes at 450°F. Reduce heat to 350°F and bake for 45 to 50 minutes longer, or until golden brown. Serve warm or cold. Makes 1 large soda bread.

✷ Irish Currant Loaf

Whole-grain flours vary considerably in their ability to absorb liquid. Start with the smaller amount of buttermilk given. If the mixture is dry and crumbly, add more.

Preheat oven to 450°F. In a large, flat bowl stir together well

 2 cups unbleached all-purpose flour
 2 cups stone-ground whole-wheat flour

1 teaspoon salt
1 teaspoon baking soda
1 tablespoon brown sugar

With your fingers work into the flour mixture

¼ cup butter, cut into small pieces

Stir into the flour mixture

½ cup dried currants

Make a well in the center of the flour mixture and pour into that well

1 ½ to 1 ⅔ cups buttermilk

Stir lightly with a fork until the dough comes together. Turn out on a lightly floured surface and knead seven or eight times until the dough is smooth. Shape into a ball and place, smooth side up, in the well-greased bottom of a Dutch oven. Brush the top of the loaf with

melted butter

Cut a cross in the top of the loaf. Cover the Dutch oven and bake in preheated 450°F oven for 5 minutes. Reduce heat to 350°F and bake for 45 to 50 minutes longer, or until nicely browned. Serve warm or cold. Makes 1 large loaf.

❄ Busy-Day Breads

Batter breads, do-ahead doughs, and make-ahead mixes for your busy schedule

Honey-Wheat Batter Bread
Butter-and-Egg Batter Bread
Buttermilk Batter Bread
Oatmeal Batter Bread
Peanut-Butter Batter Bread
Batter Brioche
Overnight Sponge Bread
Refrigerator-Risen Bread
Handy-Andy Bread Dough

Overnight Rolls
Refrigerator Rolls
Angel Biscuits
Minute-Man Muffins
Frozen Bread Dough
Make-Ahead Bread Mix
Buttermilk Baking Mix
Corn-Bread Mix

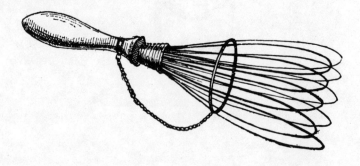

❖ BUSY-DAY BREADS

When I look around my own community, it seems that everyone is working. In my own circle of friends, the women all have either part-time or full-time jobs.

I know this is indicative of the rest of the country, so I have assembled all the bread recipes that can be made with a minimum of effort in this one chapter. Some of these are batter breads, which do not require kneading. Some are refrigerator doughs, which enable you to do most of the work ahead of time. Some divide the work detail into different segments, to fit more easily into a hectic schedule. If you are a busy baker with more than one iron in the fire, read this section diligently. It will help you fit fresh homemade bread into your busy life.

❖ Honey-Wheat Batter Bread

This exceptionally good wheat bread slices easily and makes excellent morning toast.

To soften yeast, in a medium-sized mixing bowl combine

> ¼ cup warm water
> 1 teaspoon sugar
> 1 scant tablespoon (or 1 packet) active dry yeast

Allow yeast to proof. Meanwhile, in a heavy saucepan over medium heat, stir together until butter is melted

> 1 cup milk
> 2 tablespoons honey
> 2 tablespoons butter
> 1 teaspoon salt

Let milk mixture cool just to warm, then add to yeast mixture with

> 2 cups Wheat-Bread Flour (see Pantry Mixes, p. 18)

Beat for 3 minutes. Add, ¼ cup at a time, beating well after each addition

> 1 cup Wheat-Bread Flour

Scrape down sides of bowl. Cover and let rise until doubled, about 45 minutes. Stir batter down and beat for about 30 seconds. Transfer to a well-greased 9×5-inch baking pan. Cover and let rise until almost doubled, 30 to 45 minutes. Bake in a preheated 375°F oven for 40 to 45 minutes. Cool on a wire rack. Makes 1 loaf.

❖ Butter-and-Egg Batter Bread

I sometimes call this bread Poor Man's Brioche. By all means, use some leftover slices for French toast!

Butter two 8½×4½×2½-inch baking pans. To soften yeast, in a small container, mix

> *¼ cup warm water*
> *1 scant tablespoon (or 1 packet) active dry yeast*
> *1 teaspoon sugar*

In a medium-sized mixing bowl, combine

> *1 cup scalded milk*
> *¼ cup butter*
> *3 tablespoons sugar*
> *1 teaspoon salt*

Stir to dissolve butter and sugar. Let cool until just warm. Beat into milk mixture

> *2 eggs*
> *softened yeast mixture*
> *2 cups unbleached all-purpose flour*

Beat well. Stir in, ½ cup at a time

> *2 cups unbleached all-purpose flour*

Stir until all flour is incorporated. Cover bowl with waxed paper, then a towel. Let rise 45 to 60 minutes. Stir dough down. Spoon into prepared pans. Cover and let rise 45 to 60 minutes, or until almost doubled. Bake in preheated 400°F oven for 40 to 45 minutes. Cool on wire racks. Makes 2 loaves.

❖ Buttermilk Batter Bread

When I developed a Buttermilk Batter Bread recipe for this book, I aimed for something light and tender with the unique flavor of buttermilk. Buttermilk gives it a tender crumb. Lemon zest complements the buttermilk flavor. You will love the aroma while it is baking.

To soften yeast, in a medium-sized mixing bowl combine

> *¼ cup warm water*
> *1 scant tablespoon (or 1 packet) active dry yeast*
> *1 teaspoon sugar*

Allow yeast to proof. Stir into softened yeast mixture, in this order

> *1 cup buttermilk, heated to warm*
> *2 tablespoons soft butter*
> *2 tablespoons sugar*
> *1 teaspoon salt*
> *1 tablespoon freshly grated lemon zest*
> *2 cups unbleached all-purpose flour*

Beat for 3 minutes. Add, 1 tablespoon at a time, beating well after each addition

> *6 tablespoons unbleached all-purpose flour*

Scrape batter down in bowl. Cover and let rise until almost tripled in bulk, about 1 hour. Stir batter down. Beat for 1 minute. Spread batter in a well-greased 8½ × 4½ × 2½-inch baking pan. Cover and let rise until almost doubled, 30 to 45 minutes. Bake in a preheated 375°F oven for 35 to 40 minutes. Cool on a wire rack. Makes 1 loaf.

❖ Oatmeal Batter Bread

Oatmeal brings back childhood memories, but it doesn't just have to be a part of your past. Start your morning with a slice of this bread toasted. It is easy to make with just one rising.

In a mixing bowl, combine

> *½ cup old-fashioned rolled oats*
> *½ cup raisins*
> *3 tablespoons butter*
> *3 tablespoons brown sugar*
> *1 teaspoon salt*
> *½ teaspoon cinnamon*
> *¾ cup scalded milk*

Stir to dissolve the butter and sugar. Let cool down to warm. Meanwhile, to soften yeast, in a small container combine

> *¼ cup warm water*
> *1 scant tablespoon (or 1 packet) active dry yeast*
> *¼ teaspoon sugar*

Allow yeast to proof. When milk mixture has cooled down to warm, stir in

> *softened yeast mixture*
> *1 egg*
> *1 ½ cups unbleached all-purpose flour*

Beat for 3 minutes. Add, ¼ cup at a time, beating well after each addition

> *1 cup unbleached all-purpose flour*

Add, 1 tablespoon at a time, stirring well after each addition

> *2 tablespoons unbleached all-purpose flour*

Spread dough in a well-greased 9×5-inch baking pan. Cover and let rise until doubled in bulk, about 45 minutes. Brush top of loaf with

> *2 teaspoons melted butter*

Sprinkle over the top

> *1 tablespoon rolled oats*

Bake in preheated 375°F oven for 35 to 40 minutes. Cool on a wire rack. Makes 1 loaf.

❖ Peanut-Butter Batter Bread

For peanut-butter lovers only. See directions below for the Ultimate Peanut-Butter Sandwich.

To soften yeast, in a medium-sized mixing bowl combine

1 cup warm water
1 scant tablespoon (or 1 packet) active dry yeast
1 teaspoon sugar

Allow yeast to proof. Stir in, in this order

2 eggs
1 tablespoon oil
3 tablespoons honey
½ cup creamy peanut butter, such as Jif
1 teaspoon salt
1 ¾ cups unbleached all-purpose flour or bread flour

Beat for 3 minutes. Add, ¼ cup at a time, beating well after each addition

1 cup unbleached all-purpose flour or bread flour

Scrape down sides of bowl. Cover and let rise until fully doubled, about 1 hour. Stir in

½ cup finely chopped dry-roasted peanuts

Beat for 1 minute. Spoon dough into a well-greased 9×5-inch baking pan. Cover with buttered plastic. Let rise until almost doubled, 30 to 45 minutes. Bake in preheated 375°F oven for 35 to 40 minutes. Cool on a wire rack. Makes 1 loaf.

The Ultimate Peanut-Butter Sandwich

Spread two slices of Peanut-Butter Batter Bread with creamy peanut butter. Drizzle a little honey on one of the slices. Stack slices with spread sides together to make a sandwich. Spread top of sandwich with soft butter. Place under heated broiler until top is toasted. Remove from broiler. Turn sandwich over and butter other side. Return to broiler and leave until second side is toasted. Serve with a tall glass of cold milk.

❖ Batter Brioche

These golden egg-rich rolls are embarrassingly easy to make. Simply spoon the batter into buttered muffin cups. Serve them with sweet butter and strawberry jam.

In a medium-sized mixing bowl, combine

> ¼ *cup warm water*
> 4 *teaspoons (or 1 ½ packets) active dry yeast*

Stir to dissolve. Allow yeast to proof. Stir into yeast mixture

> ½ *cup warm milk*
> ½ *cup soft butter*
> ¼ *cup sugar*
> ¾ *teaspoon salt*
> 2 *cups unbleached all-purpose flour*

Beat for about 3 minutes. Add, one at a time, beating well after each addition

> 4 *eggs*

To make a stiff batter, gradually add

> 1 ¾ *to 2 cups unbleached all-purpose flour*

Beat until batter is smooth. Transfer batter to a buttered bowl. Cover and let rise until fully doubled, about 1 hour. Stir batter down. Spoon evenly into 24 well-buttered muffin cups. The muffin cups should be about ⅔ full. Cover with buttered plastic and let rise until dough rises to the tops of the muffin cups and is almost doubled. Bake in a preheated 350°F oven for 20 to 25 minutes, or until well-browned. Let stand in pans for 2 minutes before removing. Cool on wire racks. Makes 24 brioches.

❖ Overnight Sponge Bread

This is a good bread to make when you don't want to do everything at once. The timing is pretty flexible. You can let the dough rise an additional time after all the flour has been incorporated, if you wish. As with most yeast breads, it's awfully hard to ruin it.

To soften yeast, in a large mixing bowl combine

> 2 cups warm water
> 1 scant tablespoon (or 1 packet) active dry yeast

Allow yeast to proof. Stir in

> 2 cups unbleached all-purpose flour or bread flour

Beat well. Cover and let rise on counter overnight. In the morning, stir down the sponge. Stir in

> 2 tablespoons sugar
> 2 tablespoons oil
> 2 teaspoons salt

To make a stiff dough, gradually add

> 2 ½ to 3 ½ cups unbleached all-purpose flour or bread flour

Turn out on a floured surface and knead until smooth. Divide dough in half. Shape into oblong loaves and place in well-greased 8½ × 4½ × 2½-inch baking pans. Cover and let rise until doubled, about 1 hour. Bake at 400°F for 35 to 40 minutes. Cool on wire racks. Makes 2 loaves.

✵ Refrigerator-Risen Bread

> *This is ideal for the baker who works nine to five. You can make the dough after your evening meal and bake it the following morning while getting ready to go to work.*

To soften the yeast, in a large mixing bowl combine

> 2 cups warm water
> 2 scant tablespoons (or 2 packets) active dry yeast

Allow yeast to proof. Stir in

> 2 tablespoons sugar
> ¼ cup oil
> 1 tablespoon salt
> 3 cups unbleached all-purpose flour or bread flour

Beat well to develop gluten. To make a stiff dough, gradually add

2 ½ to 3 cups unbleached all-purpose flour or bread flour

Turn out on a floured surface and knead until smooth. Shape into a ball, cover, and let rest on board 20 to 30 minutes. Knead lightly. Divide dough in half. Shape into oblong loaves and place in well-greased 8½ × 4½ × 2½-inch baking pans. Brush tops of loaves with oil. Cover loosely with plastic wrap and refrigerate for 6 to 12 hours. Remove loaves from refrigerator and uncover. Let stand uncovered 15 minutes while oven preheats. Bake at 375°F for 35 to 40 minutes. Cool on wire racks. Makes 2 loaves.

❖ Handy-Andy Bread Dough

This dough should keep fresh in the refrigerator for about three days. It is good to have on hand when you want fresh bread without the fuss.

In a large bowl, combine

2 cups scalded milk
½ cup shortening
½ cup sugar
1 tablespoon salt

Stir to dissolve. Let cool until just warm. Meanwhile, to soften yeast, in a small container combine

½ cup warm water
1 teaspoon sugar
1 scant tablespoon (or 1 packet) active dry yeast

When milk mixture has cooled down to warm, stir in

softened yeast mixture
½ cup freshly cooked mashed potatoes, cooled down to warm
4 cups unbleached all-purpose flour or bread flour

Beat this for about 10 minutes. If you tire, rest a minute, then continue. If you are using a mixer, you need only to beat the dough at medium speed for about 4 minutes. Scrape down sides of bowl. Cover and let rise until doubled in bulk, 45 to 60 minutes. Stir dough down. To make a soft dough, gradually add

3 to 4 cups unbleached all-purpose flour or bread flour

Turn out on a floured surface and knead until smooth. Place the dough in a greased bowl, turning dough once to grease the top. Cover with waxed paper, then a china plate. Use at once, or refrigerate until needed. Makes 3 loaves or 36 rolls.

To Shape and Bake One Loaf

Use one-third of dough. Shape into a ball and place in well-greased round baking pan. Cover and let rise until almost doubled in bulk, 1 to 1½ hours. This could take longer if the dough has been chilled. Bake in preheated 375°F oven for 35 to 40 minutes. Cool on a wire rack. Makes 1 loaf.

To Shape and Bake Rolls

Use one-third of dough. Divide dough into 12 pieces. Shape each piece into a round ball. Place on well-greased 10×15-inch baking sheet, evenly spaced. Cover and let rise until almost doubled in bulk, about 1 hour. Bake in preheated 400°F oven for 20 to 25 minutes, or until well browned. Cool on wire racks. Makes 12 rolls.

❖ Overnight Rolls

These are easy to make and very reliable. When you are having your family over for Sunday lunch, this is the roll to make.

The night before, in a large mixing bowl combine

3 tablespoons sugar
¼ cup shortening
1 ½ teaspoons salt
1 cup scalded milk

Stir to dissolve shortening and sugar. Let cool until just warm. Meanwhile, to soften yeast, in another container combine

¼ cup warm water
1 scant tablespoon (or 1 packet) active dry yeast

Allow yeast to proof. When milk mixture has cooled down to warm, stir in

softened yeast mixture
1 egg
1 ½ cups unbleached all-purpose flour or bread flour

Beat well. To make a soft dough, gradually add

1 ½ to 2 cups unbleached all-purpose flour or bread flour

Transfer dough to a greased bowl. Brush top of dough with oil. Cover with waxed paper. Cover this with a dinner plate. Refrigerate overnight. In the morning, remove dough from refrigerator and let stand on counter for 30 minutes to warm. Knead dough down in bowl. Divide dough into 24 equal pieces, shape into balls, and place in well-greased muffin cups. Cover and let rise 45 to 60 minutes. Before baking, brush tops of rolls with

2 tablespoons melted butter

Bake at 400°F for 12 to 15 minutes, or until golden brown. Makes 24 rolls.

❖ Refrigerator Rolls

This recipe allows you to prepare beforehand for entertaining. You can keep these rolls in the refrigerator for 3 days before shaping and baking.

In a large mixing bowl, combine

¼ cup sugar
3 tablespoons shortening
1 teaspoon salt
¾ cup scalded milk

Stir to dissolve shortening and sugar. Let cool until just warm. Meanwhile, to soften yeast, in another container, combine

¼ cup warm water
1 scant tablespoon (or 1 packet) active dry yeast

Allow yeast to proof. When milk mixture has cooled down to warm, stir in

softened yeast mixture
1 egg
1 ½ cups unbleached all-purpose flour or bread flour

Beat well. To make a soft dough, gradually add

1 ½ cups unbleached all-purpose flour or bread flour

Brush top of dough with oil. Cover with waxed paper. Cover this with a dinner plate. Store in refrigerator until needed. When needed, remove dough from refrigerator and shape into cloverleaf rolls with buttered hands. Place in well buttered muffin cups. Cover and let rise until doubled, about 2 hours. Bake at 400°F for 12 to 15 minutes. Makes about 20 rolls.

Shaping Cloverleaf Rolls

To shape cloverleaf rolls the old-fashioned way, divide the amount of dough needed for one roll into three parts. Shape each part into a round ball. Then place all three balls in one buttered muffin cup. To make them more quickly, shape the amount of dough needed for one roll into one ball. Place this in the buttered muffin cup and cut a cross deeply into the ball, using a kitchen shears. However, the old-fashioned method produces a roll that will break apart more easily for buttering and eating.

✹ Angel Biscuits

Angel Biscuits are a Southern specialty. The dough, risen by both yeast and quick leaveners, produces a very light biscuit. The mixing can be done ahead of the baking to suit your schedule.

To soften yeast, in a small container combine

3 tablespoons warm water
1 scant tablespoon (or 1 packet) active dry yeast

Let yeast stand while preparing the dry ingredients. In a large bowl, sift together

>   1 cup unbleached all-purpose flour
>   1 tablespoon baking powder
>   1 teaspoon baking soda
>   1 ½ teaspoons salt

Stir into sifted ingredients

>   ¼ cup sugar
>   4 cups unbleached all-purpose flour

With pastry blender or two knives, cut into dry ingredients

>   1 cup shortening

Make a well in the center of the dry ingredients. Into that well pour

>   softened yeast mixture
>   2 cups buttermilk

Gently mix with a wooden spoon just until dry ingredients are moistened. Dough will be soft. Scrape down sides of bowl. Cover with waxed paper and then a china plate. Chill for at least 1 hour and up to 24. When ready to bake, preheat oven to 400°F. Remove enough dough to make desired number of biscuits. On a lightly floured surface, knead gently two or three times. Roll to ½-inch thickness. Section with a floured biscuit cutter. Place biscuits about 1 inch apart on an ungreased baking sheet. Bake 12 to 15 minutes at 400°F, or until golden brown. Serve warm. Makes 36 biscuits.

�֎ Minute-Man Muffins

If you like hot bran muffins for breakfast, keep this mixture on hand. It produces muffins in minutes. The recipe can be doubled, if you wish.

Sift together and set aside

>   3 cups unbleached all-purpose flour
>   ½ teaspoon salt
>   2 ½ teaspoons baking soda
>   ¼ cup sugar

To melt butter, in a large mixing bowl stir together

> 1 cup boiling water
> ¼ cup butter

Stir into butter mixture, in this order, blending well after each addition

> 3 cups Kellogg's All-Bran cereal
> ½ cup oil
> ½ cup honey
> 2 eggs
> 2 cups buttermilk

Add sifted dry ingredients to bran mixture and stir lightly just until dry ingredients are all moist. Batter may be stored in refrigerator in an airtight jar or other container for up to 10 days. To bake, spoon batter into greased muffin cups, filling each about two-thirds full. Bake in preheated 400°F oven for 20 minutes, or until browned. Remove from pans and serve hot. Makes 36 muffins.

❖ Frozen Bread Dough

Bread dough can be frozen, but it is best to use it within one month. Rich doughs are not recommended for freezing. When any dough is frozen, some of the yeast action is lost. To compensate for this, you must use extra yeast. Here is a dough that has enough yeast for the thawed dough to rise normally.

To soften yeast, in a large bowl combine

> 3 cups warm water
> 3 tablespoons (or 4 packets) active dry yeast

Stir into softened yeast mixture

> ½ cup sugar
> ½ cup oil
> 1 tablespoon salt
> 4 cups unbleached all-purpose flour

Beat well. To make a stiff dough, gradually add

> 4 to 5 cups unbleached all-purpose flour

Turn out on a floured surface and knead until smooth. Invert a large bowl or stockpot over the dough to prevent its drying out and let the dough rest 15 minutes. Divide the dough into three parts. Shape each part into a loaf and place in an oiled or nonstick 9×5-inch baking pan. Cover tightly with foil and freeze immediately. After loaves are frozen, remove them from the pans. Wrap the frozen loaves tightly in plastic or foil and overwrap with a tightly closed plastic sack. Return them to freezer. Use within a month. When ready to bake, unwrap and place in a well-greased 9×5-inch baking pan. Cover and let thaw and rise. It will take about 1 hour for the dough to thaw; it will take 1 to 2 hours for it to rise. Bake thawed and risen loaf in preheated 375°F oven for 35 to 40 minutes. Cool on wire racks. Makes enough dough for 3 loaves.

Frozen Wheat Dough

Substitute Wheat-Bread Flour (see Pantry Mixes, page 18) for the unbleached all-purpose flour called for. Proceed as in Frozen Bread Dough.

Frozen Rye Dough

Substitute Bohemian Flour (see Pantry Mixes, page 18) for the unbleached all-purpose flour called for. Proceed as in Frozen Bread Dough.

If you like to make your bread from mixes, you can save a great deal of money by concocting your own. Stock your larder with these.

❖ Make-Ahead Bread Mix

Into a very large bowl, measure

12 cups unbleached all-purpose flour

Stir into flour

4 teaspoons salt
1 tablespoon wheat germ (optional)
1 tablespoon bran (optional)
½ cup sugar

Cut into flour mixture with a pastry blender

½ cup shortening

You will have a little more than 13 cups of mix. Divide the mix evenly among 4 quart-size Ziplock plastic sacks. Seal sacks. Label and refrigerate.

When ready to bake: Bring one package of mix to room temperature. To soften yeast, in a mixing bowl combine

¼ cup warm water
1 scant tablespoon (or 1 packet) active dry yeast

Stir into softened yeast mixture, in this order

1 cup scalded milk, cooled to warm or 1 cup warm water
1 package Make-Ahead Bread Mix

Mix until dough forms a ball and cleans sides of the bowl. Turn out on a lightly floured surface and knead until smooth. Place in a well-greased bowl, turning dough once to grease the top. Cover and let rise until doubled in bulk, 45 to 60 minutes. Knead dough down in bowl. Shape and bake as directed below. Makes 1 loaf or 16 rolls.

To Make a Loaf of Bread

On a lightly floured surface, press dough out to a 6×9-inch rectangle. Brush off any excess flour. Starting with a 6-inch side, roll tightly. Place seam side down in a well greased 9×5-inch baking pan. Cover and let rise until almost doubled, 30 to 45 minutes. Bake in preheated 375°F oven for 35 to 40 minutes. Cool on a wire rack.

To Make Rolls

Divide dough into 16 pieces. Shape into balls and place in well-greased muffin cups. Cover and let rise until almost doubled, 20 to 35 minutes. Bake in a preheated 400°F oven for 20 to 25 minutes, or until well-browned. Cool on wire racks.

❉ Buttermilk Baking Mix

This buttermilk baking mix is better than most. It advocates liquid buttermilk instead of dry.

Into a large bowl, sift together

> *2 cups unbleached all-purpose flour*
> *1 tablespoon baking powder*
> *1 tablespoon baking soda*
> *1 tablespoon salt*

Add to sifted mixture

> *6 cups unbleached all-purpose flour*

Stir to mix thoroughly. Cut into flour mixture with pastry blender

> *1 1/2 cups shortening*

You will have about 10 cups of mix. Divide the mix evenly among four sandwich-size Ziploc plastic sacks. Seal sacks. Label and refrigerate. When ready to bake: Bring one package up to room temperature. Use to make biscuits, pancakes, or waffles.

To Make Biscuits

Preheat oven to 450°F. Empty package into bowl. With a fork, stir in just until dough cleans bowl

> *3/4 cup buttermilk*

Toss on a lightly floured surface until no longer sticky. Knead lightly once or twice. Roll to 1/2-inch thickness. Section into rounds with a floured biscuit cutter and place rounds on ungreased baking sheet. Bake at 450°F for 12 to 15 minutes. Makes 10 to 12 biscuits.

To Make Pancakes

In a mixing bowl, beat

> *2 eggs*

Blend into eggs, in this order

   1 tablespoon sugar
   2 tablespoons oil
   2 cups buttermilk

Add to liquids, stirring just until dry ingredients are moistened

   1 package Buttermilk Baking Mix

Let batter stand 5 minutes before using. Stir lightly. Using ¼ cup batter per cake, bake on lightly greased griddle at 375°F, turning only once. Makes 16 4-inch cakes.

To Make Waffles

Mix as for pancakes. Bake in a preheated waffle iron until steaming stops. Makes 3 or 4 waffles.

❋ Corn-Bread Mix

Sift together into a large bowl

   2 cups unbleached all-purpose flour
   ¼ cup baking powder
   1 tablespoon salt

Add to sifted ingredients

   2 cups unbleached all-purpose flour
   4 cups yellow cornmeal
   1 cup sugar

Stir well. With a pastry blender, cut into dry ingredients

   1 cup shortening

You will have about 11 cups of mix. Divide the mix evenly among four sandwich sized Ziploc plastic sacks. Seal sacks. Label and refrigerate. When ready to bake: Bring one package to room temperature. Use to make corn bread or corn muffins.

To Make Corn Bread

Preheat oven to 350°F. In a mixing bowl, beat

> *1 egg*

Stir into egg

> *1 cup milk*

Add and stir just until dry ingredients are moistened

> *1 package Corn-Bread Mix*

Turn into a well-greased 8×8-inch baking pan. Bake at 350°F for 35 to 40 minutes. Makes 9 servings.

To Make Corn Muffins

Preheat oven to 425°F. Mix as for Corn Bread. Spoon into well-greased muffin cups. Bake at 425°F for 20 to 25 minutes. Makes 12 large muffins.

❉ Our Rich Heritage of Bread

*Breads brought to the melting pot of
America from countries all over the world*

❖ OUR RICH HERITAGE OF BREAD

When I was a youngster, it was fashionable to deny one's heritage. Even though both my parents spoke German fluently, they made no attempt to pass this knowledge on to their children. I am glad to see families more recently transplanted to our shores showing interest in maintaining their heritage. This chapter preserves some of their recipes. They come from people whose friendship has enriched my life here in the Midwest.

Occasionally a so-called foreign food becomes Americanized. Recently I was chatting with a charming lady about her upcoming trip to Germany to visit relatives who remain there. I asked her if she ever baked German bread. At first she said no. Then she brightened a bit and said, "Oh, yes, I make a stollen, but it is with an American recipe!" And so it is that some of the more festive foreign breads have become part of the greater culture that pours from the melting pot called America.

❖ Yorkshire Pudding

From her English beginnings, Winifred Martin brought to our small community the tradition of a family Sunday dinner of roast beef and Yorkshire Pudding. This serves four hungry eaters, the number most of us have to contend with. If you do not have beef drippings for preparing your pans, you may use shortening. Avoid using oils.

In a mixing bowl, with a wire whisk, whip

> *2 eggs*

Add alternately, about one-third at a time, beating well after each addition

> *½ cup unbleached all-purpose flour*
> *½ cup milk*

At some time during the addition (it is not critical when this is done), add

> *¼ teaspoon salt*

Continue to beat until mixture bubbles. Let this batter stand for about 1 hour. In the meantime, prepare the baking pan. Place in a 9×9- or an 8 ×8-inch baking pan

> *2 tablespoons beef roast drippings (fat only)*

Heat the pan in a 450°F oven until fat begins to bubble. When the pan is hot, add to batter

> *1 ½ teaspoons cold water*

Beat again until batter bubbles. Remove pan from the oven and pour in the beaten batter. Return to 450°F oven and bake for 20 to 25 minutes, or until golden brown and cooked through. If oven is opened prematurely, the pudding may fall. Serve immediately. Makes 4 generous servings.

❖ Chinese Steamed Bread

> *Shuiho Lee was born in Taiwan and has lived here in our community for the last 10 years. She uses a tiered bamboo steamer for making steamed bread. If you do not have one, you can substitute a vegetable or fish steamer. In a non-tiered steamer, the loaves can be steamed one at a time rather than all at once.*

To soften the yeast, in a mixing bowl, combine

> *1 ¾ cups warm water*
> *1 ½ teaspoons (or part of 1 packet) active dry yeast*
> *6 tablespoons sugar*

To make a stiff dough, stir into softened yeast mixture, 1 cup at a time

> *5 to 6 cups unbleached all-purpose flour, sifted before measuring*

Scrape dough down in bowl. Cover with a moist cloth and let rise until doubled or tripled in bulk. Turn dough out onto a floured surface and knead lightly. Divide the dough into six equal parts. Roll each part into a 5×10-inch oval, using oil to lubricate both your hands and the dough. Brush the top of the ovals with oil. Let rise for 30 minutes. Place risen ovals on waxed paper on the rack of a steamer. Steam for 15 minutes. The bread can be cut into smaller pieces after steaming. Serve for breakfast with butter and jelly. Makes 6 steamed loaves.

Breads from the Philippines

Mercedita Osorio Wells was born in Mey Cauayan, Bulacan, in the Philippine Islands. She has lived in the United States for eight years, the last three in our small community. Merci learned how to make bread from her grandmother. She shared three of her recipes with me.

❖ Puto

This bread calls for raw rice that is soaked and then ground. Filipinos use a stone grinding tool called a gilingngan that roughly resembles a large mortar and pestle. Merci has adapted this to the blender. When I use her recipe, I grind the soaked rice in a food processor.

In a large bowl soak overnight

> 2 cups raw rice
> 4 cups water

The next day, drain rice, reserving soaking water. Place rice in a blender and cream to a smooth texture, adding a little of the soaking water, 1 tablespoonful at a time, until the rice is the texture of thick cream, or slightly melted ice cream. It may take 1 to 1½ cups of the water, depending on the rice. Mix the creamy rice with

> 1 ½ cups sugar
> 1 teaspoon baking powder
> 1 egg

Steam the mixture. In the Philippines this was done in a bamboo steamer lined with cheese cloth. Merci now uses an egg poacher to make small individual breads in 15 to 20 minutes. The mixture can also be steamed in two 8-inch cake pans. Doing it this way takes 30 minutes or longer. Serve the steamed bread warm with butter and freshly grated coconut. Makes 12 to 16 servings.

❖ American Puto

In a large bowl, mix together

>   4 cups biscuit mix, such as Bisquick
>   2 cups milk
>   4 eggs
>   1 ½ cups sugar
>   1 tablespoon mayonnaise

Steam and serve as described above.

❖ Pan De Sal

Sometimes Merci uses fast-acting yeast for these delicious rolls. I particularly like them rolled in bread crumbs.

In a large bowl, combine

>   2 cups scalded milk
>   ½ cup (1 stick) margarine
>   ½ cup sugar

Let cool until just warm. To soften yeast, add

>   1 scant tablespoon (or 1 packet) active dry yeast

Let stand 5 minutes. Stir in

>   2 cups unbleached all-purpose flour

Mix well. Let stand 10 minutes. Add, in this order

>   1 teaspoon salt
>   ½ teaspoon baking powder
>   ½ teaspoon baking soda
>   3 cups unbleached all-purpose flour

Turn out on a floured surface and knead until smooth and elastic. Place in a greased bowl, turning dough once to grease the top. Cover and let rise until doubled in bulk, about 1 hour. Punch dough down and divide into three parts. Divide each part into ten pieces. Roll each piece into a ball and roll in cornmeal or fine bread crumbs. Place on ungreased baking sheets. Cover and let rise until almost doubled, 20 to 25 minutes. Bake in preheated 350°F oven for 15 to 20 minutes, or until brown. Serve warm. Makes 30 rolls.

✳ Paratha

This recipe for delicious Indian bread comes from Meena Verma Roy. Meena graduated from Visva Bharati University in Bengal. She later moved to London, where she attended gourmet cooking classes while studying the Montessori Method of Teaching.

In a large bowl, mix together

⅞ cup (1 cup minus 2 tablespoons) whole-wheat flour
a sprinkle of cumin seeds (about 25 grains, optional)
a sprinkle of celery seeds (about 25 grains, optional)

With your fingers, rub into the flour mixture

2 tablespoons melted butter or margarine

To make a soft dough, add

2 to 3 tablespoons water

If needed to make the dough soft, add more water, 1 teaspoon at a time. Knead well. Divide the dough into four parts and shape each into a ball. Cover the balls of dough with a cloth. On a surface lightly floured with whole-wheat flour, roll the balls of dough, one at a time, into a 4-inch circle. Fold the dough twice to make a quarter of a circle. Roll this triangular shape until the length of the sides is about 6 inches. Heat a heavy skillet until hot but not smoking. Place the triangle of dough in the heated skillet and cook for about a minute. Turn over and cook for an additional minute. If the dough cooks too quickly, reduce the heat. Brush the top of the dough with

1 teaspoon melted butter or margarine

Turn the paratha again. The bread should puff and brown as it cooks. Repeat with remaining balls of dough. Makes 4 paratha.

❖ Challah

Natalie Smith has a reputation among her friends for making the best challah. She has been working on the recipe for years, refining it as she goes along. Natalie graciously shared her secrets with me. For the Sabbath, Natalie bakes her challah in the form of a simple braid, preferring that to the double braid some bakers use. For the holidays of Yom Kippur and Rosh Hashonah, she bakes a high crowned loaf, creating bowknot rolls with the rest of the dough. She usually makes this recipe in her Kitchenaid mixer, but on occasion has whipped it up in her food processor. She uses Ceresota unbleached all-purpose flour, and cautions us not to use fast-rising yeast.

To soften yeast, in a small bowl combine

> ½ *cup warm water*
> 3 *scant tablespoons (or 3 packets) active dry yeast*
> 1 *tablespoon honey*

Allow yeast to proof. In a large bowl, beat

> 5 *egg yolks*

The eggs should be nice and large. If yours look skimpy, add another yolk. Stir in, in this order

> ¾ *cup oil*
> 1 *tablespoon salt*
> *pinch of saffron*
> 4 *tablespoons honey*
> *softened yeast mixture*
> 1 *cup unbleached all-purpose flour*

Let this sponge rest for 5 minutes. Add, 1 cup at a time, beating well after each

> 4 *cups unbleached all-purpose flour*

Add alternately, dividing ingredients into thirds

> 2 *cups water*
> 3 *to 4 cups unbleached all-purpose flour*

The amount of flour needed will depend on the size of the egg yolks. If using a mixer, such as a Kitchenaid, you will add all of the flour. If mixing it in a bowl with a wooden spoon, you may reserve some to knead in by hand. Scrape down dough in bowl. Cover and let rest 10 minutes. Knead on a lightly floured surface or in a Kitchenaid mixer for 10 minutes. If kneading by machine, Natalie advises that you also knead a short time by hand. Place kneaded dough in an oiled bowl, turning dough once to oil the top. Cover with waxed paper and then a towel and allow to rise until doubled, 1 to 1½ hours. Shape and bake as directed below.

To Make Braids

Divide dough into three parts. Divide each part again into three parts. Roll each part to a rope 16 to 18 inches long. Braid three ropes together, pinching ends together to seal. Place on a greased baking sheet. Repeat with remaining dough. Cover and let rise until almost doubled, 45 to 60 minutes. Before baking, brush braids with a mixture of

> *1 egg yolk*
> *1 teaspoon water*

Sprinkle tops of loaves with

> *poppy seeds*

Place loaves on center rack of preheated 325°F oven. Bake for 10 minutes. Raise heat to 350°F. Bake an additional 25 to 35 minutes or until well-browned.

To Make Braid-Crowned Loaf

Use one-third of the dough. Shape into a round ball. Place in a well-greased round baking pan. Use a small amount of additional dough to make a very thin braid. This will take about one-twelfth of the total dough, or one-fourth of one of the thirds. Use this braid to encircle the top of the ball of dough, forming a crown. Cover and let rise until almost doubled, 45 to 60 minutes. Before baking, brush top of loaf with egg glaze, as described above. Bake in a preheated 350°F oven for 35 to 45 minutes, or until well-browned.

To Make Bowknot Rolls

Divide one-third of dough into 12 pieces. Shape each piece into a rope 12 inches long. Shape loosely into a knot, curving the loose ends toward one another. Cover and let rise until almost doubled, 30 to 45 minutes. Before baking, brush tops of rolls with egg glaze, as described above. Sprinkle tops with

sesame seeds

Bake in a preheated 350°F oven for 25 to 30 minutes, or until well-browned.

❖ Vortlimpor, Christmas Rye Bread

Marge Carlson married into her Swedish family. Soon after the wedding, Marge's father-in-law told her there was nothing he would like better than to have his favorite rye bread with some flaming glogg. Marge knew some Swedish women who were bakers in the nearby town of Paxton and she traveled there to learn how to make the bread for Mr. Carlson.

The seeds for this bread need to be pounded until fine. I used a mortar and pestle. You can also put them into a small plastic sack and pound them with a hammer, or put them through a food processor with 1 cup of the all-purpose flour.

Stir together and set aside

4 cups all-purpose flour, sifted before measuring
2 cups medium rye flour, sifted before measuring

In a heavy saucepan, combine and heat over medium heat until the *stout is warm and the shortening begins to melt

1 ½ cups (1 12-ounce bottle) stout
1 tablespoon anise or fennel seeds, pounded until fine
2 tablespoons shortening

---

*Stout is a special kind of beer. If you can't find it, use regular beer.

Pour the warmed ingredients into a large mixing bowl and add

½ cup dark corn syrup
grated rind of 1 orange
¼ cup sugar
½ teaspoon salt

Mix well. Stir in

3 cups flour mixture

Beat this batter until smooth. To soften yeast, in a small container combine

¼ cup warm water
1 scant tablespoon (or 1 packet) active dry yeast

Mix the softened yeast mixture thoroughly with the batter. To make a soft dough, gradually add

the remaining flour mixture

Turn out on a lightly floured surface and knead until smooth and elastic. Place in a greased bowl, turning dough once to grease the top. Cover and let rise until doubled in bulk, 1½ to 2 hours. Punch dough down and again let rise until doubled in bulk, 1 to 1½ hours. Shape into two loaves, about 12 inches long. Place loaves in a well-greased 9×12-inch baking pan. Cover and let rise until doubled in bulk, about 1 hour. Perforate each loaf about five or six times with the tines of a fork. Bake in a preheated 350°F oven for 45 to 50 minutes, or until well-browned. Remove from the oven and brush the tops of the loaves with hot water. Cool on wire racks. Makes 2 loaves.

✿ Pan de Maiz con Jalapeño

I went into Zarate's Market one day to talk about making corn tortillas and came away with Melida's recipe. Melida and her husband Pedro have had their market for the last eleven years. They feature all the ingredients needed for Mexican dishes. They are also known for having sweet Spanish onions and good field-grown tomatoes when no one else in town seems able to get them.

Melida usually doubles this recipe and bakes it in a 10×13-inch baking pan for about 45 minutes. She says it's perfect for potluck suppers.

Preheat oven to 375°F. Grease a 9×9- or an 8×8-inch baking pan. In a large bowl, mix together well

> 1 ½ cups cornmeal
> 1 tablespoon unbleached all-purpose flour
> 1 ½ teaspoons salt
> ½ teaspoon baking soda

Add to dry ingredients

> 1 cup milk
> ⅔ cup melted shortening, slightly cooled
> 2 eggs
> 1 cup canned creamed corn

Mix well. Stir into batter

> *3 to 6 fresh Jalapeño peppers, seeded and chopped
> 5 green onions, white parts only, chopped
> ½ cup (about 1 medium) chopped green bell pepper

Pour half of the batter into the prepared pan. Spread over the batter

> 1 ½ cups shredded American cheese

Pour remaining batter over the cheese. Bake in preheated 375°F oven for 35 to 40 minutes. Serve warm. Makes 9 servings.

❖ Grandma Nachtigal's Zweibach

To my grandmother, a Mennonite, zweibach (twice-baked) meant one roll baked on top of another. It was not the toasted bread so often given to teething infants. Grandma's zweibach recipe resulted in delicious rolls to be served hot or cold. My favorite way to eat them was cold, dipped into a chilled puréed fruit soup that I often found in her refrigerator.

Shape your zweibach carefully. If not evenly formed, they can become lopsided during baking. A young Mennonite bride was judged by the shape of her zweibach. Grandma's, of course, were always perfect.

---

*Wear rubber gloves when seeding peppers so the oils won't burn your skin, and be careful not to touch your face. Wash the gloves before removing them.

To soften yeast, in a large mixing bowl combine

¼ cup warm water
½ teaspoon sugar
1 scant tablespoon (or 1 packet) active dry yeast

Let yeast mixture stand. In a saucepan, heat while stirring, until butter and shortening are melted

2 cups milk
½ cup butter
1 tablespoon shortening

Let milk mixture cool to just warm, then add to yeast mixture with

2 teaspoons salt
1 tablespoon sugar
4 cups unbleached all-purpose flour

Beat well. To make a soft dough, gradually add

2 to 3 cups unbleached all-purpose flour

Turn out on a floured surface and knead until smooth. Place in a greased bowl, turning dough once to grease the top. Cover with a piece of waxed paper, then a kitchen towel. Let rise until doubled in bulk, 1 to 1½ hours. Knead dough down in bowl. Cover and let rise again for about 30 minutes. Shape into rolls as follows: Remove a piece of dough about the size of a grapefruit and squeeze this dough through the opening made with your thumb and index finger. Squeeze out a piece about the size of a golf ball. Place that piece on a well-greased baking sheet. Repeat with enough pieces to cover the sheet, spacing the balls about 2 inches apart. Now squeeze out pieces of dough that are about half the size of the first ones. Flatten the bottom piece of dough, poke a small indentation in the center of it and place the smaller piece in the center, pressing firmly to seat it well. When all are formed, cover with waxed paper, then the towel. Let rise until almost doubled, about 30 to 45 minutes. Bake at 400°F for about 20 minutes, or until well-browned. Serve warm or cold with butter and homemade jam and jelly. Makes 30 zweibach.

❖ Russia-Pankakos

There are many ethnic origins of paper-thin pancakes. In our household of Mennonite heritage, they were called Russia-Pankakos. We had them for Sunday night supper with a stewed fruit soup. We would take turns baking them, so that they could be eaten immediately by those who were not cooking. Double the recipe, if you wish.

In a large bowl, beat lightly

> *2 eggs*

Stir in

> *½ cup unbleached all-purpose flour*
> *pinch salt*

Slowly beat in, avoiding beating in air

> *1 cup milk*

Bake in a hot, greased iron skillet. Pour in about ¼ cup batter. Quickly swirl pan to coat the bottom evenly. Loosen and turn pancake, cooking until brown on second side. Place on a warmed plate. Spread with butter and tart jelly. Roll up and serve. Makes about 8 cakes.

❖ Stollen

This traditional German Christmas bread resembles a giant fruited Parkerhouse roll. My version is easy to make with premixed candied fruit and golden raisins.

In a small bowl, combine several hours ahead of baking time to plump the fruit

> *1 cup mixed candied fruits*
> *1 cup golden raisins*
> *¼ cup orange juice or dark rum*

When ready to begin, in a large mixing bowl combine

¾ cup scalded milk
½ cup sugar
½ cup butter, cut into 8 pieces
1 teaspoon salt

Stir to dissolve sugar and butter. Let cool until just warm. Meanwhile, to soften yeast, in a small container combine

¼ cup warm water
2 scant tablespoons (or 2 packets) active dry yeast

When milk mixture has cooled down to warm, stir in

softened yeast mixture
2 eggs
grated rind of 1 lemon
¼ teaspoon cardamom
¼ teaspoon mace
2 ½ cups unbleached all-purpose flour

Beat until smooth. Add and blend well

plumped fruit, including any remaining liquid

To make a soft dough, gradually add

2 to 2 ½ cups unbleached all-purpose flour

Turn out on a floured surface and knead until smooth. Place in a well-buttered bowl, turning dough once to butter the top. Cover and let rise until doubled in bulk, 1½ to 2 hours. Press dough down to expel air. Divide dough in half. Working with one-half at a time, *pat or roll out into a 9-inch circle. Brush the surface of the dough with

1 teaspoon melted butter

Sprinkle with

1 teaspoon sugar

Fold the circle almost in half, letting 1 inch of the bottom extend beyond the edge of the top. Transfer to a well-buttered or nonstick baking sheet. Press lightly on the creased side of the loaf. Do not press where the two halves meet. Repeat from * for second half of dough. Cover and let rise until almost doubled in bulk, 45 to 60 minutes. Before baking, brush tops of loaves with

melted butter

Bake in a preheated 350°F oven for 30 to 35 minutes, or until loaves are golden brown. Cool on wire racks. While still slightly warm, brush with

melted butter

Cool completely. When cooled, sprinkle with

sieved confectioner's sugar

Do not slice until completely cooled. Slice thin and serve with sweet butter. Makes 2 stollen.

❉ Panettone

Originally served only at Christmas time, this rich, buttery Milanese creation has become an Italian favorite for celebrations at any time of the year.

To make a sponge, in a large mixing bowl combine

¼ cup warm water
1 scant tablespoon (or 1 packet) active dry yeast
1 tablespoon sugar
⅓ cup unbleached all-purpose flour

Cover and let this sponge rise for a full 30 minutes. Stir down. Stir into sponge

½ teaspoon salt
5 tablespoons sugar

Add, one at a time, beating well after each addition

2 eggs

Divide flour into three parts and butter into two. Beginning and ending with flour, add alternately

1 ⅔ to 2 cups unbleached all-purpose flour
½ cup softened butter

Beat well after each addition. Turn out on a floured surface and toss until no longer sticky. Knead gently until smooth, adding more flour if needed to prevent sticking. Turn into a well-buttered bowl, turning dough once to butter the top. Cover and refrigerate for 2 hours to chill the dough. Meanwhile, prepare pan. Generously butter a 2-pound coffee can. Line the bottom of the pan with a circle of waxed paper. Butter the waxed paper. Turn chilled dough out onto a lightly floured surface. Flatten to an 8-inch circle. Sprinkle on the surface of the dough

> ½ cup golden raisins
> ¼ cup chopped candied citron
> ¼ cup chopped candied orange peel
> ¼ cup chopped candied lemon peel
> grated rind of 1 lemon

Roll dough up as for jelly roll. Gently knead several times to distribute the fruit. Shape into a round ball and drop into prepared pan, smooth side up. Cover and let rise until doubled. This may take 2 to 4 hours, depending on the warmth of the kitchen. Before baking, cut a cross in the top of the loaf. Insert in the center of the cross

> 1 teaspoon butter

Bake in a preheated 350°F oven for 35 to 40 minutes, or until the top sounds hollow when tapped with a finger. Turn out of pan carefully. Lay the loaf on its side on a stack of clean kitchen towels to cool. The loaf can be quite tender and may collapse if placed upright on a rack. Turn the loaf several times while it is cooling to prevent a flat side from forming. When thoroughly cooled, dust the top of the loaf with

> sieved confectioner's sugar

Makes 1 large panettone.

✵ Kugelhopf

Both Germans and Austrians claim Kugelhopf as theirs. Bread literature gives us several variants of the spelling. It sometimes appears as Gugelhupf or Kugelhupf. Europeans usually bake this bread in a smaller mold than we do. Because the American baker most often has a bundt pan with a 10-cup capacity, I have written the recipe for that size. If you wish, you may plump the raisins in 2 to 3 tablespoons of light rum several hours before baking time. I sometimes vary the spice and use nutmeg or cinnamon instead of the allspice.

Generously butter a 10-cup Bundt pan. Sprinkle evenly over the butter in the pan

> *¼ cup finely chopped almonds*

To soften yeast, in a 1-quart container combine

> *½ cup warm water*
> *2 scant tablespoons (or 2 packets) active dry yeast*
> *1 teaspoon sugar*

Let stand 5 minutes. Meanwhile, in a large bowl, cream together

> *½ cup softened butter*
> *¾ cup sugar*
> *½ teaspoon salt*

Add, beating well after the addition

> *5 egg yolks*

Stir into the softened yeast mixture

> *½ cup evaporated milk*
> *grated rind of 1 lemon*
> *½ teaspoon ground allspice*

Divide the flour into three parts and the yeast mixture into two. Beginning and ending with the flour, add to the butter mixture alternately with the yeast mixture

> *3 cups unbleached all-purpose flour, measured by spooning gently into the cup*

Blend well after each addition. Stir into batter

> *1 cup golden raisins (drained, if plumped in rum)*
> *½ cup finely chopped almonds*

Stir in one-quarter, then fold in the remainder of

> *5 egg whites, stiffly beaten*

Carefully spoon batter into prepared pan. If needed, smooth top of batter with a flexible spatula. Cover and let rise 1 hour, or until batter almost reaches the top of the pan. Bake in preheated 400°F oven for 10 minutes. Reduce heat to 350°F and bake for 25 to 30 minutes longer, or until a metal skewer inserted in the center of the batter comes out clean. Cool 10 minutes in the pan. Turn out to cool completely on a wire rack. Before serving, dust with

sieved confectioner's sugar

Serve slightly warm or at room temperature. Makes 1 large kugelhopf.

❖ Paodoce, Portuguese Sweet Bread

The Portuguese immigrated to Hawaii in the late 1800's during the reign of the Hawaiian King Kalakaua. Their foods, which quickly became favorites in the islands, include spicy Portuguese bean soup and this sweet bread, called Paodoce. * *I've adapted the recipe from one sent to me by Joseph K. Sherrard, Coordinator of the Hotel & Restaurant Department of the University of Hawaii at Hilo.*

To soften yeast, in a small bowl combine

2 scant tablespoons (or 2 packets) active dry yeast
¾ cup warm potato water

Set aside to ferment. In a large mixing bowl, cream together

6 tablespoons shortening
1 ½ cups sugar
1 ½ teaspoons salt

Add, one at a time, beating well after each addition

4 eggs

Stir into the batter, in this order

½ cup unseasoned mashed potatoes
1 cup scalded milk, cooled down to warm

---

*Insight Guides, eds. *Hawaii* (American edition) (Englewood Cliffs, NJ: Prentice-Hall, 1984), pp. 77, 78.

softened yeast
4 cups bread flour

Beat until smooth. To make a soft dough, gradually add

2 ½ to 3 cups bread flour

Turn out on a floured surface and knead until smooth and elastic. Place in a well-greased bowl, turning dough once to grease the top. Cover and let rise until doubled in bulk, 1 to 1½ hours. Punch down dough and divide into three parts. Shape each part into a ball and place in well-greased 9-inch round layer-cake pans. Cover and let rise until almost doubled in bulk, about 1 hour. Before baking, brush tops of loaves with a mixture of

1 egg
1 tablespoon water

Bake in a preheated 350°F oven for 35 to 40 minutes, or until well-browned. Cool on wire racks. Makes 3 loaves.

❖ Potica

Potica (pronounced poh-teet'-sa) comes from Yugoslavia, where it heralds the fall harvesting of nut trees. The best Potica has the dough rolled very thin before the filling is layered into it. If you take your time, you won't find the rolling difficult.

In a mixing bowl, combine

½ cup scalded milk
¼ cup butter, cut into 4 pieces
¼ cup sugar
1 teaspoon salt

Stir to dissolve butter and sugar. Let cool until just warm. Meanwhile, to soften yeast, in a small container combine

¼ cup warm water
1 scant tablespoon (or 1 packet) active dry yeast

When milk mixture has cooled down to warm, stir in, in this order

softened yeast mixture
1 egg
1 ½ cups unbleached all-purpose flour

Beat until smooth. To make a soft dough, gradually add

1 to 1 ½ cups unbleached all-purpose flour

Scrape dough down in bowl. Cover and let rise until doubled in bulk, 45 to 60 minutes. Punch dough down with a wooden spoon. Do not knead. You want this dough to be relaxed. Turn out on a lightly floured surface and toss until no longer sticky. Divide dough in half; work with one-half at a time. *Roll out on a lightly floured surface to a circle 16 to 18 inches in diameter. At the beginning of the rolling process, check often to see if the rolling surface and the surface of the dough need a dusting of flour to prevent sticking. If dough becomes too springy to roll, cover it for a few minutes to let it relax. Brush circle of rolled dough with

2 tablespoons melted butter

Spread with

½ of Walnut Filling

Gently roll filled dough jelly-roll fashion. Place on a buttered baking sheet and curve into a loose coil or snail shape. Repeat from* for second half of dough. If baking sheet is large, both loaves may be placed on one sheet. They should be separated by a couple of inches. Cover and let rise until doubled, about 1 hour. Bake in a preheated 350°F oven for 35 to 40 minutes, or until well-browned. Cool on wire racks. While still warm, sprinkle tops of loaves with

sieved confectioner's sugar

Serve warm. Makes 2 loaves.

Walnut Filling

You can chop the walnuts in a blender or food processor, but keep your touch light. You don't want walnut butter!

In a heavy saucepan, place

>   *2 cups very finely chopped walnuts*

Stir into walnuts, in this order

>   *½ teaspoon cinnamon*
>   *½ cup evaporated milk*
>   *½ cup sugar*
>   *⅓ cup honey*

Cook over medium heat, stirring constantly, just until mixture thickens. If this gets too thick, it will tear the dough when it is spread. Remove from heat. Stir into mixture

>   *1 teaspoon vanilla extract*

Cool to room temperature.

❖ Kulich

The Russians traditionally make Kulich for Easter. The icing covering the tops of the loaves and dripping down the sides represents the melting of snow on their round-domed churches. The four loaves make an attractive centerpiece set on Easter grass with brightly colored Easter eggs nestled around their base. When you cut the breads, save the tops. They can be put back on the dwindling loaves to prevent drying out.

Several hours or the night before baking, to marinate the fruit and nuts, in a small bowl combine

>   *⅓ cup slivered blanched almonds*
>   *⅓ cup raisins*
>   *⅓ cup golden raisins*
>   *⅓ cup chopped red candied cherries*
>   *¼ cup brandy or rum*

When ready to bake, in a large mixing bowl combine

    1 cup scalded milk
    6 tablespoons butter
    6 tablespoons sugar
    1 ½ teaspoons salt

Stir to dissolve butter and sugar. Let cool until just warm. Meanwhile, to soften yeast, in a small container combine

    ½ cup warm water
    2 scant tablespoons (or 2 packets) active dry yeast

When milk mixture has cooled down to warm, stir in

    softened yeast mixture
    2 eggs
    3 cups unbleached all-purpose flour

Beat until smooth. Add

    marinated fruit, including any liquid that remains
    grated rind of 1 lemon
    grated rind of 1 orange

Mix together well. To make a soft dough, gradually add

    2 ½ to 3 cups unbleached all-purpose flour

Turn out on a floured surface and toss until no longer sticky. Knead gently until smooth. Place in a well-greased bowl, turning dough once to grease the top. Cover and let rise until doubled in bulk, 1 to 1½ hours. Meanwhile, prepare pans. Generously grease four 1-pound coffee cans. Line bottoms of pans with circles of waxed paper. Grease waxed paper. When dough has risen, press down to deflate air. Divide into four parts. Shape each part into a round ball and drop into prepared pans, smooth side up. Cover and let rise until doubled, 45 to 60 minutes. Bake in a preheated 350°F oven for 35 to 40 minutes, or until the bread sounds hollow when tapped on the top. Gently remove loaves from cans and set on their sides on wire racks to cool. Turn them now and then while cooling to prevent their developing a flat side. When the loaves are almost cool, stand them erect and frost with a mixture of

1 cup sieved confectioner's sugar
1/4 teaspoon vanilla extract
1 to 2 tablespoons milk

Allow some of the frosting to drip down the sides of the loaves. Cool completely before use. Makes 4 kulich.

Jule Kaga

This is a traditional Norwegian Christmas bread. Baked into round loaves, it is decorated with a white sugary icing and snipped candied fruits.

To soften yeast, in a large mixing bowl combine

1/2 cup warm water
2 scant tablespoons (or 2 packets) active dry yeast

Stir into softened yeast mixture, in this order

2 eggs
1/2 cup sugar
1/2 cup softened butter
1 teaspoon salt
1/4 teaspoon cardamom
1/4 teaspoon nutmeg
1/2 cup evaporated milk
3 cups unbleached all-purpose flour

Beat until smooth. To make a soft dough, gradually add

1 to 1 1/2 cups unbleached all-purpose flour

Turn out on a floured surface and knead until smooth. Place in a well-greased bowl, turning dough once to grease the top. Cover and let rise until

doubled in bulk, 1 to 1½ hours. Punch dough down. On a lightly floured surface, flatten dough into a 12-inch circle. Sprinkle over dough

1 cup raisins
¼ cup finely chopped candied citron
¼ cup finely chopped candied red cherries
¼ cup finely chopped candied green cherries

Knead dough to distribute the fruit evenly. Divide dough in half. Shape each half into a ball. Place in well-greased 9-inch round layer-cake pans. Flatten the balls slightly. Cover and let rise until almost doubled, 45 to 60 minutes. Before baking, brush tops of loaves with a mixture of

1 egg
1 tablespoon water

Bake in a preheated 350°F oven for 35 to 40 minutes. Cool on wire racks. When almost cooled, frost with a mixture of

1 cup sieved confectioner's sugar
¼ teaspoon vanilla
1 tablespoon melted butter
1 to 2 tablespoons milk

On the top of the icing, place several candied red cherry halves. Use a few snipped green cherries to suggest leaves surrounding the red cherries. Makes 2 Jule Kaga.

⁂ Granary Loaves

Recipes from the purveyors of grain, flour, pots and pans, and many other items too numerous to mention

Amaranth-Oat Bread
Fast Whole-Wheat Yeast Bread
Hearty Brown Bread
Pumpernickel-Style Rye Bread
Cracked-Wheat Bread
No-Knead Refrigerator Rolls
"White" Bread
Toasted Corn Muffins
Cheese Crackers
Tender White Bread
Hi-Lysine Cornmeal Egg Bread
American Rye Bread
Corn Crisps
Graham Nut Bread
Graham Yeast Bread
English Muffin Bread
Molasses-Walnut Muffins
Raisin-Coconut Banana Bread
Rugelach
Barley Biscuits
Corn-Flour Pancakes
12 Grain Bread
Corn Dodgers

❖ GRANARY LOAVES

In preparation for the writing of this book, I engaged in lively correspondence with bread bakers at mills and mail-order sources for my supplies. They sent me their recipes to try, and I discovered so many good ones that I decided to devote an entire chapter to them. Many more were sent than could be used here. I'm sorry I couldn't include them all.

❖ Amaranth-Oat Bread

FROM ARROWHEAD MILLS

Amaranth flour was used by the Aztecs centuries ago. It is high in carbohydrates, rich in calcium, iron, and phosphorus, and contains an unusually complete vegetable-grain protein with very little fat.

Amaranth flour combines well with other flours to make many delicious, smooth-textured baked goods, such as breads, muffins, and pancakes. If you want to use it in your favorite recipes, just use one part amaranth flour to three or four parts wheat flour.

In a heavy saucepan, combine

1 cup Arrowhead Mills Oat Flakes
2 cups water
2 teaspoons salt (optional)

Bring mixture to a boil. Reduce heat and cook until thick and creamy. Allow mixture to cool to room temperature. Meanwhile, in a large mixing bowl combine

½ cup warm water
2 teaspoons (or part of 1 packet) active dry yeast
3 tablespoons honey
¼ cup oil

Stir well. Let stand until bubbly, about 10 minutes. Stir in

cooled oat mixture
1 cup Arrowhead Mills Amaranth Flour
4 cups Arrowhead Mills Stone-ground Whole-Wheat Flour

Turn out on a floured surface and knead for 10 minutes. Place in a well-greased bowl, turning dough once to grease the top. Cover and let rise until doubled in bulk, about 1½ hours. Knead again. Let rise a second time. Punch down dough, divide in half. Shape into round loaves. Place on a lightly floured baking sheet and brush with

milk

Sprinkle with

Arrowhead Mills Oat Flakes

Bake at 350°F for 60 minutes, or until crust is golden brown. Cool on wire racks. Makes 2 loaves.

❋ Fast Whole-Wheat Yeast Bread

FROM ARROWHEAD MILLS

This bread can be made from start to finish in 1 hour, including baking. Actual mixing time is only 5 to 10 minutes.

In a small bowl, mix together

13 ounces (1 ½ cups plus 2 tablespoons) lukewarm water
1 scant tablespoon (or 1 packet) active dry yeast
1 teaspoon honey

Set aside until frothy, about 5 minutes. Meanwhile, in a large mixing bowl, combine

4 cups Arrowhead Mills Stone-ground Whole-Wheat Flour
1 teaspoon salt (optional)

Mix into yeast mixture

2 tablespoons unrefined corn germ oil or safflower oil (optional)

Make a well in the center of the flour mixture. Pour yeast mixture into the center of that well. Mix flour in from the sides, first with a wooden spoon and later with your hands. Shape the dough into a loaf. Place in an oiled or well-greased loaf pan. Cover and let rise until slightly over the top of the pan, 20 to 30 minutes. Bake at 350°F for 30 to 40 minutes. Turn out to cool on a rack. Makes 1 loaf.

❊ Hearty Brown Bread

FROM ARROWHEAD MILLS

This hearty bread uses wheat gluten to support the heavier materials incorporated into the loaf. The wheat gluten from Arrowhead Mills is extracted from wheat through a water-washing procedure. The process is entirely mechanical with no chemicals added.

To soften yeast, in a large mixing bowl combine

> *2 ½ cups warm water*
> *1 scant tablespoon (or 1 packet) active dry yeast*
> *½ cup molasses, preferably blackstrap*

In another container, mix together thoroughly

> *1 cup Arrowhead Mills Wheat Gluten*
> *2 cups Arrowhead Mills Stone-ground Whole-Wheat Flour*
> *1 cup Arrowhead Mills Stone-ground Rye Flour*
> *1 cup Arrowhead Mills Wheat Bran*
> *1 cup Arrowhead Mills Wheat Germ*
> *½ cup Arrowhead Mills Oat Flakes*
> *1 tablespoon salt (optional)*

Stir dry ingredients into yeast mixture. Turn out on a floured surface and knead in an additional

> *½ to 1 cup Arrowhead Mills Stone-ground Whole-Wheat Flour*

Place dough in a greased or oiled bowl, turning dough once to grease the top. Cover and let rise until doubled in bulk, 45 to 60 minutes. Punch dough down and divide in half. Shape into long loaves. Roll to coat surface in

> *Arrowhead Mills Oat Flakes*

Place loaves side by side on an oiled cookie sheet sprinkled with oat flakes. Cover and let rise until almost doubled, about 45 minutes. Bake in 350°F oven for about 45 minutes, or until loaves test done. Place on wire racks to cool. Makes 2 loaves.

❖ Pumpernickel-Style Rye Bread

FROM ELAM MILLS

All of Elam's flours are stone ground and are consistently good to use. Elam's recipes never call for salt. I have suggested an amount, just in case you wish to use it.

In a large bowl, combine

1 cup scalded milk
1 tablespoon shortening
2 tablespoons molasses
(1 teaspoon salt)

Stir to dissolve shortening. Let cool until just warm. Meanwhile, to soften yeast, in a small container combine

¼ cup warm water
1 scant tablespoon (or 1 packet) active dry yeast

When milk mixture has cooled down to warm, stir in, in this order

softened yeast mixture
1 tablespoon caraway seed
3 cups Elam's Stone-ground Whole-Rye Flour

Turn out on a lightly floured surface and knead just until smooth. Resist the temptation to knead in too much flour. Place in a well-greased bowl, turning dough once to grease the top. Cover and let rise until doubled in bulk, about 1 hour. Knead dough down in bowl. Shape into a ball and place in a well-greased round pan. Cover and let rise until almost doubled, about 1 hour. Bake in a preheated 350°F oven for 45 to 50 minutes. Cool on a wire rack. Makes 1 loaf.

❖ Cracked-Wheat Bread

FROM ELAM MILLS

Elam's cracked-wheat cereal is delicious in a loaf of bread.

In a large mixing bowl, combine

> 1 ½ cups Elam's Cracked-Wheat Cereal
> 2 cups boiling water

Mix well. Stir into cereal mixture

> 3 tablespoons shortening
> ¼ cup honey
> ⅛ teaspoon baking soda
> (2 teaspoons salt)

Stir to melt shortening. Let cool until just warm. Meanwhile, to soften yeast, in a small container combine

> ⅔ cup warm water
> 2 scant tablespoons (or 2 packets) active dry yeast

When cereal mixture has cooled down to warm, stir in

> softened yeast mixture
> 3 ¾ cups Elam's Stone-Ground 100% Whole-Wheat Flour

Cover with a damp cloth. Let rise until doubled, 1 to 1½ hours. Stir down. Stir in

> 1 cup Elam's Stone-Ground 100% Whole-Wheat Flour

Turn dough out on a surface floured with additional whole-wheat flour. Knead until smooth, adding flour as needed. Place in a well-greased bowl, turning dough once to grease the top. Cover and let rise 30 minutes. Punch down. Let rest 10 minutes. Shape into two loaves. Place in greased 8½× 4½×2½-inch baking pans. Cover and let rise until almost doubled, 1 to 1½ hours. Bake in preheated 350°F oven for 45 to 50 minutes. Turn out to cool on wire racks. Makes 2 loaves.

❖ No-Knead Refrigerator Rolls

FROM GREAT GRAINS MILLING COMPANY

Great Grains stone-ground whole-wheat flour is milled from hard red spring wheat grown in northeast Montana. It absorbs a little more liquid than some of the flours you may have used from other mills. This recipe makes good rolls. I have also used it for two loaves of bread which I baked for 45 minutes at 350°F.

To soften yeast, in a large bowl combine

> ½ *cup warm water*
> 2 *scant tablespoons (or 2 packets) active dry yeast*

Stir into softened yeast mixture

> 1 ½ *cups warm water, preferably from boiled potatoes*
> ½ *cup brown sugar*
> 1 ½ *teaspoons salt*
> ¼ *cup oil*
> 1 *egg*
> 3 *cups Great Grains' Stone-ground Whole-Wheat Flour*

Beat well. To make a stiff dough, gradually add

> 1 ½ *to 2 cups Great Grains' Stone-ground Whole-Wheat Flour*

Kneading is not necessary. Transfer dough to a clean, well-greased bowl. Cover with waxed paper, then a damp towel. Refrigerate. It will keep for 3 days. Punch down dough when needed and re-cover. When ready to bake, shape into rolls and place on well-greased baking sheets. Cover and let rise until doubled in bulk, 1 to 1½ hours. Bake for 15 to 20 minutes in a preheated 350°F oven. Serve warm or cool on wire racks. Makes 24 to 36 rolls, depending on the size of the rolls.

❖ "White" Bread

FROM THE GREAT VALLEY MILLS

I put quotes around white *because Steve and Susan Kantoor of the Great Valley Mills suggest trying two cups of either stone-ground whole-wheat flour or rye meal in place of the first two cups of hard white flour called for. I happen to like the recipe as originally written. It is a delicious bread, due, I am sure, to the use of their very good unbleached hard white flour.*

To soften yeast, in a large bowl combine

2 cups warm water
2 scant tablespoons (or 2 packets) active dry yeast

To the softened yeast mixture add

1 tablespoon salt
⅓ cup honey
1 egg
1 cup milk
3 tablespoons melted butter

Add, 1 cup at a time, stirring well after each addition

8 cups Great Valley Mills Unbleached Hard White Flour

Turn out on a floured board and knead until smooth. Place in a lightly oiled bowl, turning dough once to oil the top. Cover and let rise until doubled in bulk, 1 to 1½ hours. Punch dough down. Divide dough into four parts. Lightly knead each part separately. On a lightly floured surface, roll each into a triangle, pushing any air bubbles out to the sides. Roll each triangle into a loaf, starting at the wide end of the triangle, and pinching the point under. Place on a lightly greased baking sheet. Brush the tops of the loaves with

melted butter

Cover and let rise until almost doubled, 45 to 60 minutes. Bake in a preheated 350°F oven for 35 to 45 minutes, or until brown. The loaves should be hollow-sounding when tapped and the sides will be slightly cracked. Cool on wire racks. Makes 4 loaves.

✻ Toasted Corn Muffins

FROM THE GREAT VALLEY MILLS

In addition to their regular cornmeal, the Kantoors offer a toasted cornmeal, used in this recipe. When these muffins are baking, the aroma is heavenly. And they taste as good as they smell.

Preheat oven to 350°F. Grease a 12-cup muffin pan. In a mixing bowl, beat together

> *1 egg*
> *¼ cup oil*

Stir in, in this order

> *3 tablespoons sugar*
> *½ teaspoon salt*
> *1 tablespoon baking powder*
> *1 ¼ cups buttermilk*

Add

> *1 cup Great Valley Mills Toasted Corn Meal*
> *1 cup Great Valley Mills Unbleached Soft White Flour*

Mix until smooth. Spoon into prepared muffin cups. Bake at 350°F for 20 minutes, or until golden brown. Do not overbake, as this tends to dry out the muffins. Serve warm. Makes 12 muffins.

✻ Cheese Crackers

FROM HECKERS & CERESOTA FLOURS

These crackers may be rich, but that didn't stop the first woman who tested them from eating the whole batch!

Sift and set aside

> *2 cups Hecker's or Ceresota Unbleached All-purpose Flour*

In a mixing bowl, cream together until light

> *1 cup lightly salted butter*
> *2 cups (8 ounces) grated sharp cheddar cheese*

Gradually blend in

> *sifted flour*

Wrap and chill the dough for 1 hour. On a lightly floured surface, roll to ¼-inch thickness. Cut into 2-inch squares. Place squares on an ungreased baking sheet. Brush tops of squares with a mixture of

> *1 egg yolk*
> *1 tablespoon milk*

Bake in a preheated 325°F oven for 15 to 20 minutes, or until golden brown. Cool on wire racks. Makes 42 crackers.

❖ Tender White Bread

FROM HECKERS & CERESOTA FLOURS

The people at the mill say they got this recipe from a friend, who got it from a friend, who got it from a friend. . . . I'm happy that they sent it to me, so I can share it with you. . . .

To soften yeast, in a large bowl combine

> *1 cup warm water*
> *2 scant tablespoons (or 2 packets) active dry yeast*

Stir into softened yeast mixture

> *6 tablespoons sugar*
> *1 tablespoon salt*
> *2 cups buttermilk*
> *½ cup melted shortening, cooled to warm*
> *4 cups Hecker's or Ceresota Unbleached All-purpose Flour*

Beat well. To make a soft dough, gradually add

> *3 to 4 cups Hecker's or Ceresota Unbleached All-purpose Flour*

Turn out on a floured surface and knead until smooth. Place in a well-greased bowl, turning dough once to grease the top. Cover and let rise until doubled in bulk, 1 to 1½ hours. Knead dough down in bowl. Shape into a ball. Cover and let rest 10 minutes. Divide dough in half. Shape into loaves and place in well-greased 9×5-inch baking pans. Cover and let rise until almost doubled, 45 to 60 minutes. Bake in a preheated 425°F oven for 15 minutes. Reduce heat to 400°F and bake for an additional 15 to 20 minutes. Turn out on racks to cool. Makes 2 loaves.

❖ Hi-Lysine Cornmeal Egg Bread

FROM KWC INTERNATIONAL CORPORATION

Crow's hi-lysine corn is grown not far from my home. I have been using this cornmeal for some time, as it is whole grain, all natural, and has a higher protein content than ordinary cornmeal. Use it in all your cornmeal recipes. If you cannot find it in your area, write to KWC International at 3806 North Vermilion, Danville, IL 61832.

In a large bowl, combine

1 cup Crow's Hi-lysine Corn Meal
2 teaspoons salt
¼ cup sugar
¼ cup margarine
1 ½ cups scalded milk

Stir to dissolve sugar and margarine. Let cool until just warm. Meanwhile, to soften yeast, in another container combine

½ cup warm water
2 scant tablespoons (or 2 packets) active dry yeast
½ teaspoon sugar

When cornmeal mixture has cooled down to warm, stir in

softened yeast mixture
3 eggs, beaten
2 cups unbleached all-purpose flour or bread flour

Beat well. Let stand 15 minutes. To make a stiff dough, gradually add

3 ½ to 4 ½ cups unbleached all-purpose flour or bread flour

Turn out on a floured surface and knead until smooth and elastic. Place in a greased bowl, turning dough once to grease the top. Cover and let rise until doubled in bulk, 45 to 60 minutes. Turn out on a lightly floured surface and knead briefly. Divide into three parts. Shape into oblong loaves and place in well-greased 8½ × 4½ × 2½-inch baking pans. Cover and let rise until almost doubled, 30 to 45 minutes. Bake in 350°F oven for 35 to 40 minutes. Cool on wire racks. Makes 3 loaves.

❖ American Rye Bread

FROM KENYON CORN MEAL COMPANY

Kenyon's Rye Meal gives this loaf a nice texture.

Stir together and set aside

4 cups Kenyon's Rye Meal
2 cups unbleached all-purpose flour or bread flour

In a mixing bowl, combine

1 cup scalded milk
4 tablespoons molasses
2 tablespoons shortening
2 teaspoons salt

Stir to dissolve molasses, shortening, and salt. Let cool until just warm. Meanwhile, to soften yeast, in a small container combine

¼ cup warm water
1 scant tablespoon (or 1 packet) active dry yeast

When milk mixture has cooled down to warm, stir in

1 tablespoon caraway seed (optional)
softened yeast mixture
¾ cup warm water
3 cups flour mixture

Beat well. To make a stiff dough, gradually add

2 to 3 cups flour mixture

Turn out on a floured surface and knead until smooth. Place in a well-greased bowl, turning dough once to grease the top. Cover and let rise until doubled in bulk, 1 to 1½ hours. Divide dough in half and shape into long loaves. Place on a well-greased baking sheet that has been sprinkled with cornmeal. Cover and let rise until almost doubled, about 1 hour. Before baking, brush tops of loaves with a mixture of

1 egg white
1 tablespoon water

With a sharp knife, cut three diagonal slashes down the top of each loaf. Bake at 375°F for 40 to 45 minutes. Cool on wire racks. Makes 2 loaves.

❋ Corn Crisps

FROM KENYON CORN MEAL COMPANY

These easy-to-make corn crackers are good plain or with your favorite dip.

In a medium-sized bowl, stir together

1 cup Kenyon's Stone-ground Corn Meal
½ teaspoon salt
1 tablespoon oil
⅞ cup boiling water

Make small balls of this mixture, using 1 tablespoonful of dough for each. Place on a well-greased baking sheet. With moistened fingers, press out to 3-inch rounds. Bake in 400°F oven for 15 to 20 minutes, or until well-browned. Makes 24 crisps.

❖ Graham Nut Bread

FROM KENYON CORN MEAL COMPANY

This large loaf of quick bread slices well for sandwiches.

Preheat oven to 325°F. Butter a 9×5-inch baking pan. In a large bowl, stir together until well mixed

> 2 cups Kenyon's Graham Flour
> 1 cup unbleached all-purpose flour
> 1 cup sugar
> ½ teaspoon salt
> 1 tablespoon baking powder
> 1 cup chopped nuts

In another container, beat together

> 1 egg
> 1 ½ cups milk

Add milk mixture all at once to dry ingredients, stirring just until dry ingredients are moistened. Spoon into prepared pan. Bake at 325°F for 1 hour, or until a wooden pick inserted in the center comes out clean. Cool in pan 5 minutes. Turn out on a wire rack to cool completely. Makes 1 loaf.

❖ Graham Yeast Bread

FROM KENYON CORN MEAL COMPANY

The Graham flour from Kenyon is stone-ground whole-wheat flour sifted to remove some of the larger particles of bran.

In a large bowl, combine

> 1 cup scalded milk
> 5 tablespoons brown sugar
> 2 teaspoons salt

Stir to dissolve brown sugar and salt. Let cool until just warm. Meanwhile, to soften yeast, in another container combine

1 cup warm water
1 scant tablespoon (or 1 packet) active dry yeast

When milk mixture has cooled down to warm, stir in

softened yeast mixture
1 cup unbleached all-purpose flour or bread flour
2 cups Kenyon's Graham Flour

Beat well. Stir in

3 tablespoons melted shortening, cooled slightly

To make a soft dough, gradually add

2 to 3 cups Kenyon's Graham Flour

Turn out on a floured surface and knead until smooth. Place in a well-greased bowl, turning dough once to grease the top. Cover and let rise until doubled in bulk, 1 to 1½ hours. Punch dough down in bowl and let rise again until three-fourths as high as before, about 45 minutes. Knead dough down in bowl. Divide dough in half and shape each half into a ball. Cover and let rest 10 minutes. Shape into loaves and place in well-greased 9 × 5-inch baking pans. Cover and let rise until doubled in bulk, 30 to 45 minutes. Bake in 400°F oven for 35 to 40 minutes. Turn out on racks to cool. Makes 2 loaves.

❖ English Muffin Bread

FROM SASSAFRAS ENTERPRISES*

I have often looked at my bread crocks from Sassafras on the kitchen shelf and thought they would be great pots to bake English Muffin Bread in. But I never got around to figuring out the ratio of ingredients. Then I found a recipe from Sassafras that did all the work for me. The resulting loaves are perfect for slicing into English muffin rounds.

To soften yeast, in a large bowl combine

1 1/2 cups warm milk
1 scant tablespoon (or 1 packet) active dry yeast
1 tablespoon sugar

Allow yeast to proof. Stir in

2 cups unbleached all-purpose flour
1 teaspoon salt
2 tablespoons soft butter

Beat until smooth. To make a stiff batter, stir in

1 3/4 to 2 cups unbleached all-purpose flour

Cover and let rise until doubled in size, about 1½ hours. In a small container, combine

1/4 teaspoon baking soda
1 tablespoon warm water

Stir to dissolve baking soda. Stir down the batter and stir in the dissolved baking soda, mixing until well blended. Divide batter and fill two baking crocks that have been generously buttered and coated with about 2 teaspoons cornmeal. Sprinkle tops of batter with additional cornmeal. Cover and let rise until dough reaches tops of crocks, about 30 minutes. Bake on lower shelf in a preheated 350°F oven for 30 to 35 minutes, or until light golden brown. Remove from crocks and, if desired, return to oven for a few minutes to give loaves additional color. Let loaves cool on a rack. Makes 2 loaves.

❖ Molasses-Walnut Muffins

FROM SUN-DIAMOND GROWERS OF CALIFORNIA*

Rich with molasses, these muffins offer a nice flavor change for breakfast.

Preheat oven to 375°F. Grease a 12-cup muffin pan. Sift before measuring

> 2 cups unbleached all-purpose flour

Resift with

> 3 ½ teaspoons baking powder
> 1 teaspoon salt

In a mixing bowl, cream together

> ¼ cup shortening
> ½ cup molasses

Beat in

> 1 egg

Add

> sifted dry ingredients
> ½ cup milk

Stir to a soft batter. Lightly mix in

> ¾ cup chopped Diamond Walnuts
> ½ cup snipped Sunsweet Prunes

Spoon into prepared muffin cups. Bake at 375°F for 15 to 20 minutes, just until browned. Serve hot. Makes 12 muffins.

---

*From *Diamond Walnut Recipe Favorites,* used with permission of the Sun-Diamond Growers of California.

✣ Raisin-Coconut Banana Bread

FROM SUN-DIAMOND GROWERS OF CALIFORNIA*

This bread's tropical taste derives from the combination of banana, coconut, golden raisins, and nuts.

Grease an 8½ × 4½ × 2½-inch baking pan. Preheat oven to 350°F. In a large bowl, mix together

> 1 ½ cups all-purpose flour, sifted before measuring
> ½ cup sugar
> 2 teaspoons baking powder
> ½ teaspoon baking soda
> ½ teaspoon salt
> ½ cup Sun-Maid Seedless Golden Raisins
> ½ cup chopped walnuts
> ½ cup shredded coconut

In a small container, beat

> 2 eggs

Stir into the eggs

> 1 cup mashed, very ripe banana
> ¼ cup oil

Add the liquid ingredients to the flour mixture, stirring just until the flour is moistened. Pour the batter into the prepared pan. Bake at 350°F for 50 to 55 minutes or until a pick inserted in the center comes out clean. Let stand on a wire rack 10 minutes before removing from the pan to cool completely on the rack. Makes 1 loaf.

---

*From *The Sun-Maid Cookbook,* © 1980, Sun-Maid Growers of California and the Benjamin Company, Inc. Used with permission of the Sun-Diamond Growers.

❋ Rugelach

FROM SUN-DIAMOND GROWERS OF CALIFORNIA*

"Miniature Danish rolls" describes these flaky little swirls perfectly. Serve them warm with coffee.

In a mixing bowl, mix together

> *1 cup butter or margarine, softened*
> *1 package (8 ounces) cream cheese, at room temperature*

Stir together and add to cheese mixture

> *2 cups all-purpose flour*
> *⅛ teaspoon salt*

Knead by hand or beat until well mixed and smooth. Divide dough in half. Wrap each half separately and refrigerate until dough is well chilled, several hours or overnight. Combine and set aside

> *⅔ cup chopped Sun-Maid Zante Currants or Sun-Maid Puffed Seeded Muscat*
>   *Raisins*
> *½ cup chopped walnuts*
> *½ teaspoon cinnamon*
> *2 tablespoons sugar*

On a lightly floured board, roll each dough half into a 12×8-inch rectangle. Sprinkle each rectangle with half of the currant mixture to within about ¼ inch of the edges. Preheat oven to 350°F. Starting with the 12-inch side, roll dough into a long tube. Moisten the edge with water and pinch seam lightly to hold in place. Cut into 1-inch-thick slices and place on a lightly greased baking sheet. Bake for 18 to 20 minutes, or until pastry is very lightly browned. Remove from pan and cool slightly on wire rack. Makes 24 rolls.

---

*From *The Sun-Maid Cookbook,* © 1980, Sun-Maid Growers of California and the Benjamin Company, Inc. Used with permission of the Sun-Diamond Growers.

✻ Barley Biscuits

FROM WALNUT ACRES

Paul Keene, one of the founders of Walnut Acres, sent me numerous recipes using the flours packaged at his Pennsylvania plant. What a wonderful way to explore the world of whole-grain baking! After experimenting, I selected three to share with you here.

Sift together into a bowl

> *1 cup Walnut Acres Barley Flour*
> *½ teaspoon salt*
> *2 teaspoons baking powder*

In a small container, beat together

> *1 egg*
> *2 tablespoons oil*
> *½ cup milk*

Add the milk mixture to the dry ingredients and mix lightly. Dough should be soft, but thick enough to hold its shape. If needed, add a little additional barley flour. Drop by spoonfuls onto a lightly greased baking sheet. Bake in a preheated 375°F oven for 12 to 15 minutes. Makes 10 biscuits.

✻ Corn-Flour Pancakes

FROM WALNUT ACRES

These cakes, made with 100 percent corn flour, have a smooth, mellow corn taste. Serve them hot with maple syrup, or cold as a knapsack snack at hiking time.

Sift together into a bowl

> *1 cup Walnut Acres Corn Flour*
> *1 ½ teaspoons baking powder*
> *½ teaspoon salt*

In a small container, beat together

1 egg
1 teaspoon honey
1 ½ tablespoons oil
⅔ cup buttermilk

Add the buttermilk mixture to the dry ingredients and stir until smooth. Let stand a minute or two. If needed, thin with a little buttermilk. Fry on a hot, oiled pancake griddle. Turn once. Makes 8 pancakes.

❖ 12-Grain Bread

FROM WALNUT ACRES

The flour used for this bread contains whole wheat, rye, corn, brown rice, buckwheat, soy, oats, barley, millet, sunflower seed, sesame seed, and flaxseed. Notice the unique method for softening the yeast.

In the bottom of a dry bowl, place

1 level tablespoon (about 1 packet) active dry yeast

In a small container, stir together

1 ⅓ cups warm water
2 tablespoons blackstrap molasses

Pour the sweetened water over the yeast. Do not stir. Set aside to foam, about 10 minutes. Stir into softened yeast mixture

1 ½ teaspoons salt
2 tablespoons oil
1 cup Walnut Acres 12-Grain Flour

Beat for 150 strokes. To make a soft dough, gradually add

2 ½ to 3 cups Walnut Acres 12-Grain Flour

Turn out on a floured board and knead for a full 7 minutes. Place in an oiled bowl, oiling the top of the dough. Cover with a damp cloth and let rise until doubled. Punch dough down and shape into a loaf. Place in a well-greased 9×5-inch baking pan. Cover and let rise until almost doubled, 30 to 45 minutes. Bake in a 350°F oven for 45 to 50 minutes. Remove from pan and cool on a wire rack. Makes 1 loaf.

❖ Corn Dodgers

FROM WAR EAGLE MILL*

Zoe Medlin, author of The War Eagle Mill Wholegrain Cookbook, *says, "If you don't want to heat your oven or build a fire in the cookstove, try these for on-top-of-the-stove cornbread. The pioneers cooked them next to the fireplace on a griddle placed at an angle."*

In a bowl, stir together

> *1 ½ cups War Eagle Corn Meal*
> *½ cup whole-wheat flour or unbleached all-purpose flour*
> *2 teaspoons baking powder*
> *1 teaspoon salt*

In a small container, mix

> *1 egg*
> *1 cup milk*
> *1 tablespoon honey*

Add liquid ingredients to dry and mix. Grease a frying pan or griddle with oil or bacon fat. Over moderate heat, drop mixture by tablespoonfuls onto griddle and fry until brown, turning once. Split and serve with lots of butter. Makes about 24 corn dodgers.

---

*From *The War Eagle Mill Wholegrain Cookbook,* © 1976, by Zoe Medlin, used with permission of Zoe Medlin Caywood.

❋ When There Is Leftover Bread

Bread crumbs, croutons, melba, and a few selected recipes for cooking with leftover breads

❈ WHEN THERE IS LEFTOVER BREAD

Some bakers are completely organized. As soon as their bread cools, they wrap it, storing any extra loaves in the freezer. They never have leftovers. I am not among the very organized. I am likely to leave leftover bread in the bread bowl while I bake something new. Thus, I am never without. I think if I were, I would bake some just to fill the void.

❈ TO MAKE BREAD CRUMBS

There are many easy ways to make bread crumbs.

1. Place chunks of bread into the workbowl of a food processor fitted with the metal blade. Run briefly until the bread is reduced to the size crumb you desire.

2. Use a blender to do the same job.

3. Rub pieces of bread through a coarse sieve.

4. Rub pieces of bread through a hand-held grater.

5. Crumble coarse bread with your fingers.

6. Dry bread slices until crisp in a 300°F oven, and roll on a board with a rolling pin.

Bread crumbs can be used fresh, or spread on a dry baking sheet and dried in a 200°F oven for 10 to 15 minutes. Raise the temperature to 300°F or 350°F if you wish to toast your crumbs. Stir them a couple of times while baking, so that they will toast evenly. The time varies with the bread used. Cool completely before storing. Any excess crumbs are best stored in a jar in the freezer. Crumbs made from homemade bread will not keep well at room temperature or in the refrigerator.

Some Suggestions for Using Bread Crumbs

1. *For fancy vegetables:* Sauté a small quantity of bread crumbs in butter, with or without finely chopped herbs. It will take about 1 tablespoon butter for each ¼ cup of crumbs. Use to garnish steamed vegetables.

2. *For au gratin dishes:* Mix plain or toasted crumbs with grated cheese to top casseroles before baking. Dot with butter, if desired.

3. *For baked meats:* Dip cutlets of chicken or veal first in melted butter, then in seasoned bread crumbs. Bake in a 350°F oven until the juices run clear when meat is pierced with a fork. For a variation of this, cut meat into bite-sized pieces. After dipping the pieces into melted butter, quickly sauté them over medium-high heat, transferring the sautéed pieces to a baking dish. Then stir some bread crumbs into the butter remaining in the pan, adding seasonings as you stir the crumbs. Spoon the crumbs over the meat and place the dish in a 350°F oven to finish cooking through while you assemble the rest of the meal. Cooked this way, the meat is very succulent.

4. *For a tasty bread:* Use a plain bread dough after the first rising, enough for one 9×5-inch loaf. Roll out to a 6×9-inch rectangle. Cover with a layer of seasoned sautéed bread crumbs, about ¾ cup crumbs before sautéeing. Roll as for jelly roll. Place in a well-greased 9×5-inch loaf pan, seam side down, and let rise until almost doubled. Bake at 375°F for 35 to 40 minutes, or until well-browned.

5. *For fantastic rolls:* Use a plain bread dough after the first rising. Roll small balls of the dough first in melted butter, then in plain or seasoned bread crumbs. Place on a baking sheet and let rise until almost doubled. Bake at 400°F for 20 to 25 minutes, or until golden brown.

❖ Croutons

Croutons can be made plain, buttered, or seasoned. Use them to top salads and soups just before serving. Mix them with chopped onions and moisten them with milk or broth to provide a quick stuffing for fowl or meat.

Remove the crust from a loaf of bread. Cut ½-inch slices into ½-inch cubes. You can also slice the bread and cut it into various shapes with miniature cookie cutters.

For plain croutons: Bake the cut pieces of bread on a dry baking sheet at 300°F for about 10 minutes, or until dry and crisp.

For buttered croutons: Melt ¼ cup butter in a heavy skillet. Toss ¾ cup cubed bread in this, stirring to coat all sides. Spread on a baking sheet and bake at 300°F for about 10 minutes, or until crisp and browned.

For seasoned croutons: Sauté 2 pressed garlic cloves in a mixture of 2 tablespoons butter and 2 tablespoons olive oil just until they become translucent. If you wish, add some finely chopped herbs. Add ¾ cup cubed bread. Toss to coat, spread on a baking sheet, and bake at 300°F for about 10 minutes, or until crisp and browned.

For sautéed croutons: Prepare croutons as for buttered or seasoned croutons, but do not bake. Instead, toss them in the skillet over medium-high heat until toasty brown on all sides.

❖ Melba Toast

You can make melba toast from a variety of breads. A cheese bread makes particularly tasty toast. If I plan ahead to make melba, I bake bread in a baguette shape. I usually leave the crusts on, but you can trim them if you prefer. Melba toast is a perfect base for canapes.

Slice bread as thin as possible, ⅛ inch or slightly less. If your bread is difficult to handle, try freezing it first just until it begins to firm, but not until it is frozen solid. Spread cut slices on a dry baking sheet. Bake in a 250°F oven for 10 minutes. Turn slices over. Bake an additional 10 minutes, or until crisp and dry. Turn off the oven, leave the door ajar, and cool the toast in the oven to dry completely. Cool completely before storing. Store in Ziploc bags or in an airtight cookie jar.

❋ Cold Corn-Bread Soup

If you like to eat Sunday dinner in the middle of the afternoon, you probably have no room left for supper. Cold Corn-Bread Soup, made from that dinner's leftover corn bread, might be all you'll want.

Use a water tumbler to prepare your soup. Break enough corn bread into the glass to fill it two-thirds. Pour enough buttermilk or sweet milk over the corn bread to fill the glass. Eat with a spoon. Very simple. Very satisfying.

❋ Milk Toast

Milk Toast is too often reserved only for the invalid. There is no reason why it cannot be eaten by hardy, healthy individuals.

Toast two slices of white or light whole-wheat bread. Spread them generously with sweet creamery butter. Break them in coarse chunks into a flat soup bowl. Pour over them milk which has been heated to just below the scalding point. Dust the top of the dish with either salt and pepper *or* sugar *or* cinnamon-sugar. A grating of fresh nutmeg is good on any variation. Very nutritious and filling.

❋ Mabell's Fried-Egg Sandwiches

When I was growing up, a fried-egg sandwich always meant a fried egg between 2 slices of buttered bread. The first time I visited my husband's hometown, his mother made her favorite fried-egg sandwiches for lunch. Now they are also mine.

Trim the crust from a slice of homemade bread. Feed the crust to the birds or save for crumbs. Spread both sides of the bread with soft butter. Use a small biscuit cutter or a juice glass to cut a circle about the size of an egg yolk out of the center of the piece of bread. In a skillet over medium heat sauté the slice of bread and the cut-out round until browned on one side. Turn both over. Break an egg over the hole, letting the white of the egg spread out over the browned top of the bread. After cooking long enough to brown the bottom of the bread, turn it again to cook for a short time longer. The egg yolk may be broken or left whole, according to your preference. Salt and pepper to taste. Serve at once on a warm plate with the round of bread to the side. It can be used to soak up any soft egg yolk left on the plate when the sandwich is gone.

❖ Bread Tarts

Bread Tarts are a simple, easily prepared dessert. Good for the fresh fruit season.

Cut the crusts from slices of homemade bread. Thinly butter both sides of the bread with soft butter and lay the slices out on baking sheets. Sprinkle with cinnamon-sugar. Arrange overlapping thin slices of peeled fresh fruit on the slices of bread. Plums, peaches, nectarines, and pears are best for this tart. The fruits may be assorted or all the same. Sprinkle the fruit with more cinnamon-sugar. Dot the top of it all with small slivers of butter. Bake in a preheated 400°F oven for 20 to 25 minutes, or until lightly browned. Serve plain or with a spoonful of good vanilla ice cream.

❖ Cinnamon Toast

You can sprinkle cinnamon-sugar over buttered toast and be done with it, but this is much better.

Brush the tops of bread slices with melted butter. Sprinkle liberally with cinnamon-sugar. If desired, dash a few drops of Meyers's dark rum over the top and grate some fresh nutmeg over all. Bake in a preheated 400°F oven for 8 to 10 minutes, or until lightly browned. Serve with steaming bowls of old-fashioned oatmeal.

✨ Orange Toast

This is a little more complicated, but worth mentioning. In case you were beginning to wonder, I really don't own stock in the Meyers's rum company.

Combine

    ¼ cup orange juice
    ¼ cup melted butter
    ¼ cup sugar
    1 tablespoon Meyers's rum

Cut the crusts from slices of homemade bread. Cut the slices into strips about 1½ inches wide. Quickly dip them into the orange juice mixture and lay them out on buttered baking sheets. Bake in a preheated 400°F oven for 5 to 7 minutes, or until toasted lightly. Serve with bowls of hot chunky tomato soup.

✨ Open-Faced Cheese Sandwich

My favorite way to make this combines sharp well-aged cheddar with sweet marmalade.

Simply cover a slice of any white bread with a slice of very sharp cheddar cheese. In the center of the cheese, place 1 tablespoon Three-Fruit Marmalade, or a marmalade of your choice. Bake in a 350°F oven until the cheese is melted. The marmalade will melt to cover the top of the cheese. Eat with knife and fork, accompanied by a cold glass of milk.

✨ Bread-Crumb Griddlecakes

In a mixing bowl, soak together for about 30 minutes

    1 cup soft bread crumbs
    1 cup buttermilk

Stir into bread-milk mixture

1 tablespoon sugar
2 tablespoons melted butter
2 eggs

Sift together and add, stirring just until dry ingredients are moistened

½ cup unbleached all-purpose flour
½ teaspoon baking soda
⅛ teaspoon salt

If the batter is too thick to pour, thin it with a small quantity of buttermilk. Bake on a lightly greased griddle at 375°F, turning only once. Serve with butter and warm maple syrup. Makes 8 cakes.

❖ Bread-Crumb Muffins

I like to use whole-grain bread to make the crumbs for these.

Preheat oven to 375°F. Grease a 12-cup muffin pan. In a mixing bowl, soak together for about 30 minutes

1 ¼ cups soft bread crumbs
1 cup milk

Mix together

½ cup brown sugar
½ teaspoon cinnamon
¼ teaspoon nutmeg

Remove ¼ cup brown sugar-spice mixture and reserve for topping. Stir into soaked crumbs

2 eggs
remaining brown sugar-spice mixture
¼ cup melted butter

Sift together and stir into crumb mixture, just until dry ingredients are moistened

> *1 1/4 cups unbleached all-purpose flour*
> *1/4 teaspoon salt*
> *2 teaspoons baking powder*

Spoon into prepared muffin cups. Sprinkle the top of each muffin with

> *1 teaspoon reserved brown sugar-spice mixture*

Bake in preheated 375°F oven for 20 to 25 minutes, or until nicely browned. Serve warm. Makes 12 muffins.

❖ Dutch Cottage Cobbler

> *My Uncle Durb liked to make Dutch Cottage Cobbler for breakfast. When he was in a hurry he would simply toast a piece of bread, butter both sides of the hot toast, tear it into his bowl, and pour the sauce over it. It was delicious!*

Cut into strips and sauté on all sides until golden brown

> *4 thick slices any white bread, crust removed*

in

> *6 tablespoons butter*

Arrange sautéed bread in four sauce dishes and pour warm fruit sauce over bread. Thick cream can be added at the table. Makes 4 servings.

Fruit Sauce

Drain, reserving juice

> *1 quart home-canned fruit**

To each cup of reserved juice, stir in

> *1 1/2 teaspoons cornstarch*

---

*If you have no home-canned fruit, you may substitute commercially canned fruits.

Return drained fruit to juice. Heat over medium heat, stirring constantly, until the sauce is thickened. Sweeten to taste. The amount of sugar needed to sweeten the sauce varies with the fruits used and the syrup in which they were canned.

❖ Brioche Bread Pudding

Bread pudding is a comforting dessert of English origin. It is also one of the best ways to use up day-old bread. This version lends an elegance to an otherwise homey dish. Use a casserole that will look pretty making the trip from oven to table. In this pudding, as in my other desserts of this type, I like to use my own homemade vanilla extract.

Preheat oven to 325°F. Butter a 2-quart casserole. In a mixing bowl, toss together

> 1 cup dried currants
> 2 tablespoons Meyers's Dark Rum

Toss again with

> 5 cups loosely packed day-old brioche bread cubes

Transfer to buttered dish. Using the same bowl, with a wire whisk beat

> 3 eggs

Beat into eggs

> 3 cups milk
> ⅓ cup sugar
> ¼ teaspoon salt
> 1 ½ teaspoons vanilla extract, preferably homemade
> ⅓ cup orange marmalade

Pour milk mixture over bread cubes and currants. Place casserole in a large, flat pan. Place on oven rack. Add almost-boiling water to pan to reach halfway up side of casserole. Bake at 325°F for 1¼ hours, or until knife inserted near the center comes out clean. Serve warm with Rum Sauce. Makes 8 servings.

Rum Sauce

In a heavy saucepan, combine

½ cup butter
1 cup brown sugar
⅓ cup Meyers's Dark Rum

Heat to boiling, stirring all the while. Remove from heat. Stir in

¼ teaspoon freshly grated nutmeg

Serve warm. Makes 1 cup.

✷ Homemade Vanilla Extract

If you want to lighten the extract, use vodka instead of bourbon. If you like it heavier, use brandy.

In a 1-cup jar with a porcelain or white-coated lid, place

2 vanilla beans, split

Fill the jar with

bourbon

Cover with the lid and let stand for at least 2 weeks before use. As you use the extract the bourbon can be replenished until the beans are exhausted. Then start over.

✷ Brioche Custard Casserole

This gold-toned casserole makes a delightful supper when served with a mixed salad of greens and citrus fruits dressed with a basil vinaigrette. A glass of chilled blush wine rounds out the service quite nicely.

Preheat oven to 350°F. Butter a 2-quart casserole (I use a flat one that is about 10 inches square). In the bottom of the casserole, place

4 cups day-old brioche bread cubes

Scatter over the bread

½ cup finely diced baked ham
1 cup (4 ounces) shredded sharp cheddar cheese

Mix together and pour over cheese

2 eggs
1 cup light cream or half and half
½ teaspoon salt
¼ teaspoon paprika
¼ teaspoon dry mustard
dash freshly ground pepper
1 tablespoon finely chopped chives

Bake at 350°F for 30 to 35 minutes, or until set in the center. Serve at once. Makes 4 servings.

❖ Creole Brandied Bread Pudding

One taste of this delectable pudding will make you think you are in the French Quarter of old New Orleans, dining in a secluded courtyard. I like to bake it in a rectangular glass lasagna dish to insure that each serving has a browned top.

The day before baking, in a small bowl combine

1 cup raisins
2 tablespoons brandy

On baking day, in a buttered 3-quart casserole place

4 cups bread cubes

Scatter the brandied raisins over the bread cubes. In a large-sized mixing bowl, beat

5 eggs

Beat into eggs in this order

1 cup brown sugar
1 teaspoon cinnamon
½ teaspoon nutmeg
¼ cup melted butter

Slowly stir into the egg mixture

5 cups hot milk

Pour milk mixture over the bread cubes and raisins. Let stand 10 minutes. Place casserole in a shallow pan filled with enough water to reach up the side of the dish to a depth of 1 inch. Bake in a preheated 350°F oven for 1 hour, or until custard is set. Serve warm with Brandy Sauce. Makes 12 servings.

Brandy Sauce

In a heavy saucepan, beat

2 eggs

In a small container, mix together

1 cup sugar
2 tablespoons cornstarch

Stir sugar mixture into eggs. Add slowly, stirring constantly

2 cups hot milk

Heat over low heat, stirring constantly, until thick. Remove from heat and stir in

½ cup brandy

Serve at once.

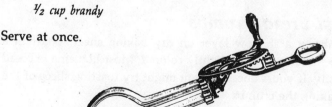

❖ Apple Brown Betty

This old-fashioned recipe is as American as apple pie, but easier to make, because it uses toasted bread crumbs instead of a crust.

Preheat oven to 350°F. Butter a 9×12-inch baking dish. Spread over bottom of baking dish

> *1 cup toasted bread crumbs*

Layer over bread crumbs

> *8 cups (about 4 pounds) peeled, cored, and thinly sliced baking apples, such as Mutsu or Granny Smith*

Mix together and sprinkle over the apples

> *2 tablespoons Meyers's Dark Rum*
> *2 tablespoons water*

Mix together and sprinkle over the apple mixture

> *1 cup brown sugar*
> *1 teaspoon cinnamon*
> *1 teaspoon nutmeg*

Mix together and spread over the top of the sugar mixture

> *6 tablespoons melted butter*
> *1 ½ cups toasted bread crumbs*

Bake at 350°F for 35 minutes, or until top is well-browned. Serve warm with a dollop of vanilla ice cream. Makes 12 servings.

To Toast Bread Crumbs

Lay bread crumbs in a shallow layer on dry baking sheet. Toast in a 350°F oven for 5 minutes, or until lightly colored. Most homemade bread will crumble easily. If yours does not, you might try toasting slices of the bread before making the crumbs.

✣ Bread-Crumb Kisses

This recipe was born as much from a need to use extra egg whites as it was from a desire to whittle down a backlog of bread.

Preheat oven to 300°F. Grease and have ready two baking sheets. In a large bowl, beat until frothy

   3 egg whites

Add to the beaten whites

   ¼ teaspoon vanilla extract
   ¼ teaspoon cream of tartar

Beat while gradually adding

   1 cup sugar

When the egg-white mixture is quite stiff, fold in gently

   ½ cup toasted bread crumbs
   1 cup semi-sweet chocolate morsels

Drop by slightly rounded teaspoonfuls onto a prepared baking sheet. Bake about 20 minutes at 300°F. Cool on wire racks. Makes 72 kisses.

✣ Jeanette's French Toast for Any Number

Jeanette Groves and I share a love for good food served without a lot of fuss. Here, she shares her recipe for French toast. It is a speciality she likes to serve for Sunday brunch when entertaining weekend guests at her "fishing cabin" in the Michigan woods.

   The recipe makes enough toast for two persons. Multiply for as many as you wish to feed.

Use a wire whisk to beat this batter. In a medium-sized bowl, beat together

   ¼ cup milk
   2 tablespoons unbleached all-purpose flour

Add and beat in, in this order

> *2 eggs*
> *1 tablespoon Meyers's Dark Rum*
> *1 teaspoon orange juice (optional)*

Dust top of the batter with

> *about ⅛ teaspoon cinnamon sugar*

Stir this in. Slice homemade bread, sourdough preferred, into ½-inch slices. If loaf is large, cut slices in half. Soak several pieces in the batter while the oil is heating in the pan. Pour ¼ inch oil in a heavy cast-iron pan and heat over medium-high heat. When oil is hot, transfer soaked bread to pan. Cook quickly, turning once, until browned on both sides. Transfer cooked pieces to heated platter and place in preheated 275°F oven. This will keep the toast warm while the rest cooks, and will cook any soft egg that remains. Repeat cooking with remaining toast slices. The toast can be kept in the oven for up to 10 minutes. Serve with sweet creamery butter, warmed maple syrup, and thick country bacon. Makes 2 generous servings.

❖ Embellishments

*Jams, jellies, syrups, and glazes to make
your breads sing*

EGG GLAZES

WASHES

SWEET GLAZES

HONEY BUTTER

WHIPPED HONEY BUTTER

MAPLE BUTTER

HOMEMADE MAPLE SYRUP

BLUEBERRY SYRUP

PEANUT-BUTTER SYRUP

LEMON CHEESE

GARLIC BUTTER

MUSTARD BUTTER

FRESH HERB BUTTER

MUSTARD MAYONNAISE

PESTO MAYONNAISE

BARBECUED BREAD SPREAD

VERY BERRY JAM

FREEZER-FRESH STRAWBERRY JAM

APRICOT-PINEAPPLE MARMALADE

CONCORD GRAPE JAM

TART CHERRY JAM

HERBAL LEMON JELLY

RHUBARB PRESERVES

THREE-FRUIT MARMALADE

APPLE BUTTER

PEAR BUTTER

❖ EMBELLISHMENTS

Homemade bread is so very good, how could it possibly be better? By glazing it, of course. The simple act of brushing an egg glaze over a loaf before it is introduced to the oven makes it shine with pride. Sweet glazes applied to cooling sweet buns render them irresistible. Freshly made syrups help whet your appetite for pancakes and waffles. Both sweet and savory butters enhance the flavor of your loaves. These descriptions are intended to make you hungry enough to turn the page.

Egg Glazes

For a shiny brown crust mix together and brush on the loaf before baking

> *1 egg*
> *1 tablespoon water or milk*

For a shiny crust that is not quite as dark mix together and brush on the loaf before baking

> *1 egg white*
> *1 teaspoon to 1 tablespoon water*

For a shiny crust that is quite dark mix together and brush on the loaf before baking

> *1 egg yolk*
> *1 teaspoon water or milk*

A pinch of sugar or salt may be added to any of the Egg Glazes.

Washes

For a crisp crust brush water on the loaf before baking.

For a dark crisp crust mix together and brush on loaf before baking

> *1 teaspoon instant coffee or Postum*
> *1 tablespoon water*

For a smooth, shiny crust brush milk on the loaf before baking.

For a soft crust with a rich appearance brush melted butter on the loaf after baking.

Sweet Glazes

Sweet glazes, for drizzling or painting on bread or rolls as they cool, are made by mixing confectioner's sugar with flavorings and a small amount of liquid. Before measuring confectioner's sugar, stir it in a sieve held over a bowl. This will easily remove any lumps that might mar the smoothness of your glaze.

To make a simple confectioner's sugar glaze combine

> *1 cup sieved confectioner's sugar*
> *¼ teaspoon vanilla extract*
> *1 to 2 tablespoons hot milk*

This glaze can be made richer by adding

> *1 to 2 tablespoons melted butter*

To make a coffee-flavored glaze substitute hot coffee for the milk.

To make a lemon-flavored glaze combine

> *1 cup sieved confectioner's sugar*
> *1 to 3 tablespoons lemon juice*

This glaze can be made richer by adding

> *1 to 2 teaspoons grated lemon rind*
> *1 to 2 tablespoons melted butter*

The following butters and syrups provide a variety of toppings for waffles, pancakes, and French toast.

❖ Honey Butter

Cream together until well blended

½ cup soft butter
¼ to ½ cup honey

Chill to store.

❖ Whipped Honey Butter

Make honey butter, using ½ cup honey. After mixture is smooth, gradually beat in

½ cup whipping cream

Continue beating until soft and fluffy. A little grated orange or lemon rind can be added to this butter, if desired. This does not store well.

❖ Maple Butter

Beat until smooth

½ cup butter

Gradually beat into the butter

¼ to ½ cup pure maple syrup

Chill to store.

❖ Homemade Maple Syrup

My mother kept a small bottle of Mapleine flavoring right next to her bottle of vanilla extract. On the occasions when we were unexpectedly out of maple syrup, she would whip up a homemade version. It was always warm, because it was freshly made, and the small amount of butter she mixed into it made it nice and smooth.

In a heavy saucepan, heat until boiling

1 cup water

Stir into boiling water

1 ¾ cups sugar
¼ cup brown sugar

Reduce heat and simmer, stirring constantly, until the mixture loses its cloudy appearance. Remove from heat and stir in, in this order

½ teaspoon Mapleine or other maple flavoring
1 to 2 tablespoons butter

Serve warm.

❖ Blueberry Syrup

In a heavy saucepan, combine

2 cups blueberries
½ cup sugar
¼ cup water

Heat over medium heat, stirring frequently, until thickened, 5 to 10 minutes. Remove from heat and stir in

1 teaspoon lemon juice

Serve warm.

❖ Peanut-Butter Syrup

In a heavy saucepan, blend together

¼ cup peanut butter
¼ cup honey
2 tablespoons butter

Heat over medium heat, stirring constantly, until mixture is smooth. Serve warm. Refrigerated leftovers of this syrup are good for spreading on hot toast.

❖ Lemon Cheese

Lemon cheese, or lemon curd, a traditional English spread, is especially good on a plain muffin. This same mixture can be spooned into prebaked tart shells and topped with whipped cream for a satisfying dessert.

Using a stainless-steel whisk, in the top of a double boiler beat

> *4 eggs*

Whisking all the while, gradually add

> *¾ cup sugar*
> *grated peel of 2 lemons*
> *½ cup freshly squeezed lemon juice*

Place over simmering water and cook, stirring constantly, until mixture is quite hot. Add, ½ tablespoonful at a time, stirring after each addition until it is melted

> *6 tablespoons butter*

Continue to cook, stirring, until smooth. Remove from heat and pour into sterilized jars. Cool completely before covering. Chill to store. Makes 2 cups.

These savory butters are good brushed on breads, sandwiches, and grilled meats. They can also serve as a base for various canape toppings.

❖ Garlic Butter

Cream together until smooth

> *½ cup softened butter*
> *2 to 4 finely minced or pressed garlic cloves*

✵ Mustard Butter

Cream together until smooth

½ cup butter
1 tablespoon prepared mustard

You may add a dash of Worcestershire sauce or a dash of hot pepper sauce to this butter, if you wish.

✵ Fresh Herb Butter

In a small bowl, cream together

½ cup butter
1 tablespoon finely chopped chives
1 tablespoon finely chopped Italian parsley
1 to 2 tablespoons finely chopped herb of your choice, such as basil, oregano, summer savory, dill, or thyme

If you wish, you may add a dash of lemon juice or a small amount of grated lemon rind to this butter.

There are two mayonnaise mixtures that I like to use for sandwiches. A bowl of each with a selection of breads, cheeses, and sliced cold meats makes an easy smorgasbord.

✵ Mustard Mayonnaise

In a small container, mix together

1 cup mayonnaise
2 to 4 tablespoons mustard

❉ Pesto Mayonnaise

In a small container, mix together

> 1 cup mayonnaise
> ½ to 1 cup Pesto Sauce (see page 260)

I like to spread the following mixture on a loaf of French bread that has been split in half lengthwise. Slather the mixture thickly on the cut sides and wrap the two long pieces in crumpled foil, with their tops exposed. Then place them in a hot (400°F) oven until the cheese mixture melts and browns slightly. If the pieces do not brown as quickly as you would like, transfer them to the broiler unit for a short while to finish them off. The bread can be cut or pulled into serving pieces.

❉ Barbecued Bread Spread

Mix together until well blended

> ½ cup butter
> 1 cup shredded very sharp cheddar cheese
> ¼ cup mayonnaise
> 1 or more minced or pressed garlic cloves
> ½ teaspoon herb salt, or 1 to 2 tablespoons chopped fresh herbs

Jams and Jellies

My personal collection of jam and jelly recipes is not extensive, but it does contain a few I think are worthy of sharing with you here.

❉ Very Berry Jam

This works equally well with raspberries or blackberries. Throw in a few slightly underripe berries for added pectin. If all of your berries are ripe, you might chop the pulp from one small apple and add it to the pot. You won't notice the apple in the finished product.

In a large stainless-steel pot or enameled preserving kettle, combine

> *4 cups crushed garden berries*
> *4 cups sugar*
> *1 tablespoon fresh lemon juice*

Stir and cook over low heat until the sugar is dissolved. Raise heat and simmer, stirring from the bottom until the mixture thickens. Ladle into hot sterilized jars and seal. Process in a boiling water bath for 10 minutes. Fills four ½-pint jars.

❖ Freezer-Fresh Strawberry Jam

> *I have made strawberry jam many different ways over the years. This method produces the freshest-tasting, reddest jam of all . . . and it is the easiest.*

Wash and remove caps from

> *1 quart fresh garden strawberries*

Crush berries, one layer at a time, to measure 1¾ cups. If needed, add more berries. Place crushed berries in a large glass bowl. Add

> *4 cups sugar*

Stir thoroughly. Let stand 10 minutes. In a side bowl, combine

> *1 tablespoon lemon juice*
> *1 pouch liquid pectin (3 ounces)*

Stir lemon-juice mixture well. Now stir this into strawberry mixture and continue stirring for 3 minutes. Some sugar crystals may remain; that is okay. Ladle into sterilized 1- or 1½-cup jars with screw lids, leaving ½ inch space at the top. Cover at once with lids and seal. Let stand at room temperature for 24 hours. Place in freezer to store. To defrost for use, transfer to refrigerator. Makes a little more than 2 pints.

❖ Apricot-Pineapple Marmalade

This can be made any time during the year from items readily available on your grocer's shelf.

Cut into small pieces

2 6-ounce packages dried apricots

Place in a stainless-steel or enameled preserving kettle. Cover with

3 cups water

Let stand 8 hours. Add

3 cups sugar
1 20-ounce can crushed pineapple
grated rind of 1 lemon
juice of 1 lemon

Simmer over medium heat, stirring occasionally, until sugar dissolves. Raise heat and boil gently, stirring to prevent sticking, until mixture thickens. Ladle into hot sterilized jars and seal. Process 10 minutes in a boiling water bath. Fills six ½-pint jars.

❖ Concord Grape Jam

I think the only way to keep the skins intact in an old-fashioned grape jam is to make it yourself.

Slip the skins from washed, stemmed concord grapes. Set aside.

Simmer grape pulp until seeds begin to separate. Add water only if grapes are not juicy enough to prevent sticking. Force cooked pulp through a sieve and discard seeds.

Combine cooked pulp with reserved skins and measure. Add an equal amount of sugar. Cook at low heat until sugar dissolves, stirring to prevent sticking.

Cook at high heat, stirring often, just until mixture begins to sheet when dropped from a metal spoon.

Ladle into hot sterilized jars and seal. Process 10 minutes in a boiling water bath. Yield varies with the amount of grapes processed.

❖ Tart Cherry Jam

If I'm not careful, the birds in my backyard will clean the cherry tree before I harvest enough for this jam!

In a stainless-steel pot or enameled preserving kettle, combine

4 cups tart cherries, washed and pitted
3 cups sugar

Stir over low heat until sugar is dissolved. Increase heat and simmer, stirring from the bottom to prevent sticking, until mixture thickens. Ladle into hot sterilized jars and seal. Process in a boiling water bath for 10 minutes. Will fill about 4 ½-pint jars.

❖ Herbal Lemon Jelly

This is the only jelly I use to preserve the fresh flavor of herbs from the summer garden. There are other jams and jellies that marry well with herbs, but for the most part, I guess I like them plain. As my good friend and herbalist Rhoda Scott says, "We don't need to put herbs into everything!"

Squeeze the juice from

2 large lemons

Add enough water to the juice to make 3½ cups in all. Place in a large stockpot, preferably stainless steel, with

finely minced zest of 2 lemons
7 cups sugar

Bring to a boil over high heat, stirring all the while. Add

2 pouches liquid pectin (6 fluid ounces)

Boil 1 minute at a full rolling boil, stirring all the while. Remove from heat. Stir and skim the cooked jelly. Ladle into hot sterilized jars in which you have placed, per jar

1 sprig of washed fresh herb of your choice (my favorites are basil and thyme)

Seal with melted paraffin. Store in a cool, dark place. Fills 7 ½-pint jars.

❖ Rhubarb Preserves

This is so easy, it can be made any time there is a little "extra" rhubarb.

Place in stainless-steel or enameled preserving kettle

2 cups very thinly sliced fresh garden rhubarb
juice and grated rind of 1 lemon
1 tablespoon finely chopped crystallized ginger
½ cup water
4 cups sugar

Bring to a boil, stirring occasionally. Continue to boil, stirring frequently, until the rhubarb is translucent and the mixture has reached the jelling stage. It usually continues to boil along and then all of a sudden begins to boil more furiously. When that happens, remove it immediately from the heat and continue to stir. Otherwise it may burn. You can test the liquid with a candy thermometer, reaching 220°F. After removing from the heat, stir it a little and then ladle into hot, sterilized jars and seal. Process in a boiling water bath for 10 minutes. Fills 4 ½-pint jars.

❖ Three-Fruit Marmalade

Here is a marmalade recipe for fruits easily found at the market. The combination makes a nicely colored and flavored spread. It tops broiled English muffins beautifully.

Peel, taking with the peel a very thin layer of the white pith that lies
underneath

> 2 oranges
> 2 lemons
> 1 grapefruit

Cut the peel into very thin strips. You should have about 2 cups thinly
sliced peel. Place in a heavy stockpot, preferably stainless steel, with 2
quarts water. Heat mixture to boiling and boil for 5 minutes. Remove from
heat and let this mixture stand for 4 hours. Peel the remaining white pith
from the fruit and discard. Slice the fruit over a bowl, so as to catch all the
juice. Tear or cut the slices into small pieces, discarding any seeds and core
material. You should have a little more than 3 cups fruit and juice. Add
to the reserved cooked peel. Bring to a boil and boil gently for 30 minutes.
This is to cook the peel until tender. Add to the hot mixture

> 8 cups sugar

Process one-half of this fruit-sugar mixture at a time. Cook in the stockpot,
stirring over high heat until mixture reaches a temperature of 220°F. Use
a candy thermometer to determine the temperature. This is the jelling
point; do not overcook. The mixture may still appear to be liquid—It will
just begin to drop from a spoon more thickly than it did at the beginning.
The marmalade will jell more after it sits. Skim off foam and ladle into hot
sterilized jars, leaving ½-inch headspace. Seal. Process in a hot-water bath
for 10 minutes. Makes 4 pints.

❋ Apple Butter

*Some cooks use an exotic ingredient when a plain one is really better. For this recipe,
use plain old apple-cider vinegar. It gives just the right tang to the finished product.
Do not substitute anything more regal.*

In a heavy stockpot, preferably stainless steel, combine

> 1 quart apple cider
> 6 pounds tart cooking apples, cored and quartered, with blossom and stem ends
>   removed

Bring to boiling over high heat. Reduce heat and simmer, covered, stirring often, until apples are tender. This will take about 30 minutes. Force the mixture through a sieve or food mill. Return mixture to pot. Stir in

¼ *cup apple-cider vinegar*
4 *cups brown sugar*
1 *teaspoon cinnamon*
½ *teaspoon cloves*

Simmer uncovered, stirring often, until thick enough to spread on bread. This may take 2 hours. To test thickness, spoon some onto a china plate. If ready, the butter will hold its shape and will not weep a thin liquid around its edge. The mixture will also begin to mound on the spoon when drawn from the pot. Ladle hot apple butter into hot, sterilized jars, leaving ½ inch headroom. Seal. Process 10 minutes in a boiling water bath. Makes 6 pints.

❖ Pear Butter

Firm ripe or slightly underripe pears should be used for this. If you grow your own, you can cut firm pieces from windfalls to make up enough for a batch.

Wash and quarter

4 *pounds firm ripe pears*

Remove the stems and blossom ends from the quarters. You can also remove the seeds, if you wish. It doesn't matter. Place the fruit in a large stainless-steel pot or enameled preserving kettle with

1 *quart apricot nectar*

Bring to a boil. Reduce heat and cook, stirring occasionally, until fruit is tender. Force fruit through a food mill. Return to pot with

2 *cups sugar*
1 *teaspoon ginger*

Place over medium-low heat and cook, stirring often, until thickened. Ladle into hot, sterilized jars. Seal. Process in a boiling water bath for 10 minutes. Makes 4 pints.

❊ Access

*Sources for supplies and a bibliography of
bread*

❊ SOURCES FOR SUPPLIES

*This listing is alphabetical. These suppliers all give good service and are known for standing
behind their products.*

Arrowhead Mills
Mail Order: no
Retail: yes
110 S. Lawton
Hereford, TX 79045
(806) 364-0730

Grain, flour, seeds, nuts, cereals, granolas, unrefined oils, bread mixes, cookbooks.
Arrowhead Mills' products can be found in many health-food stores.

The Birkett Mills

Mail Order: yes
P. O. Box 440
Penn Yan, NY 14527
(315) 536-3311
Retail: yes
163 Main Street
Penn Yan, NY 14527

A full line of buckwheat products, including seeds for sprouting, groats, kasha, grits, and pancake mix. Also wheat in the form of bran, flour, wheat germ, pastry flour, and graham flour.
If you like buckwheat, write to these people.

Brookside Farm

Mail Order: yes
Tunbridge, VT 05077
Retail: no

Maple syrup.
Henry and Cornelia Swayze have several grades of syrup, including one they call cooking syrup. It is darker and stronger than the others and is recommended for cooking as well as topping for hearty buckwheat cakes.

Deer Valley Farm

Mail Order: yes
R.D. 1
Guilford, NY 13780
(607) 764-8556
Retail: yes
Same address

Extensive listing including flours, grains, seeds, leaveners, sweeteners, and seasonings.
The folks at Deer Valley are proud of being a New York State Certified Organic Farm.

Elam's

Mail Order: yes
2625 Gardner Road
Broadview, IL 60153
(312) 865-1612
Retail: yes
Same address

Flours, cereals, and bread mixes.
I usually use the stone-ground flours from Elam's in my own pantry mixtures of Wheat-Bread Flour and Bohemian Flour.

Great Grains Milling Co.

Mail Order: yes
P. O. Box 427
Scobey, MT 59263
(406) 783-5588
Retail: no

Stone-ground whole-wheat flour and golden wheat flour.
Both of these flours are excellent.

Great Valley Mills

Mail Order: yes
687 Mill Road
Telford, PA 18969
(215) 256-6648
Retail: yes
Same address

Extensive listing including flours, meals, cereal, mixes, sweeteners, cast-iron cookware, meats, and cheeses.
Susan and Steve Kantoor's bread flour (unbleached hard white) is absolutely amazing!

H. Roth & Son (also known as Lekvar by the barrel).

Mail Order: yes
1577 First Avenue, Box F
New York, NY 10028
(212) 734-1111
Retail: yes
1577 First Ave, corner of 82nd St.

Phone orders are handled 9:00 A.M. to 6:30 P.M. EST, Tuesday through Saturday. Laszlo Roth claims to have 6,000 items in his retail store, many more than are listed in the catalogue.

If you are looking for a special ingredient for an old-world recipe, check with H. Roth.

Jaffe Bros.

Mail Order: yes
P. O. Box 636
Valley Center, CA 92082-0636
(619) 749-1133
Retail: yes
28560 Lilac Road
Valley Center, CA 92082
(warehouse)

Flours, grains, seeds, unsulphured dried fruits, unsweetened coconut.
Six varieties of dates alone!

Kenyon Corn Meal Company, Inc.

Mail Order: yes
Glen Rock Road
Usquepaugh Village
West Kingston, RI 02892
(401) 783-4054
Retail: yes
Same address

Flours, meals, mixes, syrups, preserves, and jellies.
They give afternoon tours of the grist mill March 1 through December 24.

The Little Old Bread Man
Mail Order: yes
500 Independence Ave., S.E.
Washington, D. C. 20003
(202) 544-6858
Retail: no

Baguette pans, sourdough loaf pans, and large baking sheets.
I have used the Little Old Bread Man's pans for years. They can often be purchased at a gourmet cookshop.

Maid of Scandinavia
Mail Order: yes
3244 Raleigh Ave.
Minneapolis, MN 55416
Retail: yes

Six Minneapolis-area locations. Check the phone book when you get to town.
Extensive listing including pans, utensils, cookbooks.
The most extensive listing of baking pans and utensils that I know of.

Mari-Mann Herb Co.
Mail Order: yes
RR 4, P. O. Box 7
Decatur, IL 62521-9404
(217) 429-1404
Retail: yes

Gingerbread House
N. End of St. Louis Bridge Road
Decatur, IL 62521
and at
Vinegar Hill Mall
Springfield, IL
(217) 522-7444

Herbs, mixes, essential oils, potpourris, and jellies.
There are a lot of herbalists, but none could be more personable than Maribeth. If you can, visit the Gingerbread House in the summer and tour the herb gardens.

Paprikas Weiss Importer
Mail Order: yes
1546 Second Ave.
New York, NY 10028
(212) 288-6117
Retail: yes
Same address

Spices, meats, cheeses, cookbooks, various imported foods.
They are famous for their Hungarian paprika.

Sassafras Enterprises, Inc.
Mail Order: yes
East Bank Center
429 W. Ohio Street
Chicago, Illinois 60610
(312) 670-5000
Retail: yes
Same address. This is a warehouse. Call the office number to order
products and arrange for pickup at the warehouse.

Stonewear baking utensils, baking stones, tiles, bowls, cookbooks.
Sassafras has a toll-free number to call for product information, 1-800-537-4941.

Walnut Acres
Mail Order: yes
Penns Creek, PA 17862
(717) 837-0601
Retail: yes
Same address

Extensive listing including flours, grains, cereals, leaveners, sweeteners, dried
fruits, nut butters, juices, meats, and cheeses.
*Paul Keene, the cofounder of Walnut Acres, has long been in the front ranks of the organic farm
movement.*

War Eagle Mill
Mail Order: yes
Rt 5, Box 411
Rogers, AK 72756
Retail: yes
Same address. 13 miles east of Rogers, Arkansas, off Hwy 12 on Hwy 98.

Stone-ground flour and cornmeal.
The water-powered grist mill is open all year round. Tours are conducted and there is a gift shop on the premises.

Williams-Sonoma
Mail Order: yes
P. O. Box 7456
San Francisco, CA 94120-7456
(415) 652-9007
Retail: yes
Flagship store:
576 Sutter Street
San Francisco, CA 94102

There are also 27 retail outlets all over the United States.

Serving and cooking equipment, foodstuffs.
For a listing of trendy goods, order their catalog. Chuck Williams, the owner, is a respected cook and recipe developer.

❖ A BIBLIOGRAPHY OF BREAD

Here is a reading list for your research, reading, and baking pleasure. Some titles are out of print. Your local library or library system should be helpful in supplying those that are no longer available for purchase. I have learned something from each.

Alston, Elizabeth. *Muffins.* New York: Clarkson N. Potter, 1985.
A small hardback book with 60 sweet and savory muffin recipes.

Amendola, Joseph, and Lundberg, Donald E. *Understanding Baking.* Chicago: Medalist Publications, Inc., 1970.
An easy-to-read manual for the commercial baker. Material about ingredients used in baking, and explanations about the physics and chemistry involved in the process.

Asquith, Pamella Z. *The Quintessential Croissant.* Millbrae, CA: Celestial Arts, 1982.
An attractive paperback devoted entirely to the croissant.

Autry, James A., ed. *Better Homes and Gardens All-time Favorite Bread Recipes.* Des Moines: Meredith Corporation, 1979.
An affordable basic bread book. Good for the beginning collector.

Baggett, Nancy. *The 60-minute Bread Book.* New York: Putnam's, 1985.
160 recipes, many utilizing the newer fast-rising yeasts.

Bailey, Adrian. *The Blessings of Bread.* New York: Paddington Press, Ltd., 1975.
An easy-to-read history of bread illustrated with old drawings and photographs. There is a section of basic recipes.

Balsley, Irol Whitmore; Wood, Larhylia Whitmore; and Whitmore, Nanna Carson. *Homestyle Baking.* Philadelphia: Dorrance & Company, 1973.
A large book of baking recipes, many for breads.

Baylis, Maggie, and Castle, Coralie. *Real Bread.* San Francisco: 101 Productions, 1980.
An attractive paperback in a square format with recipes emphasizing whole grains.

Beard, James. *Beard on Bread.* New York: Knopf, 1980.
A book of bread from the dean of American cookery. A must for any collection.

Bencivenga, Marguerite, and Brauer, Barbara Swift. *Bake Bread.* San Francisco: Owlswood Productions, 1975.
An inexpensive paperback with some interesting recipes.

Better Homes and Gardens editors. *Bread Cook Book.* Des Moines: Meredith Press, 1963.
A bookful of the standard recipes. Essential for a complete collection.

Betty Crocker's Breads. New York: Golden Press, 1974.
An inexpensive large paperback with recipes for rolls, loaves, and sweet breads.

Boater, Debbie. *The Bread Book.* Dorchester: Prism Press, 1979.
An attractive inexpensive paperback by an English author.

Brown, Edward Espe. *The Tassajara Bread Book.* Boulder: Shambhala, 1970.
A bread book by the former head cook at the Tassajara monastery.

Bumgarner, Marlene Anne. *The Book of Whole Grains.* New York: St. Martin's Press, 1976.
This covers growing, harvesting, and grinding your own grain. Includes recipes.

Casella, Dolores. *The New Book of Breads*. Port Washington, NY: David White, 1979.
A general bread book with some emphasis on whole grains and on sourdough.

———. *A World of Breads*. New York: David White, 1974.
A very complete book of bread with 600 recipes from all over the world.

Clayton, Bernard Jr. *The Breads of France*. Indianapolis/New York: Bobbs-Merrill, 1978.
A beautiful book giving the classical and regional breads of France by an experienced author and bread baker.

Corley, Sherrill, ed. *Bread and Soup Cookbook*. Melrose Park: Culinary Arts Institute, 1978.
An attractive book combining those two favorites, bread and soup.

Cunningham, Marion. *The Fannie Farmer Baking Book*. New York: Knopf, 1984.
This covers all types of baking, but has a good section on bread. Written by the author of the revised edition of The Fannie Farmer Cookbook.

Cutler, Carol. *Carol Cutler's Great Fast Breads*. New York: Rawson, 1985.
One hundred recipes for breads that take from 30 minutes to 2 hours to prepare.

Cutler, Kathy. *The Festive Bread Book*. Woodbury, NY: Barron's, 1982.
A first book by a bread-baking teacher. Includes breads from many different countries.

Davenport, Rita. *Sourdough Cookery*. Tucson: HP Books, 1977.
An attractive large-format paperback with color photographs of the breads included.

David, Elizabeth. *English Bread and Yeast Cookery*. New York: Penguin, 1982.
The history and lore of English breads with recipes adapted for the American kitchen. A must for the serious student.

De Gouy, Louis P. *The Bread Tray*. New York: Dover, 1974.
An exhaustive collection of recipes, more than 500.

Dworkin, Floss, and Dworkin, Stan. *Bake Your Own Bread and Be Healthier*. New York: Holt, Rinehart and Winston, 1972.
A cookbook full of recipes stressing the nutritional aspects of baking your own.

Farm Journal food editors. *Breads Like Mother Used to Make*. Philadelphia: Countryside Press, 1971.
A selection of recipes from their 1969 book, Homemade Bread.

Field, Carol. *The Italian Baker*. New York: Harper & Row, 1985.
A beautiful book bringing you the classic and regional breads of Italy, based on two years research with the bakers of that country.

Fiske, Rosalie Cheney, and Potee, Joanne Koch. *The Bread Bakers' Manual.* Englewood
Cliffs: Prentice-Hall, 1978.
Seventy-five bread recipes by two experienced bakers.

Franklin, Linda Campbell. *Breads and Biscuits.* New York: Tree Communications,
1981.
A homespun book with 75 old-fashioned bread recipes.

Good, Phyllis Pellman, and Pellman, Rachel Thomas, eds. *Breads from Amish and
Mennonite Kitchens.* Lancaster, PA: Good Books, 1982.
Hand-calligraphed booklet of authentic old-world recipes.

The Great Cooks' Guide to Breads. New York: Random House, 1977.
A collection of 50 breads from some of America's leading food authorities.

Greene, Diana Scesny. *Whole Grain Baking.* Trumansburg, NY: The Crossing Press,
1984.
An attractive paperback with a good number of easy-to-follow bread recipes.

Gross, Sue Anderson. *Bagels, Bagels, Bagels.* St. Charles, IL: Kitchen Harvest Press,
1974.
A 16-page booklet devoted to the bagel.

————. *Old World Breads.* St. Charles, IL: Kitchen Harvest Press, 1976.
A booklet by the same author that is twice as long, with good basic recipes.

Gubser, Mary. *America's Bread Book.* New York: William Morrow, 1985.
Three hundred recipes collected on journeys throughout the United States.

————. *Mary's Bread Basket and Soup Kettle.* New York: William Morrow, 1974.
An extensive book of soups and the breads to accompany them.

Hechtlinger, Adelaide. *Cooking with Bread.* Brattleboro, VT: Stephen Greene Press,
1970.
A small paperback with 54 recipes for using leftover bread.

Herbst, Sharon Tyler. *Breads.* Tucson: HP Books, 1983.
A large-format paperback book with color photographs. Up to the usual standards of HP Books.

Hobson, Phyllis. *Making Breads with Home-grown Yeasts and Home-ground Grains.* Char-
lotte, VT: Garden Way Publishing, 1975.
A small paperback packed with useful information.

Holloway, Malcolm. *"How to" Book of Bread and Breadmaking.* London: Blandford Press,
1981.
A small book by an English author telling how to make traditional breads, buns, and yeast cakes.

Holm, Don, and Holm, Myrtle. *The Complete Sourdough Cookbook.* Caldwell, Idaho: Caxton Printers, 1972.
A folksy book full of recipes and the lore of sourdough.

Home Baked Breads. Middlesex: Rochester Folk Art Guild, 1978.
A spiral-bound paperback with 22 good recipes.

The Hoopeston Cook Book. Hoopeston, IL: The First Presbyterian Church Young Women's Missionary Society, 1930.
A treasure trove of good recipes, including many for bread.

Hunt, Bernice. *Great Bread!* New York: Penguin Books, 1980.
One hundred breads from an enthusiastic baker.

Jacob, H. E. *Six Thousand Years of Bread: Its Holy and Unholy History.* Garden City, NY: Doubleday, Doran & Co., 1945.
An extensive history. I would have liked larger print and more illustrations.

Jacobs, Patricia. *The Best Bread Book.* Los Angeles: Corwin Books, 1978.
A charming book by an English baker.

Johnson, Ellen Foscue. *Garden Way Publishing's Bread Book.* Pownal, VT: Garden Way Publishing, 1979.
A large paperback arranged as an almanac of bread baking.

Johnson, Hannah Lyons. *Let's Bake Bread.* New York: Lothrop, Lee & Shepard, 1973.
Step by step instructions in the art of baking bread for juvenile readers. Well illustrated with black and white photographs.

Jones, Judith, and Jones, Evan. *The Book of Bread.* New York: Harper & Row, 1982.
This won the A. T. French Company Tastemaker Award for the best cookbook with a 1982 copyright. A must for any collection.

———. *Knead It, Punch It, Bake It!: Make Your Own Bread.* New York: Crowell, 1981.
More than 30 recipes in a book geared for juveniles, fifth grade and up.

Kutner, Lynn. *Bountiful Bread: Basics to Brioches.* New York: Irena Chalmers, 1982.
An attractive book with good basic breads.

Laffal, Florence. *Breads of Many Lands.* Essex, CT: Gallery Press, 1975.
A friendly book with a nice collection of recipes.

Lerner, Anne. *Breads You Wouldn't Believe.* Radnor, PA: Chilton, 1974.
One hundred nineteen recipes, from batter breads to sourdough, all written in paragraphs.

London, Mel. *Bread Winners.* Emmaus, PA: Rodale, 1979.
Two hundred breads collected from 45 bakers.

Mathiesen, Elva. *Sourdough.* Providence, RI: Mathiesen Editions, 1974.
A small paperback with good information about sourdough with recipes.

Mc Cay, Clive M., and McCay, Jeanette B. *The Cornell Bread Book.* New York: Dover, 1980.
A book of recipes based on the high-protein "Cornell formula." The original booklet of recipes was published in 1955. This is a Dover reprint, revised and expanded by Jeanette McCay.

Medlin, Zoe. *War Eagle Mill Whole Grain Cook Book.* Rogers, AK: Self-published, 1976.
A wonderful little book filled with old-fashioned recipes.

Meyer, Carolyn. *The Bread Book: All About Bread and How to Make It.* New York: Harcourt Brace Jovanovich, 1971.
For children. The story of bread with enough recipes to spice the text.

Miller, Byron S. *Variety Breads in the United States.* St. Paul, MN: American Association of Cereal Chemists, Inc., 1981.
A discussion of common bakery breads, with commercial formulation and some home recipes.

Moore, Marilyn. *Baking Your Own: Recipes and Tips for Better Breads.* Hoopeston, IL: Prairie Craftsman, 1982.
This is the first book by the author of the one you are reading.

Morgan, Sarah. *Bread.* Austin: Encino Press, 1975.
A collection of 100 well-researched recipes.

Moxon, Lloyd. *The Baking Book.* New York: Delair Publishing, 1981.
A baking book by a scientist who is also an accomplished baker.

Nichols, Nell B., ed. *Homemade Bread.* Garden City, NY: Doubleday, 1969.
A collection of recipes from farm and ranch kitchens across the country, collected by the editors of Farm Journal magazine.

Noble, Phyllis, ed. *The Book of Bread.* New York: The Seabury Press, 1975.
A 96-page spiral-bound book presenting 38 breads by the parishioners of the Episcopal Church of St. Stephen and the Incarnation.

Nordstrom, Jane. *The Barmy Bread Book.* Santa Fe: The Lightning Tree, 1974.
Recipes from a baker hooked on using diastatic malt in bread dough.

————. *More Barmy Breads: Little Breads and Tea Loaves.* Santa Fe: The Lightning Tree, 1980.
The same—devoted to rolls, sweet rolls, and crackers.

Norman, Ursel. *A Basket of Homemade Breads.* New York: William Morrow, 1974.
A whimsically illustrated book with 26 recipes for bread.

Ojakangas, Beatrice. *Food Processor Bread Book.* Skokie: Publications International, 1980.
A large paperback devoted to making machine breads.

——. *Great Whole Grain Breads.* New York: E. P. Dutton, 1984.
Well-organized recipes by a knowledgeable baker.

Olney, Judith. *Judith Olney on Bread.* New York: Crown, 1985.
Innovative recipes by an imaginative cook. This is an attractive book for gifting.

Orcutt, Georgia, and Taylor, Sandra, eds. *Breads, Rolls & Pastries.* Dublin, NH: Yankee Books, 1981.
More than 200 recipes with good New England flavor.

Ortho Books editors. *Breads.* San Francisco: Ortho Books, 1985.
A large paperback with breads by the bakers at the California Culinary Academy.

Pappas, Lou Seibert. *Bread Baking.* Concord, CA: Nitty Gritty Productions, 1975.
A nice collection of recipes by a baker who knows the territory.

Peck, Paula. *The Art of Fine Baking.* New York: Simon and Schuster, 1961.
A general baking book with one chapter on breads and coffee cakes.

Pelton, Robert W. *Natural Baking the Old-fashioned Way.* Cranbury, New Jersey: A. S. Barnes and Co., 1973.
A quaint book filled with old family recipes, including some for homemade yeast.

Pillsbury editors. *Hearty Soups and Breads Cookbook.* Le Sueur, MN: Pillsbury Publications, 1985.
A nice easy-to-use paperback.

Parsons Bread Book. New York: Harper & Row, 1974.
A celebration of the art of baking bread and the great bakers of New York City by students at Parsons School of Design. Beautifully illustrated with black and white photographs.

Pomeranz, Yeshajahu, Ph.D., and Shellenberger, J. A., Ph.D. *Bread Science and Technology.* Westport, CT: Avi Publishing, 1971.
The title says it all.

Powell, Kay Emel. *The Superstone Country Kitchen Stoneware Cookbook.* Evanston, IL: Sassafras Press, 1982.
A useful cookbook of recipes using the stonewear made by Sassafras Enterprises.

Quick Bread Winners from Betty Crocker. Minneapolis: General Mills, 1985.
An easy-to-use paperback from Betty Crocker's Kitchens.

Roberts, Ada Lou. *Favorite Breads from Rose Lane Farm.* New York: Hearthside Press, 1960.
A charming book by an old-fashioned baker.

———. *Sourdough Breads and Coffee cakes.* Mineola: Dover, 1983.
The same as the above.

Robertson, Laurel. *The Laurel's Kitchen Bread Book.* New York: Random House, 1984.
A good book of whole-grain breads by a devotee of whole-food cookery.

Sandler, Sandra. *Home Bakebook of Natural Breads and Goodies.* Harrisburg, PA: Stackpole Books, 1972.
An extensive collection of whole-grain recipes.

Sher, Gail. *From a Baker's Kitchen.* Berkeley: Harris Publishing, 1984.
More than 100 bread recipes from a professional baker.

Solomon, Hannah. *Bake Bread!* Philadelphia and New York: Lippincott, 1976.
A well-illustrated book for older children, fourth through sixth grades.

The Southern Heritage Breads Cookbook. Birmingham: Oxmoor House, 1983.
From the people at Southern Living *magazine, recipes with a Southern flavor.*

Standard, Stella. *Our Daily Bread.* New York: Bonanza Books, 1970.
More than 300 recipes, divided into two sections: one for white flour, one for whole grains.

Sultan, William J. *Elementary Baking.* New York: McGraw-Hill, 1969.
A textbook with a section on breads. Good illustrations for shaping buns and braids.

Sumption, Lois Lintner, and Ashbrook, Marguerite Lintner. *Breads from Many Lands.* New York: Dover, 1982.
A Dover reprint, originally published as Breads and More Breads, *by the Manual Arts Press of Peoria, IL.*

Sunset editors. *Sunset Cookbook of Breads.* Menlo Park, CA: Lane Publishing, 1977.
A large paperback with some of the wonderful breads from the kitchens of Sunset *magazine.*

Sylvester, Natalie G. *The Home-baking Cookbook.* Grosset & Dunlap, 1973.
This is an absolutely delightful book filled with recipes and drawings of antique baking utensils.

Tarr, Yvonne Young. *Super-easy Step-by-Step Book of Special Breads.* New York: Vintage Books, 1975.
A small number of recipes with lengthy directions, broken into their various steps.

Taylor, Barbara Howland. *Mexico: Her Daily and Festive Breads.* Claremont: The Creative Press, 1969.
No recipes here, but wonderful photographs and stories about the breads of Mexico.

Teubner, Christian. *Christmas Baking: Traditional Recipes Made Easy.* Woodbury, NY: Barron's, 1983.
One chapter on breads in a lovely book with a color photo on every other page.

Time-Life Books editors. *Breads.* Alexandria: Time-Life Books, 1981.
A well-done book by the editors at Time-Life.

Time-saving Yeast Breads. Milwaukee: Universal Foods Corporation, 1983.
A small booklet of recipes using the new Red Star quick-rise yeast.

Uprisings. Hendersonville, NC: The Mother Earth News Books, 1983.
Whole-grain recipes collected from small independent bakeries.

Voth, Norma Jost. *Festive Breads of Christmas.* Scottsdale, PA: Herald Press, 1983.
A little book filled with the lore and recipes of Christmas. A nice stocking stuffer for the baker on your list.

Wade, Carlson. *The Bread Book.* New York: Drake, 1973.
More than 200 recipes with the ingredients given in an unusual format.

Wiener, Joan, and Collier, Diana. *Bread.* Philadelphia and New York; Lippincott, 1973.
A nice collection of bread recipes.

Williams, Vera B. *It's a Gingerbread House: Bake it! Build it! Eat it!* New York: Greenwillow Books, 1978.
A small book for children with complete instructions for baking and building a house of gingerbread.

❊ Index